The Gap Between God and Christianity

The Gap Between God and Christianity

The Turbulence of Western Culture

THOMAS M. STALLTER

RESOURCE *Publications* · Eugene, Oregon

THE GAP BETWEEN GOD AND CHRISTIANTIY
The Turbulence of Western Culture

Resource Publications
An Imprint of Wipf and Stock Publishers
199 W. 8th Ave., Suite 3
Eugene, OR 97401

www.wipfandstock.com

PAPERBACK ISBN: 978-1-6667-1240-7
HARDCOVER ISBN: 978-1-6667-1241-4
EBOOK ISBN: 978-1-6667-1242-1

JANUARY 7, 2022 9:01 AM

To Nathan, Erin, and Megan,
God's gifts, who make me proud to be a dad.

And to Sharon, my wonderful and loving wife, gift of God,
who inspires my work and fills my life with joy.

Contents

LIST OF FIGURES

Preface

I HAVE BEEN A LONG TIME in coming to this point of writing down my concerns for us in the body of Christ. And the journey has been a circuitous one. I have been a teacher, first in Africa for nearly two decades, and these last 23 years in a Christian college and seminary setting. After our first ten years of Central Africa experience, we came back to the US for further training, this time in intercultural studies. When we returned to Central Africa, it was to a different country. But it was almost like a different world. Not that the African peoples were all that different, it was me. I had been looking at their culture from the outside, and I thought I knew quite a bit about them. I could answer what, how, and when they did what they did, but only in the more obvious activities could I answer why. But now, I had a new awareness. I could suspend my own cultural perspective and preferences enough to see theirs more clearly. I began to see the reasons behind their behavior. It was like looking through their eyes, beginning to see their situation from the inside. What's more, I started to see values and understandings in their culture that they could not put into words themselves, things they took for granted that affected their day-to-day lives, things they attached to the expression of their faith that didn't belong there.

On our way to Africa that first time, we spent eighteen months in France for language studies and later had numerous trips back to France during our years in Central Africa. We began to see how their language was connected to their culture in ways that made it odd to use it in French-speaking Africa. The two cultures and the people's experience in them were vastly different, which loaded the vocabulary differently in each situation. In our last assignment in the country of Chad, our teammates were German. We were learning about yet another culture. Later, in my early studies for teaching in the US, I began to study other cultures, especially Japanese. I had significant encounters with Native Americans during those years and taught South Korean doctoral students for over twenty years, working closely with Korean colleagues. As I compared these groups and Central Africans to our culture, the differences were enormous. The behavior in these various cultures was controlled by their values and belief systems. It made sense to them though they seldom thought about why they did what they did. All this made the continued study of our US Anglo-American culture even more relevant.

Those years of experience in Central Africa were beneficial in helping me understand my own culture. Nothing brings your own culture under the microscope like studying another culture, living among its people, adapting to their ways of survival and social interaction, learning to think in their language, situating yourself in their world. And then, nothing cements the nature of a topic, such as the disquieting control culture has over people, in your own heart and brain like preparing lectures and discussions and teaching it to others over the years.

I began to take our culture more seriously. What about values we take for granted that control us, that we are not conscious of, that we cannot put into words? Who is paying attention to their influence? Why do we do what we do, and then, ultimately, what do we attach to the expression of our faith that does not belong there? Is it true that culture's influence on our Christian behavior often escapes our attention? Well, of course, it is.

Politics make the world look simple. Governments make sweeping generalizations across the globe and decisions for world economics and peaceful co-existence. But cultural anthropology and intercultural communication studies point out the extensive and significant differences that make these goals difficult to attain and the superficial agreements we make problematic to sustain. Like the rest of us, politicians take our Western cultural values for granted and attribute them to people of non-Western groups. If another country becomes democratic, learns our language, and trades commodities with us, we assume it makes them like us. But, below the surface, nothing could be further from the truth.

I feel, and am considered by most to be very conservative in my theological thinking, really, but I am among those who habitually analyze culture and communication. We can be seen as those who upset the applecart and possibly are branded as pessimistic or critical by those outside our field. I suppose some of us are. However, I want you to know that I am on your side, the side of all who want to own God's purposes more holistically in our lives and to see God's Word penetrate the lives of people around us in our world.

But decades of observing Western Christianity in the United States and Europe, non-Western Christianity in Africa and Korea, and years of teaching applied cultural anthropology and intercultural communication give me pause. I feel a deep concern for today's churches, Christian schools, and mission agencies that we have ignored this monster of culture and that ours has played tricks on us, invading our way of thinking about God, godliness, and ministry.

We are up against critical cultural blindness and take far too much for granted in how communication works. It is disquieting, to say the least. What damage has it already caused? How are we to move forward? We must become sensitive to the dangers and our complacency toward understanding in these matters. I am encouraged to see a new wave of interest in part of our problem. There are those talking about our Western approach to the Middle Eastern text of the Bible. I applaud them, and though I may not add much to these brilliant efforts, I hope that my perspective will touch some who have not yet seen the value of these studies. One of my aims is to help us see beyond our cultural limitations to the application of these fresh understandings in our culture-bound lives.

Though the urgency of the thoughts in this book is mine, the concept of a culturally relevant yet culturally independent faith has always been God's intention. It has been around for as long as human societies have existed. To disregard it in our day is to be distracted from essential considerations and remain at a distance from God and the peace and blessings of his grace. It gives me a sense of determination that I trust will not detract from the content. Along the way, you will find that I reemphasize previous points. That is an intentional part of my teaching strategy showing through. I will say things and later connect them with another aspect of our topic. Then I will remind you of the importance of that concept at yet another point of our discussion. We average people tend to learn something only the second or third time we read it and need to see it in various constructions to get the whole idea.

Teaching intercultural studies in a college and seminary with an earnest desire to prepare men and women for cross-cultural ministry, I have stressed the themes in this book with my students. Their positive responses to these ideas and their successful culture discovery experiences during internships confirmed the need to continue to develop these seeds of intercultural thinking. Discussions were even more invigorating at the doctoral level with experienced cross-cultural workers. The applications began to jump out of international settings and spotlight us and how our culture affects us.

When people move from one cultural system to another, they get caught in the dissonance created by the collision of the two systems for survival. Many are not aware of what is happening. They have brought their own culture to the host situation, and it is not working for them. The host people wonder why they are so strange. Culture shock is a real possibility for these sojourners in a foreign land. But awareness can change all this.

A similar problem confronts Christians when they read the Bible or implement its teachings in their own culture. They do not realize the powerful influence of the original culture on the words and then of their own on their observations of the text or its application to their lives. The results create a gap between God and their style of Christianity. This is the crux of our discussion in this book. Our journey together may cause discomfort for some. It is a sensitive topic to talk about one's own culture and its influence on us when all along we thought we were in charge of our lives and preferences. It may give us a sort of reverse culture shock.

My thoughts in this book are somewhat introductory. There is much more to be said about the topics here. More illustrations and examples might be given. Some issues are only mentioned that deserve a book of their own. But we must start somewhere and keep things in a small enough package that people might actually read it. Our culture keeps us fairly occupied with other things. I am hoping to find a small space in busy schedules.

I write hoping that it might serve some of us in our quest to be missional people in God's way. Why else does he give another breath, but that we should seek to serve him in whatever way is open to us. These thoughts have been accumulating over the years. My hope is that they add to our desire to honor God instead of detracting. I have had many great teachers over the years, both in-person and in books. I am so grateful. I am confident they have changed me, but they are not to blame if you feel I am off the mark in my comments. They have done their best.

Finally, in setting forth the concerns of this book, I try to be careful of what I assume is common knowledge. After nearly fifty years of having my head in this cloud, I realize that much has become common to me that would not be so to someone else. Common knowledge in the field of intercultural studies is, almost by definition, uncommon to most readers.

With this in mind, I have added a glossary and appendices to help define and explain the terminology and constructs to not disturb the flow of content in the text. I am counting on the reader using them. They are not exhaustive, but I hope they will be adequate for our purpose here. Other terms not found there are defined later in the book. Biblical references are mainly in the footnotes.

ACKNOWLEDGMENTS

THERE ARE MANY PEOPLE along the way in my journey leading up to this book that I wish to thank. I am forever changed by the valuable teaching and example of Dr. Charles Smith during my years at Grace Theological Seminary. I also am grateful to Drs. Stanley Toussaint, and Howard Hendricks, and many others at Dallas Theological Seminary for inspiring me and giving me a foundation in the Scriptures.

I am indebted to Dr. Tom Julien, who, as Director of Grace Brethren International Missions, opened the way for me to study culture formally and supervised my practice of that learning during my later years in Africa. I am indebted to Dr. Donald Smith for opening the subjects of intercultural studies to me in insightful ways during my years at Western Seminary in Portland. He, and many other valuable authors, put intercultural communication in my repertoire.

I am very grateful for the encouraging friendships and powerful cultural lessons from my many Central African and Chadian brothers and sisters. I am forever appreciative of their hours of time, patience, and trust in me as an outsider. My gratitude extends to missionaries Don and Lois Miller, Eddie and Linda Mensinger, Maryann Habeggar, and Marvin and Dorothy Goodman for their help to our family as new missionaries. Many colleagues with us in mission are to be thanked for their help and camaraderie, but I am particularly grateful to our German colleagues, Frank and Karin Puhl, for their friendship, encouragement, help, and insights as co-laborers in Chad. Our supporters while in missions are to be acknowledged for their encouragement of our culture learning with additional thanks to Pastor Charles Lawson, Mike and Karen Retterer, and Don and Becky McIntosh. These all made learning about culture and ministry in Africa possible.

I am also indebted to Drs. Dave Plaster and Ron Manahan of Grace College and Grace Theological Seminary for opening the opportunity for me to teach and continue research on what I had learned formally and informally about how culture works and its influence on all of us.

I am grateful for the strong influence of Dr. Paul Hiebert during my post-doctoral work at Trinity Evangelical Divinity School and then through his many books. He added deep value to cultural anthropology for me while we shared ice cream in his living room.

I am indebted to my Korean colleagues, Drs. Stephen and Rachel Park for their friendship and collaboration at the Center for Korean Studies at Grace Theological Seminary. I had many enjoyable years teaching Korean students, both pastors and missionaries. They impressed on me many things about Korean culture that shaped my thinking and changed my perspective.

Over the years of teaching Central Africans, Americans, Koreans, Native Americans, and many other nationalities, I am grateful for many inquisitive students who asked provoking questions and responded to mine with insightful comments. I am better for it.

Perhaps most of all, I am beholden to my wife, who has always believed in what God was doing in our lives and encouraged and inspired me. Her tireless work with many suggestions in editing these pages was really quite amazing.

List of Abbreviations

ESV   English Standard Version of the Bible
NIV   New International Version of the Bible
US   United States
USA   United States of America

Introduction

Perfect goodness can never debate about the end to be attained, and perfect wisdom cannot debate about the means most suited to achieve it. The Freedom of God consists in the fact that no cause other than Himself produces His acts and no external obstacle impedes them—that His own goodness is the root from which they all grow and His own omnipotence the air in which they all flower.[1]

C. S. Lewis

These words of C. S. Lewis are followed in my mind with the words, "So, let God be God." We allow so much to come between us. We, as Western[2] Christians, condone and even encourage and champion the very things that create distance between us and his goodness, between our plans and his destiny for us, between our weakness and his strength. Not only have we created distance between us, but we seldom free him from our cultural and personal expectations for his being and doings. We want to know him but are prisoners of our needs for social and personal survival. We tend to lock God into ways we expect him to meet these needs, and, in the end, the struggle to know God as he truly is continues. Is there a trusting of God that frees him to be God and then frees us

1. Lewis, *Problem of Pain*, 23.

2. I will use the terms "Western" and "non-Western" a great deal in this book to refer to two major kinds of cultural systems. Descriptions of these categories of cultural values are delineated in the Glossary.

1

of our long struggle for identity, worth, and wellbeing? Well, of course, there is. And it is not some secret that only certain people can discover.

We do not live in a perfect world, even though that is how God created it. We gave it up in Eden for what we thought would be better. Now we seek that perfection, if only in terms of emotional, physical, rational, or social survival, where it is not to be found. Though we can have God's perspective while in this world, we cannot make it a perfect place or our role in it faultless. Perfection is yet to come. We must seek to live godly lives in the world as we have it, changing what we can and moving on with this purpose when we cannot change some aspect of our lives in our present situation. Our efforts in this will be to some extent within the confines and dictates of our human culture, and that is where many of our decisions will be made. The weighty encouragement is that God is not unaware of our situation; he is at work in it to our great benefit if we give back to him what we took on ourselves in Eden—if we allow him to be God once more.

There is mystery in God's being, but not in his intentions for us. We, as Christians, believe Jesus spoke about the very nature of a relationship with God having to do with choosing a narrow gate, the way that leads to life—life like we could never know it on our own. But he also talked about the wide gate, the way that leads to eternal death. There is no room for political correctness. There is a choice to make, and Jesus is the only way to God.[3] We become God's children only when we choose his road. Those who do usually start out okay and even with passion. But too many of us lose that first love and slip into a third way we have created. We try to walk on the narrow road but hold on to the benefits offered by our culture, the other road, the broad one. We become distracted by the world around us. These excursions cause other distractions to come between God and us—other ways of survival for the self. We strain to be biblical Christians, but we are weighted down and exhausted. We are anxious and insecure because we are trying to get to the destination God planned for us by another road, one we believe can meet the demands of self and culture and still please him.

We don't want to admit it, but we are lost. We try to get directions from others, but it is confusing. They don't seem to understand that we have needs and are up against the strong pull of our old ways of survival. We want Christ to be in our lives, but we also need to survive as

---

3. Matt 7:13–14; John 14:6.

individuals and fulfill the cultural code for "Christian" success. No one seems able to tell us how to stay on the right road and still reach the complex fulfillment of our human ideals: overcoming our insecurities, the satisfaction of the self, and achieving our culture's expectations. Left to ourselves, we syncretize our faith with our cultural system for survival. We want God to be part of our new plan without realizing he wants us to be part of his. We add him into the mix, but the old system smothers his influence.

Some of the weights holding us back are easily named, but most are subtle and enabled even in the church where we expect to worship only God. Sin for us is not that often an outright rebellion against God, but rather a preoccupation with self. Humans are selfish enough without it, but there is, as we will see, a pitfall in our Western cultural system called individualism that rsahas us tethered in desperation to the survival of self. Other cultures have other struggles, but this one is ours. For us, coming to Christ means we must cut the cord. But we have subtle ways, subtle to us, but not necessarily to those around us, of tying the cord back together if we ever cut it at all. For some of us, it has become habitual, an addiction. We have so many knots in the cord, and they have been there for so long, they look normal to us. We can't seem to conquer the need to make something of ourselves that others will recognize and affirm and still be biblical people. Individualism has been drilled into us by our culture. We live among people who know no other way to manage their lives and find approval and acceptance except by personal achievement and making it known. This may feel like the way to security for us, but it is instead merciless captivity to an unrelenting master—the individualism of our culture and its expectations.

It is costly to undo, for we have institutionalized, condoned, and encouraged individualism even in the church. To walk away from self seems like social suicide. It is passing a point of no return. The road Jesus speaks of promises no recognition for self, no standing or identity among our peers that would bring feelings of affirmation, worth, and self-confidence. From a human standpoint, to follow Christ entirely is to risk all, and, as we shall see in chapter 3, that was his plan from the very beginning. We want to be Christians, but isn't it asking a bit too much? No. It is asking us to do the only thing that can help us.[4] If we stay on his road, all meaning and worth will be abundant in God himself and what

---

4. John 12:24–26; Matt 16:24–26.

he providentially brings into our lives.[5] It is not a very Western way to do things, even for a Christian—submission of self leading to fulfillment. But we have been given no other way. There is actually little real help from others on this topic. Though the books seem endless on Christian maturity, few talk about how our culture is at work against us. It has so many positive points, but someone must call our attention to its negative influence.

We will call those involved in Christianity, but whose faith is smothered by their cultural values, popular Christians in this book. They sound like Christians, believe they are Christians but have not let God have his way. They do not let him speak for himself. They can be found at every level of institutional Christianity. Those who have taken the risk and are trusting God with their lives we will call biblical Christians. They are not perfect, making them a little more difficult to find, but they have the core issues correct, have the essentials worked out, and trust God's providence in their lives. Though they exist in all walks of life and every ethnic group, they are usually not well known. Don't expect them to have a degree in theology. They may have no post-secondary education at all, but they have humbled themselves before God. They are small in number, but then, Jesus said they would be few.[6] Many of us are still popular Christians thinking we have found the way, but we are actually trying to combine God's way with culture's way.

Our cultural patterns and values seem normal to us and are the expectations of those around us. We are unsuspecting of their subtle and silent pressure to move us toward their well-worn path instead of the less used way God intends for us. How did this happen? How did so many of us who started well get so far off the road into the underbrush and bracken between the two ways Jesus talked about? What are the things that keep us in the wilderness? What choices are we making? What natural and unnatural forces are against us? And what are we missing that God in his grace and love intends for us? Unless we talk about it openly, begin to let God be God, and make hard choices, we may not find our way back. Many never do.

This struggle in the underbrush diverts us from being missional people for God in the world. The world around us weakens, the blind lead the blind, good people are persecuted, and justice is hard to find, but we

5. Luke 12:22–26; John 10:10.
6. Matt 7:14.

are preoccupied with our self-needs and the ways our culture gives us to meet them. Our message is desperately needed, but we are distracted and actually make matters worse. We discredit the real answers and dishonor their Source.

Loud voices in our society take meaning, purpose, and moral foundations from people's lives in sweeping, irrational movements and then wonder why people act without meaning, purpose, and morality. Our society is a human system turned against itself, eating at itself from the inside. It blames outward things, the things abused. But we are wrong. *We* have done this to our society, to ourselves, using the negative potential of our culture's values. A human culture that worships immediate gratification of self-needs creates its own wasteful devastation of which otherwise neutral or good things put to evil use—guns killing masses, dark dealings with money, the crippling impact of smuggled drugs, sexual disorientation, weaponized racial schemes—are only outward symptoms. What has changed is inside people, or better said, what is no longer inside people. The gap between God and humankind grows, and human judgment has filled the void with further destruction of life as God intends it. It becomes highly relevant to ask, where are the people of God in this critical hour of need? For the most part, we are in our separate churches and denominations, still under the spell of our culture's demands and expectations for us syncretized with our faith. Distracted by the needs of our institutions, few of us continue to be salt and light in the world.

We have the only answers that can save people from their self-destruction and ignorance of God, but we are looking the other way. We are prisoners of the same culture and do not realize it has us in its clutches. Our culture, like all cultures, is not bad in itself. All human beings need a cultural system, a frame of reference within which words and activity have meaning. Over time cultures develop into systems for survival and are strewn with traditional solutions to that end. This makes them helpful and essential systems developed over the generations of human experience. New generations do not have to reinvent how to survive in the world. The fact is that no one can survive without a cultural framework. But because they are human, God is on the outside, and, over time, subtly, the created thing becomes the master of its creators. Rejecting any alternatives, we know no other way to survive except to do its bidding. Until we meet Christ, we feel either satisfied or stuck with the system. But its solutions are thin and temporary, whether we realize it or not.

As Christians, we continue to suffer from culture's control because we do not recognize its silent but powerful influence on us. In the confusion of having two masters,[7] it is difficult to see the difference between God's absolutes and culture's absolutes. Culture is not all bad, which blinds our minds to what *is* contrary to God's purposes. The result is that we tend to syncretize God's ways and our cultural system rather than choose between them. We love God, but we have been married to our culture for a long time. Nicodemus's confusion is quite understandable.[8]

To be free of these cultural absolutes, we must let God be God *within* our cultural frame of reference. If Jesus is the way, we will have to discern at what points our culture can still serve us and when it is no longer relevant and even oppressive. We will have to stay on the narrow road to experience the freedom he gives—the abundant life beyond the distractions of the old system for survival. My comments to this end will be troublesome for various readers. But I am insisting that we let God be God in this life, as imperfectly as we may do that, instead of leaving our sense of wellbeing in the hands of our culture. As we have said, its solutions are thin and temporary, but God's are rich and eternal.

I fully realize that the issues I raise are not issues for every last one of us, but they are crucial for most. The credibility of our faith, a missional endeavor in our communities, and our example to the world as it looks on are at risk. I think reading my point of view will take some patience, maybe even endurance. But if we take God seriously, as I urge, we will leave popular Christianity behind us, never to return to the compartmental, polarized life we have known. We must all come to love God more than self, more than our culture, more than Christianity. Our true loyalty must be to him alone.

Some responsibility for this change rests with Christian leaders who can influence many others, but it is not theirs alone. All Christians face the same encounters with self and culture, and we must answer for our choices. Our station in life, accomplishments, or self-confidence do not change the application of the truth in our lives. In the end, we all must look the enemy in the face, even if, or especially when, it is our own. However, as those who put leaders in place, the rest of us need to see the answers to such struggles in them. The responsibilities and liabilities for those who lead God's people are enormous. They must be further along

7. Matt 6:24.
8. John 3:1–21.

in the battle with cultural absolutes to help us identify the values and understand the tactics employed against us. We all have a relationship with God to nurture and a responsibility in our society to demonstrate that loyalty. Our leaders prepare us for it, but we must all become our message.

I am comforted that God seems to take delight in using the least likely people and circumstances, even the foolish things of this world, to carry out his work. You and I are not likely from among the wise and influential of our society, but if you are reading this book, you care about his cause in the world. He uses the weak, the lowly, the despised, the nobodies in his movement among us to his ends.[9] This means, if we let God be God, we can expect him to be at work in the world in the most unlikely of situations, often using the most unlikely people, yes, using us. We will have to be alert. At this time in my life, I am less distracted by the many things that used to be my daily fare. This gives me time others may not have for musing about life, love, and ideas that matter, and for wonder at such a great God who has been so remarkably generous in his grace to allow me to be one of his. As I set out writing what I feel are urgent thoughts in a book, I don't feel a lot of choice in the matter. Each of us must do what is before us and trust God's use of it for his kingdom as he will.

I am well aware of the danger of words, for where there are many, transgression is not lacking.[10] And then the risk of putting them down on paper where anyone's eyes may fall upon them is formidable. Pages and pages of them increase the risk of misunderstanding here and there. But we are on a subject for which we must take these risks, and words are our only tools. I will endeavor to use caution, but I trust the reader to enter this realm of thought with me. And then, the idea of meaning in words carries its own danger. When we talk about things deep inside us, we have to remember that the idea or experience, when put in words, becomes a symbolic representation of those thoughts. That which is subjective becomes objective, leaving it to the reader to supply the meaning their own experience associates with those terms. This makes talking about spiritual matters difficult and dangerous because they are simply not quantifiable or specifiable in their whole or original sense in words

---

9. 1 Cor 1:26–31.

10. Prov 10:19; Eccl 5:2–3, 6:11.

alone. It is also hard to guess the degree to which we might misrepresent non-concrete ideas and concepts with words.

Some people in popular Christianity tend to talk about being "spiritual" all the time, sometimes with no more discretion than if they were talking about the price of potatoes. And the motive for doing this can be quite contrary to the actual concept. True spiritual advice is hard to find and easy to emulate. Talk about being spiritual, or displays of spiritual actions do not make a person spiritual. It is a symptom of the opposite and becomes a habit of life as the person seeks to establish and maintain this identity. We want to talk about *being* something in this book. That is very different from *doing* something but precedes the doing of anything for God. To put this into words is difficult. This book is an attempt to talk about closing the gap between God and Christianity, but I pray it does not forfeit its usefulness with ill-used words.

Talking about culture is also problematic. There is a resistance to the topic when we try to talk about it openly, especially among individualists. I will try to be sensitive, but some offense is unavoidable. Maybe the best way to learn how to swim is to jump into the deep water, but the non-swimmer is usually not convinced of that. I realize the challenge before me, and I want you to know that I will try to pull you in with me. We will all have to let go of the edge of the pool—the comfort and safety of our culture—if we are to get on the inside of God's intentions for us and begin to close the gap.

This body of thought may be wrapped up in several central ideas: Concerning the church, when the body of Christ becomes nothing more than a microcosm of the society at large through its syncretism with the surrounding culture, it is no longer the church. When relationships and motives are no different, when competition, controlling others, cliques, and celebrity personality become the motivating values, the church is gone. Culture and self are the insidious culprits. We must look at these in detail.

Concerning the biblical context, we need to look more closely at the cultural influences on the words, people, and events of the Bible. Culture and experience affect communication to such an extent that unless we know more about the culture and social context of the Bible, we may see things that are not there and miss things that are. I am aware that this can lead to a sort of "theological culture shock."[11] But the need is worth the risk.

Concerning how we read the Bible, we often come to it with assumptions and expectations about what is there, what should be there, or what must be there. We can read the Bible without ever finding out what is actually there. We prefer our opinions about what God is saying and actually speak for him ourselves. Perhaps we often do not, given our intentions, cannot let God speak for himself. If we think he needs our help or always agrees with our opinions, we do not know God. We must fix this incapacity fueled by self, culture, pet theologies, and institutional Christianity.

Another facet of our consideration of the Bible is to see it as everything there is to know about God. But its principles and generalizations and examples applied in our lives today may not look like we expect them to if we think he has stopped being God with the revelation of himself there. When we say we know all about him, that he does not, cannot, do anything that our theologies have not outlined for him, we are not letting him be God. We must approach him with the all-embracing humility that we do not know all there is to know about him and how he may work in our world and other people's lives. We must, instead, approach him with overwhelming gratefulness for what he *has* given us in his Word. We must retain a humble heart and mind allowing him to act in ways that are his own, realizing there is mystery in what we do not know.

Concerning the self, many have turned Christianity into a religion that they think will help them. Religion is an add-on like an extension to your internet browser. It acts as a shortcut adding one more avenue to the answers and results we seek while saving us the pain of undoing all our other means and methods for personal survival. Though, as a religion, it seems helpful, it is full of ritual behavior that has the appearance of something for which it is not the answer—our dilemma of self against God. We grow to mistake ritual for relationship, and, in the end, the gap between him and us grows larger. It becomes drudgery to keep up the ritual behavior because the results are so thin and do not resolve our problems for survival. The activities end up promoting our self-interest in some way until, finally, the worship is no longer of God but of inclusion and belonging, reputation, and the self in each of us. The peace and

---

11. From Rohrbaugh, "Introduction," 3.

rest, the contentment promised, is not there. How did we get here? We must get back on the path God laid out for us.

Lastly, the influence of culture on everyone and everything must be examined. We must become aware of the impact of all cultures on their members.[12] The effects of a particular culture are present in the context of God's Word, and we must attend to them because God chose to use that cultural frame of reference in revealing himself to us. Then, while we are being sensitive to our culture's influence on us, there is also the particular culture or subculture controlling the audience of our message that we cannot ignore. Culture presents a framework for relevance and yet powerful opposition in understanding and living the Christian life and talking about it to others. So, our friend is also our enemy. It has been our guide and helper all these years. What can we expect if we expose its unscrupulous side? How can we balance our desperate need for culture with our concern for its subtle and often negative influence?

These things will seem quite meddlesome to most who have not given thought to them. Especially when things are going along smoothly, these considerations are, at best, a nuisance if not quite irritating. There is always someone who wants to bring up the troublesome "facts." Someone who, if taken seriously, will spoil something really satisfying. Whenever the subject of the real nature of culture and how it works, how it influences us comes up, there is an adverse reaction. It is that way in many areas of life. When the popular idea of some belief, value, or mode of behavior is put into a realistic frame of reference, we see contradictions and react against the process. Change is unwelcome at the best of times, but this insistence on doing something about the influence of culture in our lives is an uninvited interference.

Many people react to Christianity in this way—an unwelcome intrusion into how they want life to be. In the same vein, people, especially individualists who take pride in an internal locus of control and their achievements, do not want to hear about the possibility of being highly influenced by culture or of communication being anything more than information passed on in words. When it comes to Christians, discussing these aspects of human values and the corresponding activity as affecting them in any way can cause an acute reaction—a closing and bolting of the door, a tightening of the watertight bulkhead. It is a bothersome, nagging

12. See examples in Appendix 1.

thought that must be ignored so they can get on with things. "Leave us alone"![13]

So I realize here at the beginning that I am at a significant disadvantage in my task. I am not trying to overstate my points even though I review them frequently with the reader. And I do not think I am the only one who knows some ultimate secret that has the appearance of changing everything, not by a long shot. The topics we will engage here are not new at all, and they are not secret. But, for many of my readers, they have been withheld from you from your early days in Sunday School all the way through your theological and ministry education, perhaps for the same reasons you may feel they are a nuisance.

The Scriptures and intercultural studies come together in these thoughts. But I want to shift us away from our traditional approach to the Bible. I want us to grasp an understanding of the issues that lie behind the words. An information-only approach can keep us away from being on a confident footing with God—walking by his side on a journey of common purpose. I want to move the emphasis from *knowing* to *being*. This expression of our faith must always occur within a cultural context, the only place life can be lived. What will this mean in our Western culture?

Though I am looking at the Christian life through the lens of the influence of culture, I am not trying to ignore the vast amount of scholarly research available in biblical studies. I am trying, instead, to put what we can know in these ways into perspective—into the framework of human experience shaped by culture such as God used in his revelation of himself and still takes into account with us in our day. We, for various reasons, have neglected to see how his Word should affect the influence of our cultural system and the way our experience has shaped us. We will need to let God speak for himself in these matters.

It is not that we have not accomplished anything; many theologians have truly glorified God by their remarkable efforts revealing God's wisdom and grace. It is astounding, really, quite amazing to the rest of us. They are extremely helpful, and we need them in our own efforts. But with all we have accomplished in theology and hermeneutics, most of us, in our human condition, lack an understanding of ourselves as controlled by subtle and deceptive influences. We are insensitive to a necessary adjustment to our lens in our studies. We have too little interest in the importance of the cultural context of our biblical information or our

---

13. See Hall, *Silent Language*, 181.

audience. This puts us in the dangerous position of inserting our own where it does not belong.

A part of my aim is to create a new sum by moving intercultural studies, human communication theory, and contextualization from the debit side to the credit side of the curricular account in theological schools and personal considerations. We must add a new dimension to our hermeneutics and see languages, communication, and meaning for what they actually are, historically and culturally framed and informed by social experience. In this way, we would be resolving our limitations on the ground floor of our preparations for research and ministry.

My theological training is from two very good seminaries. But I do not consider myself a theologian even though I have a strong interest in the nature of theology and have spent my years living with it, pondering it, poking at it. However, my further studies in two other seminaries of theological conservatism have been in the area of the human being in his or her culture and the effects of that on life, faith, ministry, social relations, and understanding the Bible. Thus, my perspective on theology is different from that of most. For me, theology and human culture must come together in ministry. The Scriptures are inspired by God to help culture-bound human beings. We study the Bible intensely but give little to no attention to the culture-bound human beings whose lives it must touch and whose worldviews it must penetrate.

While I am amazed at what the authors of the theologies and commentaries in my library know and reveal about God and his Word, my concern is whether we have been trained to see this wealth of information from inside the original cultural frame of reference for accurate understanding. There is a danger in separating theology (information about God and his ways) from culture (socially controlled perception, values, and behavior) in the Bible. I am also concerned that what we do know is not penetrating our modern worldview. We are not seeing the contrast between the truth of God's Word and the relentless influence of our own culture for self-survival in each of us in the routines of everyday life. I think we have, for the most part, fallen short of making these connections.

So, this is not a book of theological research but an examination of our culture's influence on us as Christians and on Christianity and the potential damage it can do to our understanding of God and his Word. Once this is established, theological scholarship is most welcome in the battle with culture to help us close the gap it has caused between God and Christianity.

Throughout the discussion, I will make assertions that are often generalizations I assume the reader will understand. Just because you can find an instance contrary to a generalization does not negate it. It shows it is a generalization instead of something true of every last element in the category of reference. There are so many variables in the context of each example as to make talking without generalizations impossible. Of course, one cannot speak only in generalizations either. Some things are true of every single one of us.

I am asking you here to read on with an open mind. Allow these thoughts to percolate for a while, ease into them. Give them a chance to show some value before you decide they are not for you. Be ready for some odd feelings, but give them time. You may catch the urgency that has come over me these years. We must not continue with a faith shaped by culture and its solutions to self-survival. The things that God has revealed to us and his continued activity in our lives today are authentic and providential. We must not pretend that they are not, however unintentional that pretense is. We must wake up to the spiritual realities of God's world—the true nature of reality. I hope we do not go on as if we had never had this conversation.

These thoughts may seem distant at first. We may be much more comfortable with our assumption of Christianity as culture neutral, that it is the same everywhere, and that it should not be affected by the local context. We may fear that to step into this way of seeing God and the world is to pass a point of no return regarding the cultural solutions we have nurtured for our spiritual and emotional survival all our lives. That would be correct. You may not want it to be true of you. But the risk is worth the trouble, the journey worth the price, and the destination is the peace of which Jesus spoke: not the absence of the human experience, good and bad, but the presence of God.[14] Once we start on this journey, we will never be the same, and we will never go back.

All this does not mean there is no mystery. There is much we do not know. The journey demands a certain tolerance for this ambiguity. We will call this "trusting the person, providence, and movement of God in the world, past, present, and future." No philosophy, common sense, logic, or theory of men can explain it away. No theologian, as skillfully as

14. Matt 11:28–30.

he may have gathered what we can know about our God or as carefully as he may have arranged and ordered this precious knowledge, is capable of making the Bible tell us what we are not given to know. There is mystery, and this book does not try to ignore that. God is God beyond our information and imagination, provident beyond our cultural expectations and preferences, gracious to us beyond our understanding and deserts, wholly other and yet present with us, moving the world to its appointed destiny and allowing us a part in his plan.

I want us to consider the effects of our own culture on the way God sets before us. The experience includes crossing cultures to enter the world of the people we meet in the Bible and understanding what God revealed to them within their context about his way of seeing the world, coming to know him, and living in his will. We must then come to see what that means for us in our own cultural system. If we really follow Jesus, the result is that we will become deviants in our own culture as people in the Bible did in theirs if they followed Jesus. That is, we will deviate from many of the norms and central tendencies of our culture. We will still look like African Americans, Anglo-Americans, or Hispanic Americans, but the understandings, beliefs, and values motivating fundamental behavior will come from a different source. The question is whether we will leave the expected values of our culture behind or try to keep them with us as part of our new life in Christ. Will we deviate from the expectations in our culture for Christ?

CHAPTER 1

Discovering the Power of Culture

Since we will be talking a great deal about culture, and most of my audience does not actually know what that is, we need to start with a basic framework for the concept. I will define culture and unpackage it in detail in chapter 4, but here let me give a simple definition that should suit our purposes at this point. Culture is a human system for survival full of values, beliefs, information, and intuitive understandings through which we view and interpret our experience in the world. It causes the resulting behavior in each particular social context to seem normal. What people do not realize is that most of the culture for any group of people is invisible. We see the behavior it causes and only occasionally interact, somewhat superficially, with the unseen levels though they are always at work to shape that behavior. This frame of reference is far more critical than we realize for life to make sense.

Let me illustrate culture at work in producing behavior. Everything begins with foundational understandings, or assumptions, about reality. These result in beliefs about what is true in light of this assumed reality. These beliefs generate values about what is good or bad to do, and these values result in choices of behavior that become normal in each culture but differ from culture to culture. We'll use a generalization from Japanese culture. Many traditional Japanese *understand* and assume everyone else understands that the world is full of nature spirits called *kami*. This is the basis of Shinto. This understanding leads to a *belief* that these spirits must inhabit natural forms such as mountains or old trees, especially old ginkgo trees. When a *kami* lives in an old tree, that tree spirit is called a *kodama*. This belief generates a *value* on the importance of showing respect and even reverence for the *kodama* in old trees. This prevalent value results in *behaviors* considered *normal* for traditional Japanese, such as showing respect or bowing to old trees or avoiding them if one is in a hurry and cannot stop to pay homage.[1]

We usually list some twenty-five to thirty potential areas of difference between cultures. But when you consider the implications of these for many areas in life, some of them covering broad ranges of activity, we can easily count hundreds of such differences at work in a culture. Think of your own Western culture as different in nearly all of these areas of assumptions, beliefs, and values compared with non-Western cultures, including biblical cultures.[2] And then, we must remember that similar behavior between two cultures does not mean similar values behind it, and similar values may not result in the same behavior. When we see some similarity between cultures, we generally assume too much. People crossing cultures need to be aware of the influence of these systems on the people of the host culture and their endeavors with them. But the most significant barrier is not the influence of their culture on the people we encounter; it is that of our own on us. It prevents us from gaining a valuable understanding of the host people in their situation.

In addition to this difficulty, many of us do not see a deviation from the expected values of our culture as necessary but try to keep them and what God gives us in the same system. We shall see that this is called syncretism, and it can influence all we do. So, for example, if Western Christians have syncretized their individualism or values on achievement with biblical truth, their message to the world is compromised whether they are working in their own culture or another. There is also the issue of local applications. These are legitimate applications in a specific culture and are necessary for all Christians. God's revelation is absolute in every way, but within each culture, its application is relative to the meanings of behavior in that culture. To take the message from God to a second culture, we have to go back to what it meant to the original audience and take that message to our modern audience without adding to it the applications it has in our own culture. The host culture must then make their

---

1. See Ono, *Shinto* and Moore and Atherton, *Eternal Forests*.
2. See Appendix 1 for examples.

own applications of a verse like "husbands love your wives."[3] So, in effect, people of every culture have their own expression of Christianity. But, if we syncretize the Gospel with our own cultural values, letting them have free reign in our expression of Christianity, it is no longer the actual message God gave us. We have some serious work, some contextualization, to do in our own culture before we can offer the true message to another culture.

We can see the enormous obstacles we are up against if we do not consider the hidden influence of culture. But that may be just our problem. The difficulty we face as Americans is understanding that we have a culture and are under its subtle but persistent control. It is nearly inconceivable for us to think that there is an invisible force influencing our lives. We believe that we are in control of our own lives. That is the meaning of the word, individualist. We are each independent and make our own decisions. But it is not so. We do not notice our culture at work even though we see the world and understand our experiences through it. It is an interpretive grid that makes life make sense, a frame of reference for navigating our social, mental, and physical survival. As with a computer, this operating system in the background makes all the programs of our lives function "normally." It gives us the expectations we need in day-to-day life. In chapter 4, we will go into detail concerning this influence of culture.

We are products of God's providence. He has provided the way of salvation through Christ for us and the peace it gives us. But my own early experience and later observations of the church in the US, Europe, Central Africa, and South Korea reveal less of that peace than we would expect. The struggles of the early Corinthian church with cultural values and personal survival continue to invade the church. My study of this influence of culture over the years gives me a perspective that brings alarm to my nervous system. How often have we thwarted God's purposes in our lives and ministries by allowing cultural values to trump his purposes? Though he provides contentment when we trust him, we continue to seek emotional and social survival through cultural channels. After all this time, after all the excellent teachers we have had in our lives, all the impressive books in our libraries, all the experiences of God's grace, we still are not much farther along than we were at the beginning of the journey in this matter of understanding the powerful and insidious influence

3. Eph 5:25.

of our culture on our lives and faith. It is time we made progress. His providence controls our circumstances; we must allow loyalty to control our choices for him.

As I share my observations in this discussion with those in ministry, the struggle may begin with our theological attitudes. There are approaches to theology that overlook fundamental limitations brought to the task by insensitivity to the influence of self and culture on us and, therefore, our theology. In addition, care must be taken to avoid loyalty to one theologian without having an open mind to see what may be on the other side. Caution must be employed that loyalties to our theological group are not disguised as an attachment to the truth. Lastly, we need some theological modesty. C.S. Lewis reminds us, "One is sometimes (not often) glad not to be a great theologian; one might so easily mistake it for being a good Christian."[4] In addition to this danger, there is much we don't know.

We need openness to consider some hidden but powerful and undesirable cultural influences in our approach to God's Word, sensitivity in our approach to God himself, and some attention to the need for proper contextualization. Only with this humility at heart can we allow that God is beyond what our culture-driven, individualist, and informational efforts can establish on their own. We must begin by recognizing the one behind, and above, and in our human experience, at work in often imperceptible ways, yet often bounded in our perception by our limited, human, culture-shaped minds.

We cannot ignore this central issue. To misunderstand the role of culture in our task is to be off course. Our own cultural frame of reference cannot become a filter leaving out essential applications in the receptor culture. Nor can Western cultural absolutes be allowed to contaminate the message. It is time to loosen the grip of our culture on our perspectives of truth and help those in our ministries understand its powerful influence on us.

If we ignore the cultural frameworks of the biblical world, we will default to our own with little question as to their relevancy to the tasks of hermeneutics and theology. We ignore the acute relevance of the original culture in applying that biblical truth to everyday life, theirs and ours. From our modern cultural perspective, we end up trying to explain what God has and, even worse, what he has not given us to know. Our cultural

---

4. Lewis, *Reflections*, 66.

predisposition is to resolve ambiguity. Being from an objective, low-context, informational, logic-bound culture, it bothers us deeply. Problems demand solutions; questions require answers. We must have a social context for these answers and solutions to work. Not knowing another, we use our own. In the passages where culture matters, this approach inevitably shapes our theological conclusions. Can we change our course?

Information about God can too commonly be an end in itself. We are often in love with our theology the way it is, and we can be very defensive of our system. But if we give no heed, we may lock God in the prison of human, cultural, and theological preferences that do not let him speak for himself. Our love affair may be spiritual adultery. In addition to overlooking culture in our theology, should not our pastoral ministries experts realize the effect of this influence on ministry to the culture-bound people of our day?

If we were fish, I would be asking that we take time to consider the water we are in and its effects on our outlook and projections of reality on the world outside the little ponds we have made for ourselves. The authors and actors of the biblical text were surrounded by a cultural atmosphere in the same way but in an entirely different body of water. To keep our analogy, it is as dissimilar as saltwater is from fresh. Only a few fish can swim in both. Our own culture is as ordinary to us as the water is to the fish. This sense of normality makes us feel like there are no real differences in other ponds, or at least none worth our attention to their details. Water is water. The word for this attitude is ethnocentrism. We allow the norms and values of our own pond to become our expectations of those in any other pond. If we extend these understandings, and we do, to the social situations of the biblical text, we cause distortion. Nothing could be more foreign to that context than twenty-first-century Western cultural expectations.

If information about God becomes an end in itself, the result is a church founded on information and *local culture* instead of on the true nature of God and the realities of his lordship in our lives within our cultures. A church based on the realities of who he *is* and *his* purposes in the world that speaks to today's cultural values can transform people's worldview within their cultures. This gives them a new frame of reference for every event and circumstance, every choice, every action. These people become holistic and relevant examples of his grace, power, and providence in everyday life in their society. Humility, grace, love, and integrity begin to be the motives of behavior instead of self-survival and cultural and social expectations. This cultural self-awareness magnifies the differences between cultural absolutes and biblical absolutes so we can see them more clearly and choose God's intentions for us. We are not perfect at living out this new understanding, but we are changed and can never go back.

The syncretism of mixing cultural absolutes with biblical absolutes or allowing our information about God to limit his providence are issues that cloud our minds and confuse our experience. We may feel safe in our little group, but it creates unrest for the thinking person where Jesus says there should be rest. In our frustration, we look for what we need with more effort but still in the wrong places. More professionalism, glitz, glamour, or gimmicks may temporarily ward off apathy, but they will not bring us closer to God's desires for us, his presence in our lives, or trusting his providence. We are mostly unaware of the contradiction of our situation, but we have allowed barriers to come between God and us, and we don't know how to get through them.

I must repeat that, as Western individualists, we firmly believe that we are in control of our lives and decisions. We reject the thought that our culture may have more influence and control over us than we realize. Many Western people are not even sure that this thing called culture exists except in other countries. We consider ourselves independent of such a force in our lives as we "take control" of our circumstances and sometimes even the people around us.

It is time to wake up. There is a God, and he is not us. He revealed himself in particular cultural situations, and they are not ours. The absolute nature and mystery around our all-powerful God in his being, his providential ways, and his grace must always be in control beyond the solutions and security of our own culture. It will demand our humility and trust. It must overshadow all our thinking about him and life in this world.

We must remember that we, none of us, are totally objective. We all speak or write in a particular time and place, the historical and cultural significance of which must and will influence our work. That influence, of course, happens outside our awareness, so it is more powerful than we expect, and there is no check on it. One of the influences of our culture on us is to strongly prefer objective, once-for-all explanations. This gives us a sense of security, and we tend to treat this or that particular theology as static information for all times and situations. We do not realize that what has been included or omitted, stressed or passed over with slight mention were choices of human beings influenced by their times and context, not to mention their personal experience and denominational absolutes. So, holding on tightly to God's Word, let's read our theology cautiously and, seeking God's help, make an effort to understand him on his terms. An awareness of our culture's influence on us is the first step.

Our motives in theology are a central concern in the process. We are approaching God, not a book. A passion for God himself, knowing him on his terms, must precede our search for information about him if we are to understand his intended message. Methodology and information come second to this attitude that should cause us to want that information. We must allow our knowledge about God to lead us to an encounter with God himself, which, in turn, may change some things in our theology. It must remain our servant instead of our master. Humility and dependence on his Spirit must surround our efforts. Cultural self-awareness will be central to this instead of unconsciously following a path of cultural legalism—allowing our culture to be the standard frame of reference.

In the end, we must live what we have learned, or we have not learned it. When we, to use an Old Testament analogy, "eat the scroll," it becomes part of who we are. When we ingest Christ, he becomes part of us. " . . . unless you eat my flesh and drink my blood . . . ."[5] We have not met him if we are not changed by an encounter with God in our theologizing. It must not be merely a profession of faith, but an engagement of truth with the self, with life, with our cultural values and beliefs, with our very worldview.

It is also necessary to call our attention in this study to the multitude of principles and generalizations in the Bible. We Western folks do not like these very much because we prefer the efficiency, clarity, and logical order of succinct facts, propositions, and information. Our culture has pushed us to prefer the objective and concrete to the exclusion of broad, many-colored descriptions and movements of thought such that indirectness is troublesome and left to the occasional poet, musician, or artist. It is considered entertainment rather than daily fare. Though we might prefer a more direct and linear style, biblical and other non-Western cultures do not agree. These cultures generally do not lend themselves to the uniformity that makes for neat little packages, all the same size that stack nicely like we might prefer. They, instead, might appear to the casual observer

5. John 6:53–59.

as untidy and cluttered. People do not click into place or "snap to grid" in universal categories as we expect them to. Despite this, we can generalize. Within that "mess," there is a system of values, an order of beliefs, and an intuitive body of unconscious assumptions that guide people in their interpretation of their experience and cause their particular interaction with the world around them. Through the lens of this framework, their world makes sense to them. It is the script for their personal and social performance. To discover the system is to understand their behavior and communication much as they do—to enter their world with them. In addition to such a cultural framework are the people's particular experiences, personal preferences, and individual personalities.

It is natural that, in the non-Western context of the Bible, we should look for generalizations and principles as God's intention in many areas of his will for us, and they will be recurring throughout our discussion. They will keep us from stereotyping our behavioral response to God's interaction with those in the original context. For example, if God had one woman selected for Isaac to marry and made this known to Abraham's servant through a sign in her behavior for which he had asked,[6] it does not mean that is the only way a wife can ever be selected or that there is only one woman that can be God's choice for each man. In some instances, God's choice and direction for the pivotal people in his plan were quite specific, but this specificity was not the norm for everyone. We also know this is not a pattern for our lives by the absence of its teaching for us in the New Testament.

This brings up a reminder of a critical introductory concept. Christians in any culture will only generally line up in their God-honoring behavior. We cannot judge the behavior of one another with a black and white template. Each has different challenges in his or her life, and God is looking at the heart of the man or woman. In addition to these broader definitions of God's guidance, we must remember, as we said earlier, that the application of a principle will look different in each culture, given the fact that the meaning for behavior is particular to each culture. When Paul tells husbands to love their wives, he does not say precisely what they should do to accomplish that. What behavior shows the respect, consideration, loyalty, and care called for is specific to the culture. The things a man would have done to show his wife he loved her then and

---

6. Gen 24.

there will, most emphatically, not be what a husband should do here and now.

My years of experience with Central African Christians and later with Korean doctoral students, and numerous encounters with Native Americans have proven over and over that the definitions of what is obedience to God's Word are highly culturally defined and fit general categories of behavior. These are high-context cultures, and all of them include honest Christians with good understandings of God's ways. But traditional Central Africans, South Koreans, and Native Americans behave very differently than we do to honor God. What it means to be honest, respect your elders, love others, or worship God is particular to each culture we encounter, and the cultural contexts of the Bible are no exception. But the generalizations and principles we must follow are very real, and though they have wider boundaries than we may feel comfortable with, those boundaries are solid and unbending. I am not saying there are no direct and specific commands of God in the Bible, but principles are far more common and most of the explicit instructions leave what behavior is called for in obedience to each person in their culture and situation.

I might add one more thing in terms of my starting point in this chapter for what follows. It may seem to some like I am one of those who trash Western, specifically the US American culture. I am not. I have lived in two other cultures and can appreciate them, but I am attached to my own. It is as valid as any other cultural system and is better than many in terms of the opportunities and freedoms it affords. However, those freedoms can easily be abused and often are. It is a human culture, to be sure, and full of both good and bad, but in good times and bad, and in God's providence, it is my culture. It has served me and challenged me in my survival as a Christian, as all cultural systems do for believers. Some are undoubtedly better than others, given the differences in the moral and social integrity of the social systems and controlling authorities. But each has its weaknesses and faults as well—all are human.

Of course, the problem, once again, is how little we really understand our culture, how it works, and how it can control us with both its good and bad influences. Edward Hall tells us, "Culture hides much more than it reveals, and strangely enough what it hides, it hides most effectively from its own participants. It is a mold in which we all are cast, and it controls our daily lives in many unsuspected ways."[7] He goes on to say,

---

7. Hall, *Silent Language*, 29.

"[I]t is frequently the most obvious and taken-for-granted and therefore least studied aspects of culture that influence behavior in the deepest and most subtle ways."[8]

Thus, I sound the alarm for us to wake up to culture's subtle but powerful influence. It is not that culture, ours or anyone's, is always defective. But it *is* always at work. We are constantly influenced without our permission in ways we not only do not expect but in ways we think are normal and positive when they are not, manipulating Christians away from God instead of toward him. What we Western people fear most as individualists is ironically upon us, and, as Western Christians, we must not allow it to rule unchallenged.

Nowhere in this book am I telling us that we must give up our culture to live for Christ or understand another culture. I am saying, as William Howell says, that we *will* need to "[S]uspend judgment on observed behavior [from another culture] until we understand how to relate it to their context rather than our own."[9] That is, our culture is a highly inaccurate lexicon for the meaning of behavior in another. Ironically, we are blind to our values and yet use them to evaluate behavior and communication in another current or the early biblical culture. Let me also say that, though I am critical of our ignorance of culture, ours, or that of others, I am not talking about everyone in our culture. I am generalizing. But I *am* talking about the vast majority of us. The more influenced people are by their culture, the less inclined they will be to finish this book.

This is not a tirade against our culture, but of its blinding effects on us, not only in our explanation of God's intentions, but of its use to interpret behavior in other cultures, either modern or ancient. It highly affects our perception, and we are unaware of it. No culture is a standard for the interpretation or evaluation of another. The criteria for that lies only in God's Word. The actors and authors of the Bible are bound to circumstances and values, situations and events, relationships and activities, moral and ethical categories that are very different from ours. This harbors the potential for confusion and misinterpretation when we attribute our cultural frame of reference to them as we read the text.

I have often pondered our human limitations, which are of some magnitude in interpreting experience and communication in other contexts. We use filters that screen incoming sensory information of which

8. Hall, *Beyond Culture*, 17.

9. Adapted, William Howell, Univ. of Minnesota Class Lecture Notes. Date unknown.

we are not aware. Since our English language lends itself to our Western way of seeing the world and our thinking style, its usage reinforces this frame of reference. It is difficult to wrap it around non-Western cognitive domains, social values, thinking styles, and even vocabulary. Using English with our own cultural frame of reference, we see and hear what we expect to see and hear and miss what we do not expect. We also know that much communication is in nonverbal forms in any culture, perhaps as much as 80 percent,[10] and more so in non-Western, high-context cultures. Most of this is outside awareness for the speaker. Many of these forms, and much of the context that gives them meaning, are missing from written communication. When communication is cross-cultural, this difficulty is magnified. In addition to all of this, our experience, both personal and collective, gives us personal associations with the words of communication such that perfect communication is not possible even in one's own culture, let alone in a context where we do not share much, if any, of their life experience.

For example, we do not have any experience regarding the social dimensions of a collective, patrilineal society controlled by honor and shame; therefore, we do not understand the account of the nativity of Jesus in the same way early readers of the Gospels would have understood it. We do not realize the extent of the social disaster described in each turn of events. We have no basis for the empathy those early readers felt for Mary and Joseph. This is not a book on the many differences of this kind between our present culture and that of people in the New Testament period, but we will look at the nativity events in more detail in chapter 3 as an example to see some of these differences in an actual situation.

This issue of the effect of experience on meaning in communication has a lot to do with our understanding of the biblical text. Human experience can be difficult and, for some, can be a nearly impossible hurdle in understanding spiritual truth outside that human experience. We must step outside ourselves and our negative or positive experiences in life. This is because associations with experiences shape us and our perception of words in communication, therefore of God, in very powerful ways. It can be a wrenching struggle to see past the stormy emotional impact of negative events and experiences in our lives. This is a barrier to the pristine and quiet calm, the natural beauty of knowing God as he

10. See Hall, "Hidden Differences," 53.

has intended, as he presents himself to us, and to know his ways outside our own struggle for emotional survival. But with God, nothing is impossible. He is there, and he is waiting. There is peace on the other side of the raging rivers of life both now and hereafter.

A theme that God has impressed on me in his schoolroom of life will be recurrent throughout the discussion. It is an emphasis on the intrusion of self between God and us. The consequences are enormous. One of its results is that when we come to the Bible, we sometimes find what we want to see there, what must, needs, or ought to be there. It is a subtle pattern of the self in operation. But the self is not the only player in the game. While we may find what we already decided was there, our culture also has strong preferences for what should be there or how it should be understood. That particular preference is becoming not so subtle in our day. And then, there is the peer pressure from our group to take a particular view of the Scriptures. Beware of self and culture and your concerns for belonging that may be hiding in your hermeneutics. It is one of the ways we do not let God be God.

CHAPTER 2

WESTERN VALUES
AND MIDDLE EASTERN TEXTS

LET US BEGIN WITH THE cultural context of the biblical authors God used to reveal himself. God reveals himself and his will to us in the stories and events of people's lives over some 1500 years, the recording of which began some 3,500 years ago. With such a gap in time, we need to know what it was like for the average person in those situations. Social anthropologists in Christian circles have spent a great deal of time ascertaining the cultural system of the New Testament period that we want to emphasize. There are differences between all cultures, and we need to know what those are between that of the New Testament and our own Western culture in the US. Sometimes cultures are organized around major "themes," as Harry Triandis would call them.[1] Some of these themes can be so powerful in the culture that Richard Lewis refers to them as "black holes" describing such a value as "an undiscussable core belief of such intense gravity that it transcends or distorts any other beliefs, values, or set of principles that enter inside the spherical boundary of its gravitational field and absorbs, indeed swallows up, the precepts held by the "victim."[2] A cultural theme is a chief attribute of culture by which most other beliefs, attitudes, norms, and values are controlled and from which they emanate. Patrilineal descent, personal honor, purity, and tradition were

1. Triandis, *Individualism*, 43.
2. Lewis, *Cultural Imperative*, 115–27.

such values in the New Testament culture of the Bible that overshadowed all notions of social relations. Individualism, internal locus of control, and personal achievement are powerful themes of American culture today, coloring all our ideas of personal identity. Collectivism, saving face, and high-context are the overriding themes in Japan and shape Japanese life. Other values are connected to these and are just as important though subordinate to the main themes. We note that Western individualistic cultures are also low-context, monochronic, and optimistic, while biblical, traditional cultures are collective, high-context, and polychronic. The Japanese face-saving value is also connected to social hierarchy, harmony, and caution in relations. What does this mean for day-to-day life in these situations? It affects everything people do, say, or think. We want to consider here how these values affect the communication of information in the text of the Bible, given that God used the Jewish cultural frame of reference of those times.

Being a collective, relational, high-context, patrilineal, traditional culture,[3] Middle Eastern communication in biblical times was more for maintaining harmony and identity, changing attitudes, expressing feelings, articulating loyalties and allegiance, etc., than exchanging linear information, winning an argument, or stating a list of propositional truths.[4] Though God revealed an organization of life and worship in the Old Testament, the purpose was to foster a relationship of trust framed by a covenant intended to bless his people and the whole world. This emphasis on relationship and loyalty flows into the New Testament, where these social values are already substantial. So the message about Jesus was relational, but we read it with individualist's eyes.

This makes a difference in how we glean information from God's Word; much of it is revealed in relational ways. Who's who in terms of status, the rank of each status in the society, and the role of expected behavior for each class is significant in collective, hierarchical, patrilineal, honor and shame, patronage oriented cultures. An author could expect, and therefore assumed, that everyone in his readership knew the social rules that went with the system. Communication used a great deal of this context. It included information, but it flowed through social and

3. See Malina, "Understanding New Testament Persons," 41–61, and *The New Testament World*, 58–80.

4. This attitude toward communication is characteristic of traditional collective cultures. For high-context, see Hall, *Beyond Culture*, 105–28.

interpersonal networks that depended a great deal on relationships for its influence.

It was an oral society in most cases. This adds further differences in communication than for Western cultures. Oral societies have a tremendous ability to remember a great deal about relationships and social events over long periods. In addition to being oral, it was a collective society where people shared many values in a formal, traditional system. This made behavior much more predictable than in our informal, individualist societies in the West today. In this oral, collective context, there was no need to mention in a conversation a great many things that everyone already knew quite well. And since language is a code under the management and control of culture, it fits the requirements of those using it in terms of their needs, not ours. That is to say, an ancient language will not reflect our expectations of a useful code in our times. A language different from ours, even a modern one, being shaped by the culture and experience of its people, has the singular characteristic of simply being "not our own," and that makes a big difference in understanding the people who use it. Foreign language dictionaries can only take you so far if you want them to fit on your bookshelf. So, beware of entrusting too much meaning to lexicons. They can define a word and give you some general usage, but they cannot tell you what the person was thinking when they used it, what personal experience they associated with it, what non-verbal cues accompanied it, or who else was in the room when they said it.

It is not that reason or logic did not exist among people at that time and place; the reasoning was built more on concrete events, indirect communication, and relational logic than on abstract thought, word-level analysis, and rational logic. It is a style not at all uncommon in non-Western settings today. This is reflected in the accounts and teaching of the Scriptures, which make less use of didactic prose and much more of the high-context indirectness of poetry, wisdom, parables, songs, and the real-life narratives of people and events to get information to us. And where there are accounts of events, they are given to us in a high-context style that leaves considerable detail for the readers to supply from their shared values and experience. The reasons for this or that act or statement or song are in the cultural, personal, and historical context, and God intentionally uses it for his purposes. There we find these non-Western values at work: high-context communication, relational logic, patrilineal kinship granting social status through ancestry, collective society granting personal identity and worth, a polychronic lifestyle, an emphasis on purity, external locus of control, and honor and shame behavioral controls. In addition, these values are lived out in a non-industrial, non-technological ancient situation of dirt floors, clay pots, wineskins, millstones, and oil lamps.

The cultures of the biblical contexts served the purpose of survival for those people to the same extent as ours does for us. No one exists without culture, and every culture is crucial to its members. Is it any wonder that we assume the normalcy and exclusiveness of our own and hang on to it as tenaciously as they did theirs? The authors God chose for his Word were not an exception. They were, with God's help, being 100 percent relevant to their readers and listeners. They did not suspend their social frame of reference for the Western reader. Many of the truths given to us in the Bible were as new to that original cultural system as they are to ours, but that was the system God chose to use to reveal those truths to the world, and we will have to respect it. Though we can understand the major aspects of many passages in our translations, we miss the finer points of how the original readers related to this or that teaching, event, or experience without knowing the original context. God uses the author, who uses his human cultural system, to make himself known, reveal his purposes, and make possible and nurture a relationship with himself. The authors make applications of that knowledge and relationship to the needs and circumstances of their situation. We know there are implications for us in our situation, but we will need to step inside their world to get the fullest contextual meaning. Armed with the original understanding of that culture and a better understanding of our own, we can make relevant applications of God's Word in our own social situations. With all this at stake, we must give our attention to the nature of cultural systems.

At this point, do we need to be cultural anthropologists to read the Bible and understand God's message for us? No, but an understanding of the cultural influence on the text and on our interpretation of the text is as important as knowing the original languages, the use of exegesis, and grammatical-historical hermeneutics to that end. In fact, without this cultural understanding, the other tools we use to get at the meaning and intention of the text have limitations. A person does not need a master's degree in exegesis to read the Bible any more than a degree in intercultural studies. But teachers and pastors must have the skills these disciplines afford to be responsible guides for translating, understanding, and teaching the text. Fortunately, the Holy Spirit is at work in our hearts and minds, for we are inadequate in ourselves even with these skills. But that does not mean we should neglect the understanding of the role of culture needed in the process.

We must remember that when we give no attention to the influence of culture in the biblical context, our own will take over to make sense of what we see there. We will have to let God be God and prepare ourselves adequately for his work. In the end, our English translations will be more faithful to the original situation, and we can lead those of our ministries to a more authentic understanding and application of the Bible. No one escapes the influence of culture, not then, not now. Our goal is to let the text speak for itself in its own cultural context and then to apply it accurately in our own. We must come to know a good deal about both of them for this to happen.

On the other side of the issue of the cultural context of the Bible is our ignorance of the effects of our own culture. It obstructs us from seeing the full implications and, therefore, the accurate applications of Scripture in our lives today. This results in syncretistic, and therefore superficial, Christianity. Dealing with this syncretism should be at the heart of ministry in the church. We must learn to exegete the controlling system of our lives to accurately apply God's Word at the points of need. How much do you know about your own culture? Can you speak to its operational values and the beliefs of what is true or possible accurately from the biblical text? We know the people in our culture may be too materialistic or selfish, but these are symptomatic of causes deeply rooted in our system for survival, cultural absolutes assumed to be normal. Not seeing and therefore not speaking to the invasion of our cultural absolutes into our reading and application of Scripture has left a significant number of us in the category of popular Christianity.

Without understanding these differences, we cannot empathize with the author, his situation or audience, and their contextual frame of reference. We must not be drawn away too much by Paul's more Hellenistic style as he stepped outside Rabbinic Judaism to convince those of other cultural contexts of God's purposes. We can easily mistake those frames of reference for our own. We need to pay closer attention to this interference in our interpretation of his writings as well. This gap between them and us is not shrinking with more prolonged exposure to the Bible but growing with new developments in technology and social change. Though some Christian social anthropologists are shedding light on these differences in our day, they are not widely read. They have yet to substantially affect the typical pastor or Bible reader.

An analogy might be when a person reads letters sent between friends. The writer and recipient share a context and experience in some larger or smaller area of life. What is commonly known between them does not need recounting. It is similar to the conversation of a couple who have been married for fifty years, much information that gives the words their contextual meaning can be assumed between them. Correspondence between friends will often use analogies and terminology from shared experiences as would golfers, scientists, fishermen, or theology teachers. If the writer and recipient are from your culture, your era, and using your language, you can deduce a great deal of information about the subjects of the letters. Your general experience in life overlaps theirs to a great extent, even if the specific events or ideas discussed are not in your personal experience and not clearly defined for you. You will be able to make an educated guess about meanings or intentions in the letters by reading between the lines.

Now, remove the common cultural frame of reference and the common experience and language. Remove the similar time frame by thousands of years. You are still able to glean some information, but now the odds are against you. You may or may not come close to the author's intended meaning or the recipient's understanding. Most likely, you are using your own experience and frame of reference, thus changing the meaning to something understandable. But if you did some research into the historical situation, the motivating cultural beliefs and social values held at the time that would lie behind interests and concerns and be the cause of behavior, you would be much better off. If you then knew the everyday or recent historical experience shared by most of the people of the time, the meaning of relationships between those of that era, and learned the language so well you could converse freely in it with a native speaker, you would come much closer to the meaning the recipient would decode on their end of the written conversation.

I have spent a good many years training students how to cross cultures for ministry. A good portion of that training has to do with adaptation in the host culture. Stress in adjusting to a new cultural frame of reference is a chief cause of failure in the missionary endeavor. It comes from trying to exert our own cultural values and assumptions where they have no meaning or, worse, negative meaning. The system of the host culture and that of the Western missionaries are frequently so different that they experience culture shock even though both cultures are found in the twenty-first century. Yet we open the Bible and, though we are crossing into ancient cultures without considering the differences. Why is that? It is because we can use our own cultural frame of reference as the interpretive system, and the people in the stories, events, and conversations of that context more than two thousand years ago cannot defend themselves or resist our ethnocentric approach. We don't have to get used to their ways, understand their feelings, learn empathy for people in an entirely different system. We simply slip them into our system, albeit dressed in different clothes. They even speak our language in our translations, a language filled with our Western cultural expectations on time, logic, and rational analysis.[5] But as teachers of the Word in ministry, we cannot afford this luxury. To us, it is appointed to study the Word in its own context and teach our people what that means in ours. Without understanding how culture works, how cultures of the Bible influenced the people of those times and places, and how ours affects us today, we are extremely handicapped. We are practicing cultural legalism. We are not letting God be God.

When God revealed himself and his will to those of the times and places of the biblical scenes, he did not use someone else's language or style of communication, someone else's social system or experience. He deeply and meaningfully used what was there—what was relevant to those to whom he spoke: their language and culture-infused style of communication and thought, their emphasis on relationships rather than on logic or personal achievement, their shared experience, and their deep but shared cultural preferences. The information we, of a much later and Westernized cultural context, seek to glean from the text is buried in this Middle Eastern value system, steeped in strange social relations, saturated with traditions foreign to us, given to us in indirect communication instead of an organized lecture format. Jesus was an expert communicator in that context, and he seldom spoke directly in answer to a question.

Western communication is more about exchanging information and accumulating accurate knowledge, facts, and figures (except in politics) and seeing relationships between these whether we are talking to people or reading a book. When we come to a verse such as "The law was given through Moses; grace and truth came through Jesus Christ,"[6] we

---

5. Agar, *Language Shock*, 61–72.

6. John 1:17.

tend to emphasize the word truth because it is measurable and objective. We are weak on words like grace because they do not have clear defining limits. We are grateful for God's grace toward us, but we are uncomfortable showing grace to others. Such is our avoidance of uncertainty. As essential as our system is for our encounters, tasks, and survival, it is opposite of and therefore detrimental to an accurate understanding upon entering the world of the Bible.

We in the West still enjoy poetry, but it is because it is rare and unusual, and goes against our everyday, mundane style, that it is so striking in its descriptions. It sees objective life at a deeper level, getting beyond the information to its meaning for someone in a particular context—in their world. A common element in life is shown to have a significance we usually do not glean from its mention in the routines of life, in everyday vocabulary, in our busy schedule. But we do not expect to speak to someone or have them respond to us in poetic language at the gas station. We expect information there, even if it is small talk about the weather or the price of the gasoline. If a conversation is serious, we expect serious and concrete information. Even our sarcasm communicates something discrete, makes a point, and results in information. We take this expectation with us to the Bible. If we find poetry there, we expect it to give us quantifiable data and that each word has been used because it adds to that. In many places in the Bible, we examine the words as the brush strokes of an artist, but we often miss the character or meaning of the finished piece of which the brushstrokes are but vehicles. Only in their combination and relation to each other overall do they reveal the purpose of the artist.

We do not often expect poetry or a parable in the Bible to be giving us an experience, taking us out of our world, bringing us into contact or relation with God in such a way as to change who we are. We tend to suppress that kind of thinking with a more practical meaning that must be the intent, for, as Western people, we are pragmatic. We may indeed actually collect all the facts and miss the meaning in its context. Word-level analysis is not unimportant, but many passages demand understanding the words in combination and in context for the overall intent and meaning. In high context passages, words have meaning in the people using them, meaning that is shaped, not by a dictionary, but by their cultural situation and the associations their experience gives them for these words or symbols. I realize this does not create a good feeling for those who want concrete, quantitative information. Yes, I know we are not used to high-context communication. We don't have a good feel for the correct meaning when the style is indirect. We will have to learn more about the context to sort it out. But to make high-context expression into low-context information is to always miss the significance intended.

Generally, in studying the Bible, our cultural bent is to collect, analyze, and organize information into a theological category. Our cultural preferences are behind this process, for our style of thought and communication is as infused by culture as was the heart and mind of the Middle Eastern person. God is bringing something to us all that is not common to either culture, but he uses one of those cultures to do it. We must remember that Jesus was sent intentionally into that particular cultural context and used it willingly to reveal God to those people. The importance of the cultural frame of reference cannot be missed, or can it?

So, there we have it. Most people of the Western mindset are influenced along the lines of a desperate need for logic, order, and information, amplified by an unrelenting fear of ambiguity. Add to that our wholesale yet unconscious acceptance of individualism as the only way people can see themselves and then our internal locus of control in dealing with the variables around us to achieve desired status and feelings of worth. We are very monochronic, direct, and objective, which intensifies a high value on pragmatic efficiency. We belong to a competitive social system framed by the right to pursue personal happiness, the need for a unique personal identity based on our achievement, and freedom of speech. Our system has high values on time and tasks put to the service of personal achievement and efficiency, tied to the ideals of democracy and capitalism. It takes work and determination to arrive at the benefits the culture offers. Instead of being holistic in our view of life, our compartmental cognitive domains only house information specific to the partitions available in the culture. These compartments are sealed off from each other unless we intentionally join information from separate domains. This is a perfectly contradictory cultural frame of reference to biblical times and places, yet it is freely used as a sieve through which we strain our reading of this critically important text.

In the West, social order differences are yet another challenge. Our compartmental views of the secular and sacred set us apart from the ancient Middle East. The holistic pagan, Jewish, and early Christian worldviews of the biblical cultures had no such divisions of life. This affects Christians in our day more than we realize, as the weight of atheism pushes religion and traditional family to the margins in our society. In the biblical contexts, the social pillars of government, economics, education, religion, and family had more or less equal functional loads for maintaining the society. In our current situation, religion and family have been relegated to the personal domain and do not function as guiding components of society.[7] Each person is, in theory, free to practice religion or decide what a family is however they like without sanction, but these social elements are not to be an influence in the public domain. In non-Western cultures, including biblical situations, all the social pillars are connected in various ways, influencing each other in life's ordinary and extraordinary affairs. In addition, the holistic system was weighted with tradition. The inevitable results of these changes in the West are a disordered society so very different from the Bible. This is yet one more difference for us in coming to the text.

This holistic social frame of reference mentioned in the last paragraph is assumed by the biblical authors and Jesus himself. Situations contradictory to this assumption are called out by Jesus as when he speaks to the incongruity of calling him Lord but not following his teachings[8] or talking about the impossibility of having two masters.[9] One master will affect everything in life. Paul confronted the people of Galatia for accepting Christ only in part.[10] In Romans, he stresses the inability to live by two standards.[11] In the Bible, we are constantly confronted by the expectation of the highest level of commitment and the lowest level of compartmentalization. Loyalty and allegiance can only be in one direction, and it must engulf, even consume, all of life. It was simply a Middle-Eastern assumption.

These are generalizations, to be sure, but they reflect the central tendencies of modern Western culture, highly contrasted with the Jewish culture within which God revealed himself. There was undeniably plenty of immorality in pagan religions in the day, but Jewish families were strong. There was no public system of education to dismantle family values. No one dreamed of any kind of evolutionary alternative to God's creation of humankind and his ultimate moral standard. They were not hearing Jesus speak to them in that kind of atmosphere. They had their problems of hypocritical religious leadership and misinterpretation of

---

7. See Pearcey, *Total Truth*, 97–121.

8. Luke 6:43–49.

9. Matt 6:24.

10. Gal 1:6, 5:1–7.

11. Rom 6:15–18.

the Law and the Prophets, etc. Still, the society was not without moral and ethical boundaries kept in place by tradition, honor, and the Law of Moses. They had a holistic religious worldview that respected the spiritual universe even if imperfectly. This made a difference in how they saw the world around them and the associations they had for, and what they understood from Jesus' words. Later the apostles will deal with syncretism in the early churches as something unnatural. Satan does not delay in his deception to create distrust of God and his ways.

So, we must approach God's Word with a careful eye on how our own cultural frame of reference affects what we see there. While information is essential and order can be good, when reading the Bible, we may be forcing the Middle-Eastern document into a Western mold, systematizing it, and wringing logical information from holistic, high-context documents. We may be squeezing information from texts intended by God to create attitude. He means to form a kind of person. Though it takes information to do that, his intention is to nurture a relationship rather than establish a body of knowledge. The purpose of the text is often to emphasize being rather than knowing or doing and a holistic understanding of the true nature of reality from the perspective of which any culture should see itself. All this is expressed in Middle Eastern ways. This qualitative intention of God in his Word should change our more quantitative expectations and preferences as we examine it without an ethnocentric frame of reference but with open minds and hearts.

So, yes. Obviously, we are to know something; there is information in the Bible, but when information is given, it is for creating a special relationship and understanding the truth about it rather than accumulating data for abstract analysis and logical systemization. And at the core of that relationship is trust in his love and power that come together in his providence. It is pure loyalty to him and selfless sacrifice to his purposes with a relevant expression in each culture that must be the result.

So, the vocabulary used has the properties of information but often goes beyond this to craft ideas, create an impression, instill an attitude, describe a relationship that words, analyzed by themselves, do not do on their own, but only in their combination and inside the culture-infused intentions of the Middle Eastern mind. In short, it is only possible to get that information accurately if we use the cultural context and shared human experience from that particular time and place as the frame of reference. The message is coded using the key of that cultural system for meaning. We must use the same key for decoding it accurately, even if some basic things seem to be clear without this decoding. If the historical fact of the death of Christ and its significance lying in God's grace toward humankind is clear, does it follow that everything else about the expected results of faith in this event and its meaning, the difference it must make for people, is equally clear using our own culture as the codebook? Can the full significance of that event be explained in terms of only our value system? Is not the significance of a teaching outside the experience of both the original cultural system and our own still explained in terms of the framework for the meaning given to us in that original system?

Our Western approach cannot help but cause us to miss the intent of some of the revelation we have that is holistically intended to create an attachment to, to build a relationship of loyalty and trust with, and to create the humility of indebtedness for the grace of the creator God of the universe. It is warm logic (I did not say sentimental) instead of cold logic, relational instead of rational, analytical, and abstract. As good and essential as they are, our hermeneutics may often lean toward pressing logical information from texts that may not intend to provide it. We stack this information in orderly systems that we feel give us intellectual clarity, removing ambiguity but perhaps deflecting the intention of the text. We must later speak to theological systems in this potential distortion of meaning.

In many passages, we are told something about the true nature of reality concerning which every culture must adjust itself at the levels of assumptions, values, and beliefs. Poetry in the Psalms, maxims of wisdom in the Proverbs, exaltation in songs such as those of Moses, Zachariah, or Mary, discerning comments and parables of Jesus, historical accounts of real people behaving in real, high-context, human situations, etc., are creating a holistic impression of great importance to relationship, trust, and maintaining an attitude that should be shared. These genres seek to create attachment and loyalty to the God who cares and controls all through his providence. His faithfulness and lovingkindness are frequently the themes contrasted with the description of him as a consuming fire. They join us with those of thousands of years ago in foreign lands under the overarching providence of God for all of creation. The information comes together in the Middle Eastern mind to create an effect, an attitude, an acknowledgment of where the power and purpose of the universe resides and how, and how much, it affects our lives and elicits our spontaneous trust and worship.

So, it becomes evident that there is a pattern. There is an expected result of knowledge: a contextual, biblical theology with a purpose. All that is revealed of God in his Word must result in becoming a certain kind of person. It begins with information about him and his greatness, grace, plans, and providence. This must lead to the understanding of its implications for our lives in his plan. Part of this realization is that he desires and has provided for a relationship with himself, wholly through his grace and that this grace sets us free from the rule of self and our culture. The pieces fit together, which results in behavior that honors God, not perfect behavior, but that which intends to honor him—behavior out of loyalty to him.

Information is only a beginning point. If we stop at this level, we will know something about God, but we will not know God. Theology must lead somewhere. It must lead to an understanding of the grace extended and relationship and loyalty intended, the fear of the Lord, and the beginning of wisdom. This relationship, built on trust, does not have to and realizes it cannot know everything about God. And so, it comes with wonder and mystery but results in freedom from fear, legalism, selfish ambition, the need to control—the struggle for survival.[12] Our culture no longer has the upper hand and becomes our servant instead of our master. Instead of influencing the truth in our lives, culture is now being influenced by the truth. We are free at last to let God be God. We do not have to make him fit our definitions. When our intention to honor God is clear, we have contentment. We place our destiny in his hands. We have no need to save ourselves and can be content to live in responsible freedom and honor him with what he brings into our lives. We are no longer committed to Christianity but to God himself, no longer to practice outward religion without the inward realities. Worship is now " . . . in spirit and in truth."[13]

12. John 8:32.
13. John 4:23–24.

CHAPTER 3

AN EXAMPLE OF OUR CULTURE AT WORK IN INTERPRETATION

LET'S LOOK AT AN EXAMPLE of attributing our cultural frame of reference to the people and events in the Bible. For this, we will examine the narrative accounts of the events of the birth of Jesus. Here I illustrate not our cultural need to collect information, analyze it, organize it, but our bent to see and hear what we expect to see and hear and not notice what we don't expect in a "common" social event. What do we miss when we only use our own cultural frame of reference to interpret the world-changing events of Jesus' birth? The subtleties of the indirect, collective, patriarchal, honor-driven society will escape us if we do not look at the events and listen to the conversations through the culturally informed eyes and ears of those who were there.

There is also an example of the control of culture and personal preferences at work as filters in this story's Jewish leaders. These filters blinded their minds to God's ways and work in the world. They wanted something else; their theology dictated another course for God. He was not allowed to speak for himself, not allowed to be God.

All cultures have social structures or hierarchies. Even Western cultures have structures though they are founded on entirely different values than those of the biblical situation, such as individualism, personal achievement, and internal locus of control with a veneer of egalitarianism. In the New Testament world of the Gospels, there was a collective, patrilineal, religious, honor and shame social structure that would conform to the following hierarchical categories:

1. God in the Heavens, Ultimate Authority

2. King, Legal Social Authority (secular at this time)

3. Religious Leaders, Religious Social Authority

4. Jewish Male Population, naturally socially honorable through patrilineal ancestry going back to Abraham with Sons of David in a particular class.

5. Jewish Female Population for which there were three categories: There were married women with male offspring who were considered socially honorable. Married women without male offspring had family honor, but their personal honor was yet to be determined. For the unmarried, their social integrity was protected by the men in their families. They awaited the social honor they would inherit from a husband and giving male childbirth. The expected qualities for them were purity, privacy, and reserve.[1]

6. Widows, Orphans, Shepherds, Beggars. These were unintentionally shamed and therefore socially marginalized people unless the beggar was such because of physical deformity. See "Sinner" below. Honorable Jews were to have limited association with them on an as-needed basis only, using mediation if possible, even though they were Jews. They were among the most vulnerable, being without attachment to someone or some social position of honor.

7. Sinners, Tax Collectors, Deformed People, Samaritans, Gentiles. These were intentionally shamed people. Deformed people, the blind or lame, were in this category since they were considered to be that way because of their intentional sin or that of their parents or grandparents, even if it could not be identified. There was to be no association with any people in this list for honorable Jews. Even though many of these were Jews, they were ostracized from the group. They were untouchables and impure. Some were hated. Others were considered animals to be ignored. The healing of the blind man in John 9 is much more than a physical miracle. It moved him from this level to category four, which was very upsetting in the Jewish system of ascribed social status.

1. Plevnik, "Honor/Shame," 106–15.

These social categories, not including economic differences in status, are highly accentuated in the everyday events of Jewish life. They are front and center in the nativity events of Mary and Joseph as God turns this social structure on its head and brings King Jesus to his people through the back door. In Matthew 1 and Luke 2, we have the birth of Jesus recorded. In the narrative, the religious elite are blinded to the significance of the events by their pride and their theological preferences. Though we clearly get the import of God's act, we Western souls may be missing quite a bit of the real story. Our social structure and value system are so different, yet we use them to understand the events. In the story, we see a surprised and obedient Mary, an honorable but bewildered Joseph, and the century's greatest romance. In fact, we have so romanticized the story in our Western tradition that neither Mary nor Joseph would recognize it as *their* story. Their memories of those days were vivid the rest of their lives, not because of romantic events, but because of the agonizing social disaster God brought them through and the great privilege, through that suffering, of playing this unimaginable role in God's plan for the universe.

Mary and Joseph were not just ordinary Jews. Their hearts were different. The Judaism of the day, still under the law of Moses, included ritual behavior—acts of worship given to them by God to be carried out with a heart of humility, devotion, and loyalty. God was looking at the heart more than the behavior in these actions.[2] But in addition to God's way for the Jews, there was the terrible weight of the oral Torah on the backs of the people, generated by the Pharisees and accompanying Jewish religious leaders.[3] Both God's will and man's interpretation of it had to be followed to maintain one's honor and place in society. Most Jews would have been sensitive to the pressing need to be seen doing the endless ritual behavior of this oral Torah for the coveted honor and inclusion in the group it provided. The eyes of the leadership were upon them and their personal survival in a collective society hung in the balance. But some, we don't know how many in that day,[4] continued to obey God from the heart, carrying out his will in their natural behavior. God identifies

---

2. Samuel reminds Saul in 1 Sam 15:22–23, and God reminds Samuel in 16:6–7, that he looks on the heart instead of on outward activity or appearance. By the time of Malachi, though the sacrifices continued, the hearts of religious leaders in Israel were far from God, Mal 1–3.

3. Matt 16:6, 12; 23:1–7, 13–33.

4. In Elijah's day there were still seven thousand as in 1 Kgs 19:14–18.

some of them, calling them "upright" or "righteous." They were not perfect people, but they were pure in heart and mind and desired to honor God in their loyalty to him. The Gospels give several examples, and we meet some of these people in the story of Jesus' birth. Zechariah and Elizabeth, and Simeon and Anna are among them.[5] Mary's song reveals her heart for God, as does Joseph's decision to take Mary for his wife.[6] These were not ordinary, conventional, outwardly obedient Jews; these were God's devoted and trustworthy agents who had eyes to see and ears to hear, who played their parts faithfully in this world-changing event of God in history.

Joseph was a son of David. Though all honorable Jewish males valued their social position, Joseph carried the additional respect of his notable inclusion in the royal family. To discover Mary's pregnancy was a heavy blow for him that could only be resolved by a swift breaking off of the engagement. We don't know Joseph's emotions at the time, only that he was a righteous man—faithful to God and honorable among his people—and intended to do the right thing, however painful. Whether his decision to do it quietly was because of his honor-bound character or his love[7] for Mary is not clear to us, but duty was before him. Only a miracle could change the determination of this honorable Jew to do the morally and socially "right" thing. When the angel told Joseph to go through with the marriage, that her pregnancy was a miracle of God, he also told him not to be afraid. He was not to be anxious about the social ramifications, the total disaster of deserting his place among his people, disgracing his family's honor,[8] and falling from his own to the last rung of the social hierarchy. He trusts the angel of God, and in that moment of decision, his human frame of reference for meaning, worth, and identity is shattered. He does not know what is ahead for him any

---

5. Luke 1:5–6; 2:21–39.

6. Luke 1:46–55; Matt 1:19, 24.

7. This would not have been of the same romantic notions of our Western culture when we use the word. We would find the love between Asian and Middle-Eastern couples a bit distant as my experience with Africans, African Muslims, and Koreans has shown. For affection in the New Testament marriage see Malina, *New Testament World*, 141. It was a family agreement and a strong commitment of loyalty that had been betrayed in Joseph's eyes. The social situation gave him no option but to end the engagement.

8. Malina talks about New Testament marriage as the fusion of the honor of two families. See Malina, *New Testament World*, 51, 143.

more than Abram knew the details of his journey when God called him.[9] But he does know he will travel that road with shame in the eyes of his friends, his extended family, and his people. They will never forget. He has become an untouchable in a collective, relational society. There is no remedy; life is never to be the same again.

Mary was young and had the status of other unmarried Jewish women, her social integrity depending on the men in her family and awaiting her personal honor. She had the qualities of physical purity, social privacy, and personal reserve, which maintained this status, but beyond this, she was one of the pure in heart and, as such, was highly favored[10] and found favor with God.[11] But from the human viewpoint, it was to bring her social and personal anguish few have ever known as she stepped into God's will for her life. She may not have understood it at this point, but she will lose all standing among her people. Her family will feel the strongest disgrace.[12] Outside of Zechariah and Elizabeth, they will see only the human side of such an event. They will shun her. She has become an untouchable, and they will avoid being seen with her. Her offspring will be scarred with her "shame" as well.[13]

When it became public that she was with child before she and Joseph were married, she lost her status of purity and reserve, all social connection with any male in her family,[14] and fell to the bottom of the social order. She was branded a sinner of the deepest shame with whom there was no association for honorable people and for which there was no remedy in the society. Joseph had suffered the same fate. One day he is a preferred and respected member of a highly collective hierarchical society, the next, he has fallen to the miserable rank of an outsider, shunned by all "respectable" Jewish people. To associate with either of them was contamination. Though foreign to us, the social consequences are so intense only angels from God can quiet their anxious hearts.

---

9. Gen 12:1.

10. Luke 1:28.

11. Luke 1:30.

12. See Malina, *New Testament World*, 46–48, 144.

13. The Jewish leaders in that oral society of collective gossip were well aware that Joseph had married a pregnant woman. The guess was that the father was a Gentile, perhaps a Roman soldier. References to this "shame" are mentioned by them, sometimes indirectly, in John 8:19, 41b, 48.

14. See Malina, *New Testament World*, 140–45.

The months before the order of Caesar came for each to register in the town of his heritage for the census were miserable for Mary and Joseph.[15] The glances of people everywhere cut like knives and gossip, the usual punishment from the highly social collective community, banished them from all social circles. Though a male typically represented his family in such situations as a national census in the patrilineal society, Joseph took Mary with him in her fragile state. It was a rough donkey ride over dirt paths for some ninety miles to Bethlehem, the City of David. We simply cannot imagine how that was for her and the weight of the risk he took with her in that state with her firstborn. But likely, he was afraid for her health and safety, and there was no one he could trust to care for her in Nazareth.[16] To be without social connections in a collective society is to be exceptionally vulnerable. Another blow is that the socially oriented people of those times usually traveled in groups for safety and mutual help on such a journey, but there is no mention of that in their case. If Mary and Joseph were alone, it would have been a sad and dangerous journey. Social ramifications being what they were in that context, if they traveled with others, they would have been, at the least, stragglers, intentionally disregarded by a group as those who disgraced the royal line of David.

In the Middle East, the collective culture highly valued extended family and, being an oral culture with a patrilineal system, remembered family history remarkably well. Bethlehem was the hometown for the family of David. Mary and Joseph would have known and been known by many people there. This kinship orientation, so foreign to us, has great importance in a collective society. On the occasion of such a massive gathering, heart-felt social obligations would have been in full swing. Few cultures value hospitality and express it as lavishly as Middle Eastern, Asian, and Central African collective cultures. And no celebration of the extended family was as rich as a homecoming of this size. This extraordinary gathering was planned by God, arranged by Caesar in his providence to fulfill the prophecy.[17] The Messiah would be born under their noses, God would come to his people, but they would not notice.

Given Joseph's previous status, Mary would not have been unattended during the days she awaited and delivered her first child. But she

15. Luke 2:1–5.

16. See Bailey, *Jesus Through Middle Eastern Eyes*, 25.

17. Isa 7:14; 8:8, 10.

was, with no shelter or bed. This is unthinkable! Not having room for one of their sons of David and his new and fragile wife about to give birth showed the strongest contempt their society could muster. Friends or family would normally have given up their own beds without a thought. But it appears that no friends or family are offering that hospitality, so they applied at the inn. But it would have been a social and financial disaster for the Jewish owner to welcome such sinners into his establishment. There was no room there—for people like that.

It must have been the talk of the town. We notice no other people mentioned as overflow in the stable where they ended their search for a room.[18] The birth of a firstborn was the joyous occasion of all the friends and family within reach. It would have been obvious that all the family was intentionally avoiding them when Jesus was born. It is an agonizingly lonely event for those of a highly relational, collective culture. The birth of a firstborn son was the highest honor for a young woman and to be celebrated with joy. In collective societies where a person's identity is tied to the group along with any feelings of worth, Mary and Joseph have lost their social frame of reference, their place in the world. They were clinging to angels' messages, angels no one else saw or heard. Though we find it hard to imagine in our Western culture, few have paid a higher price to follow God's lead. Perhaps only Elizabeth, who knew the actual score of what was very dissonant music to the people around her, could understand the difficulties Mary and Joseph faced.

Though there are no family or Jewish friends to be found, God is at work in this greatest of historical events, and his ironic providence is not finished. If the Jewish leaders are blind from their high social and religious positions, and the people turn their heads, he will alert shepherds with whom they would never associate. As the unintentionally shamed of that world, these will pay homage to the King of all Kings. There was a time when Mary and Joseph themselves would have had grave concerns about such a visit, but angels are involved again, and they welcome the shepherds into the most intimate moment of their lives. An act that, if known, would have only made the social breach with their people more profound.

This introduction of shepherds did not invoke warm, sentimental feelings among the original readers of the Gospel. Malina and Rohrbaugh

---

18. Bailey offers an interesting alternative explanation in *Jesus*, 28–33.

explain a nuance lost in translation here that Westerners are unlikely to notice.

> These old [Western] traditions account for a certain idyllic quaintness in the use of the metaphor that does not square with the real view of shepherds in Jesus' day. By this time, actual shepherds were a despised occupational group. They were generally ranked with ass drivers, tanners, sailors, butchers, camel drivers, and other [dirty and] scorned occupations. Being away from home at night, they were unable to protect the honor of their women; hence, they were presumed to be dishonorable men. Often they were considered thieves because they grazed their flocks on other people's property.[19]

Shepherds were not clean and smelled like their animals. Luke is telling a story, this aspect of which was repulsive to his audience. They would get the true and shocking picture of what had happened. It would not be, in the least, socially acceptable to invite shepherds into your home, let alone offer them proximity to your newborn child. Again, it was unthinkable. But there is no one to complain or shun the shepherds. Everyone else was looking the other way. God has chosen Mary and Joseph from among their people for the greatest possible honor while their countrymen paint them with the greatest shame imaginable. He is putting the last first and the first last.

A few days later, no friends or family are mentioned as present at his circumcision and naming or at his presentation as the firstborn at the temple. Simeon was waiting to see the Messiah, and the Holy Spirit revealed to him that it would happen before he died. We notice that God is involved again in this recognition of his Son. Anna joined him in this. We notice that the arrival of the Messiah is only recognized by the righteous and devout.[20] God reveals his great act to those who already have eyes to see. The proud and self-righteous, those whose hope is in their own honor among their people, do not see. Jesus begins his life on earth not impressing those who thought they were righteous but, as he grew older, deeply affecting those who knew they were not.

The events of Jesus' birth seem to make quiet and humble scenes for us, but as we see, they were not that for Mary and Joseph. However, the real shame lies elsewhere. These activities were actually bringing

---

19. Malina and Rohrbaugh, *Social-Science Commentary,* 179.

20. Luke 2:25–38.

enormous disgrace on the Jewish leaders. The irony of this shame on these leading people in their social system is outside Western social understandings. And God is not finished dealing with their proud hearts. Before the child is two years old, he will alert pagan astrologers of the East, and they will come in full recognition of the arrival of the King of the Jews. Zoroastrian priests[21] whose veneration of the Christ child will come weighed down with costly gifts of Arabian currency[22] brought a great distance as they followed the God-miracle of the star. Pagans will bow while the proud religious elite and fellow Jews ignore the prophets and close their eyes to God's movement in their midst. These of high standing are shamed by the lowest of any people in their social categories as these pagan Gentiles, the dogs of the earth, give sacrificial homage to the long-awaited King.

Again, not long ago, neither Mary nor Joseph would have imagined the despair of losing all social standing or that they would welcome Gentile astrologers into their home to see and pay homage to their firstborn son. They are shunned by their people and family, but God's providence continues to work in this unique event in the history of the world, and they are at the center of it. The gifts received at the hands of these strange visitors will pay for their escape from Herod in an unplanned journey to Egypt. God will save them from the mad wrath of Herod that their countrymen will suffer, bringing the greatest of sorrows. It is a grim reminder of his protection when the angel of death passed over their families in Egypt, but this time the angel does not pass over. The faith of Jewish leadership in God's promised Messiah has been relegated to a theological box labeled "political deliverer." They have ignored much of his revelation to them and given reign to their social preferences. God is being held to these human expectations. Once their theology was in

---

21. "Magi" is a term, used since at least the 6th century BCE, to denote followers of Zoroastrianism or Zoroaster. The earliest known usage of the word Magi is in the trilingual inscription written by Darius the Great, known as the Behistun Inscription. See Zaehner, *Twilight of Zoroastrianism*, 163; Boyce, *A History of Zoroastrianism*, 10–11; Gershevitch, "Zoroaster's Own Contribution," 12–38; Beck, "Zoroaster, as perceived by the Greeks."

22. Although gold, frankincense, and myrrh were products of Arabia in that day, they were widely traded in the Middle East for the commodities Arabia lacked. The Arabian tribal, and later Muslim, caravans headed to the north and north-east out of Makka (Mecca) and Yathrib (Medina) through the Arabian Hijaz to Palestine, Syria, and Persia were commonplace. This was Arabian currency and worth even more outside Arabia.

place, they limited God's activity to the categories they had created. They no longer allowed God to be God. There is a certain danger in theology that becomes standard in a group. It has a numbing effect on the mind. God has been "figured out," and we may feel we know what he can and cannot do. He is no longer God, but God as we define him and his activities. Their suffering will be unimaginable and widespread, as the greatest act of God's grace is treated as nothing, even as a ridiculous tale spun by Mary to cover her tracks.

So, our romantic tradition leaves out a few very sensitive details in the nativity story. We, as individualists, cannot feel the dependence on the group that Mary and Joseph so desperately needed and lost. The irony of God in his providential movement in this patrilineal hierarchy is beyond our experience and opposite our resilient social preference for the achievement of the self-made person. The awful anxiety of shame is not in our repertoire of dreadful emotions, attached as we are to our innocence and guilt vantage point. Honor and duty are rare words in our vocabulary. We do not get our personal identity and feelings of worth from the group, but theirs, as first-century Jews, are deeply and irreparably injured by these events in their lives. All this would have crushed the ordinary Jew, but Mary and Joseph knew what only Zechariah and Elizabeth, the shepherds, Simeon and Anna, and the strange pagans knew about the event that carried them through an utterly impossible situation. Mary had been chosen, as Abram was, that through her, all the nations of the earth might be blessed with the possibility of knowing God's grace.

There is one last detail to mention that has to do with the economic situation in the context. Mary and Joseph, though of the line of David, were peasants in the land. Since most people managed life through subsistence farming or underpaid trades, they had no possibility of "getting ahead." The assumption of limited good gave them little hope of correcting their lack of means, so the vast majority remained poor. In our Western world of unlimited good and democratic egalitarianism combined with capitalism, very few people reading this book have any idea of what it means to be in generational poverty. There was wealth in that context, but it was in the hands of the few, those who oppressed the workers, foreclosed on land to settle debts through corrupt courts, and owned slaves.[23] Mary and Joseph were among the honest poor who were often God's choice for his plan in the world. Mary refers to her "humble state" and

---

23. See Kotter, *For the Least of These*, for an economist's insights into NT poverty.

how God has "lifted up the humble." She contrasts herself, "the hungry," with "the rich," whose advantages have gained them but emptiness.[24] In the irony of God's ways (ironic to us, but proper with God), he does not elect the rich controllers of the society to be part of or even know about his doings in this, the greatest of all events in human history.[25] But this does not mean Mary and Joseph, after the debilitating circumstances of Jesus' birth, will live happily ever after in terms of social or economic freedom. Their wealth will not be of this world. When they return to Nazareth, Joseph, and later Jesus himself, will work at a peasant's trade, honest but not lucrative. Their family's social rejection will be aggravated by dirt floors and cracked pottery, the village well as the center for gossip, and the poor health that accompanied poverty in that day.

That is the Christmas story. Now we must ask why God would do such a thing. Why bring his son into the world in such a fashion? We see he shamed the Jewish elite to the core of their self-made status, but there is more. Here again, our culture does not help us. We have little sensitivity for personal honor in the collective group and what it meant for survival in that situation. In bringing his son into the world with such great paradox, God makes it simply impossible for anyone of that context to follow this man for personal gain. All human honor has been stripped from the central participants.

In the days ahead, no one would gain personal status; there would be no glory, no social recognition, no celebrity status for those who chose to follow him. The proud would not be among them. It was all the opposite. It would take the full sacrifice of everything collective people hold dear for their social survival, identity, worth, and personal honor to follow Jesus. They would be less than nobodies among their own people; they would be untouchable. God is asking would-be followers to go all in, to risk everything in their trust of him. It would certainly call for genuine faith in the face of social disaster. Only those with eyes to see beyond themselves and their culture would step out. Jesus called it counting the cost. It was a price unknown in our Western society today. It would not be more notable when a social celebrity or a wealthy person followed Jesus. It would be the same sacrifice for all in that society. Former things would truly pass away. The lesson would be repeated at the end of his

---

24. Luke 1:48, 52–53.

25. Notice Paul's words to the church at Corinth later in 1 Cor 1:26–30.

ministry, like two bookends around his coming to earth, the irony of the creator God washing the feet of men. So must we all.

From our Western cultural viewpoint, we see the nativity story as a romantic adventure. Joseph is the ultimate romantic hero, and Mary finds her prince lost in his love for her. They should live happily ever after, but instead, they were trusting God in the face of desperate personal struggle. And the irony of God in the person of Jesus did not stop with his birth. To follow Jesus later would be seen as following a homeless man with a dark and questionable past, making outrageous claims about himself, having a reputation for peculiar behavior, and no prospects for advancement, a loner of no notice to "successful" people. It would be to identify with an untouchable. To unbelievers of that day, he was one more cultic leader claiming to be the Messiah, one that would be publicly shamed and executed as a criminal for his outrageous claims. If we could get the story through their eyes, we would see the oxymoron of "Christian celebrity." We who trust Christ have gone through the narrow gate,[26] taken the road "less traveled by."[27] If we are looking for self-advancement in this, we are on the wrong road. Every caution must be taken lest we mistake Christianity as an opportunity for personal achievement and the attainment of social recognition, identity, and worth. Authentic personal identity and feelings of worth will be found, must only be sought, in our relationship with God himself and those he brings into our lives.

This is the story of God entering his creation, stooping down to the most humble human level to rescue humankind from themselves and the ruin they have brought upon all of creation. He goes around the proud elite and elects the humble. Taking them to the very bottom of the human social order, he allows them to become despised in the eyes of the world to bring about the most significant event in the history of the world. God's ways do not always look like they could be God's. Only eyes of faith can see his movement. The proud never look in that direction. They resent this intrusion into their world and hate the one God sent until one day they can finally rid themselves of him, and the seed dies. But, to their dismay, that seed burst through the soil of death with life and, through that event, God touches the untouchable everywhere and brings forgiveness, new life, hope, meaning, worth, and identity in Christ that is available to all. While he elects particular actors in his story, he brings the hope of

26. Matt 7:13–14.

27. Frost, "Road not Taken," 72.

salvation to all who choose it. Collective people will have to step outside their group. Individualists will have to step outside their achievement. All will have to bow low to enter by the narrow gate, but they who enter will forever thank him for the gate.

The Christmas story shows us God's grace beyond what we could imagine on our own. That grace is ignored at the time of Jesus' birth, even by the religious leaders. God's grace is being treated as nothing again in our day. As the Western world continues to spiral down its post-Christian trajectory, honest and humble believers, the Marys and Josephs, the Simeons and Annas of the society, will be harder to find. Our proud individualist culture sets itself up against him, still ridiculing his grace. It hangs on even for many who claim Christ, causing a gap between God and Christianity. The majority simply will not allow God to be God. But still, those few who enter the narrow gate, though they may not look like much in the world's eyes, walk on. They know something; they see something others do not. They are willing to pay the price to have the vast riches of God's grace in their lives now and for eternity.

CHAPTER 4

WESTERN CULTURE
AS A SYSTEM FOR SURVIVAL

WE HAVE SEEN THAT THE biblical world was very different from our own today. This affects the natural meaning and intention of the communication and events in the Bible for the people then and our interpretations of them in the West today. As we have been saying, these differences are deeper and more complex than just time and place. The primary differences are the cultural context and personal experience of people at that time. To forget that is to miss much of the significance of the message enrobed in that cultural system. So, how does culture work?

I often talk about culture in the classroom as a system of solutions to the common human problems of survival. These common problems have to do with protection from the elements and enemies, procurement of food and water, and how to relate to people in the group in terms of love, intimacy, friendship, and respect. They include maintaining social status, having feelings of belonging and well-being, and attaining what one cannot produce for oneself. People need to achieve self-awareness and feelings of security, meaning, and purpose for life. Finally, they need to relate to the supernatural to stay right with it. But this commonality of problems is deceptive. The universal and desperate need for survival causes us to assume too much similarity between other cultural groups and our own. Each system of solutions is particular among its people. That difference is not from choosing different solutions from a standard list of options for all peoples; it is based on differences in worldviews

53

which generate different understandings of what is real, different beliefs about what is then true or possible, and then different values on what is therefore important or necessary to do about the problems for survival people face.[1] All this results in the various behaviors we see from culture to culture. Each system is then transferred to the younger generation, so it is perpetuated as the legitimate and default operating system for shared behavior—the activities that will fulfill its interpretation of personal and social survival.

Culture is powerful, and most of it is invisible. Yet, it is the frame of reference through which all people interpret their experience, determine meaning and significance, and on which they depend far more than they realize for their physical, emotional, rational, and social survival. In each new generation, the system begins as moldable clay for children. It slowly hardens into granite by the late teens, becoming an unmovable foundation upon which adults build and live their lives, interpret their experiences, and survive in their world. It is easy to see the importance of culture. It serves an extremely useful, necessary, and vital purpose. People cannot exist without it. As Clifford Geertz explains, "People unmodified by the culture of particular places do not in fact exist, have never existed, and could not in the nature of things ever exist."[2] But, despite how instrumental it is, we are unaware of culture's presence and power. We know how things ought to be and how they ought to work, and we ignore the stranglehold of this feeling on our approach to other cultures, including those in the context of God's Word.

It is a largely unknown field of study for Western people, and what is unfamiliar is often threatening. You may not be quite at ease with these thoughts yet, but allow me to talk about how culture works and see if you can begin to appreciate its influence on you and me in our lives and ministries. When we see culture's effects on all we do and say, we will begin to grasp its impact on the people in the Bible, on its inspired authors, and on our reading of it today.

I want to begin with a model of the components and functions at work in any culture and then get to a working definition. As we have seen, there are various elements to culture. There is the understanding of the boundaries of reality, what is real and what is not possibly real. In intercultural studies, we call this our worldview. We belong to a cultural

1. This compartmentalization of the parts of culture was first delineated by Kwast, "Understanding Culture," 397–99.

2. Geertz, *Interpretation of Cultures*, 35.

group or sub-group that assumes or understands these realities as we do; for whom to question them borders on insanity. Paul Hiebert says it is the "fundamental cognitive, affective, and evaluative presuppositions a group of people makes about the nature of things, and which they use to order their lives . . . maps of reality . . . thought to be true, desirable, and moral by a community of people."[3] He would refer to it as "deep culture" as opposed to the visible aspects of culture we can see, which he calls "surface culture."[4] Edward Hall adds details of the depth and resilience of this aspect of culture:

> There is an underlying, hidden level of culture that is highly patterned—a set of unspoken, implicit rules of behavior and thought that controls everything we do. This hidden cultural grammar defines the way people view the world, determine their values, and establish the basic tempo and rhythms of life . . . . One of the principal characteristics of PL [primary level] culture is that it is particularly resistant to manipulative attempts to change it from the outside. The rules may be violated or bent, but people are fully aware that something wrong has occurred. In the meantime, the rules remain intact and change according to an internal dynamic all their own."[5]

Examples of worldview understandings might be a round earth, the force of gravity, God's existence and creation of the world, human pleasure is preferable to pain, and general ideas about the meaning and purposes of life. But they might as easily include the assumption that the world is full of nature and ancestral spirits, the suspicion of the evil eye, the power of witchcraft and magic, or the acceptance of limited good in the next culture.

People of every culture bow to something greater than themselves and attempt to stay right with the supernatural. Even if the answer is to deny the supernatural exists, they will bow to that materialistic explanation of the universe and defend it with tenacity. They might bow to a philosophy that man himself is the supreme being and has the final word on morality or to nature as the decisive force in life. People insist the view of their group must be true, as the alternatives are unthinkable. Sometimes Christians seem to bow to God on the outside, but they are kneeling to the self on the inside. These are issues of worldview. These

---

3. Hiebert, *Transforming Worldviews*, 25–26.

4. Hiebert, *Transforming Worldviews*, 33, 316.

5. Hall, *Dance of Life*, 6–7.

understandings are at the heart of culture and give people a version of meaning, purpose, normality, and moral conscience in life. They are the deeper understandings upon which the rest of the culture or subculture is constructed.

Then there is the part of our understanding of what is true or possible within those worldview boundaries. These may be referred to as beliefs. They vary a little more for people of the same group than do the worldview understandings. They can range from ideas that humans cause climate change, or all people have a right to pursue personal happiness, to views that God is active in the universe, or that legalism is the opposite of godliness. Beliefs legitimize behavior and are based on the worldview. They may legitimize the espousal of views from the existence of UFOs and Martians to the conviction that church steeples keep evil spirits away (a belief once explained to me by an elderly woman in Central Africa). Beliefs are not all true, as you can see by the contradictions that can exist between them, but they are just as powerful in people's lives, whether they are true or false. Satan uses false worldviews and beliefs to blind the minds of people.[6]

Another part of culture deals with attitudes of value we give to whatever beliefs tell us is true or possible. Given our belief that humankind is endowed with the ability to reason and appreciate, we say education is important, which is the expression of a value. Given what they believe is true about the importance of harmony in relationships, Asians feel the indirectness and ambiguity of their high-context style are more considerate than directness and objective clarity in communication. Given our Western belief that people have personal rights based on our espousal of individualism, we may attribute importance, efficiency, and fundamental necessity to self-reliance and self-assertion, which become highly valuable in our need for social survival. You can see that adjectives are indicators of values we hold. When we say an item, behavior, or concept is important, efficient, beautiful, kind, or admirable, we express values concerning these entities and the attitudes attached to those values. These are called instrumental values because they are means of achieving goals or ideals in life called terminal values. Of course, these values can be negative or positive and have intensity and relevance given each person's personality and experience in their culture.[7] Values describe the

6. 2 Cor 4:3–4.

7. Rokeach, *Understanding*, 1–11.

reasons or causes of behavior and are based on beliefs about what is true or possible.

These parts or categories of culture become a frame of reference for interpreting our experience, selecting appropriate behavior, and attributing meaning to life and communication within our cultural group or subgroup. We have now mentioned the fourth part of a culture based on these worldview understandings, beliefs, and values, the resulting behavior. It is the part we can see and from which we can deduce if we are from the same cultural system, certain motivations for this or that behavior, and the meaning of this or that expression. Though this is accomplished to a very useful extent in our own culture or subculture, we are at a real disadvantage when the frame of reference behind the behavior does not come from our group. It becomes difficult to interpret the meaning of the behavior or communication and its cause or value for the people we observe. Causes for behavior come from understandings, beliefs, and values that are below the surface. Only behavior based on these can be observed. Figure 4.1 gives us a model of the visible and invisible parts of culture.

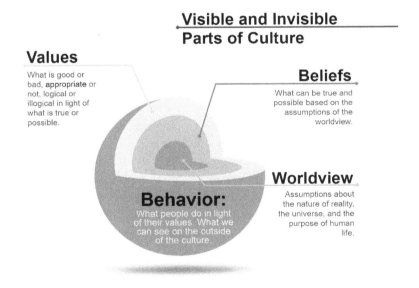

Figure 4.1. The Visible and Invisible Parts of Culture.

In this simple model, each layer is supported by the one below it, and all rest on the core of the worldview. What people value is based on their beliefs of what is true or possible, and what is true or possible is based on what is assumed that reality permits or reveals. People in every culture live their lives based on their cultural system but are hardly aware there is a system at all. It is a very natural, intuitive system and the only one the members know for surviving in social, physical, mental, and emotional life.

I mentioned that this is a simple model of culture. There are extended descriptions at each level that define what is in that category and how it functions.[8] We will get to this complexity more as we go along. This model is good at showing the basis each level rests on that finally results in behavior. Other models are better at delineating cause and effect, as in the tree model in figure 4.2, or the flow of development of behavior that is finally the result.[9] I have often used a definition of culture by Louis Luzbetek to add detail to the models. I have enumerated and emphasized its parts here:

> By viewing a way of life as a society's design for living, we mean that culture is (1) a *plan* (2) consisting of a set of *norms, standards*, and associated *notions* and *beliefs* (3) for *coping* with the various demands of life, (4) *shared* by a social group, (5) *learned* by the individual from the society, and (6) organized into a *dynamic* (7) *system* of *control*.[10]

Luzbetak's terminology is a little different from what we mentioned above. He speaks of culture as being shared, learned, organized, dynamic, and a system of control. This is an accurate definition, and each part of it is a crucial element. I am, in this book, emphasizing culture as a system of control as he has it. We can attempt a more succinct definition as follows: culture is a learned and shared, integrated system of values, beliefs, and assumptions (real or unreal) for understanding, coping with, and relating to the world, which results in behavior that is characteristic of a group of people. Still, if one thinks of norms as perceptions of reality everyone in the group should understand, standards and notions as explicit and implicit values, and finally, beliefs as we defined them; Luzbetak's definition here fits our description and adds some important aspects to it.

The system tethers people to their group's social values, beliefs, and understandings, like the sun's gravity, holds the planets in their orbits.

8. Appendix 1 gives three cultural value profiles for comparison.

9. See Appendix 2.

10. Luzbetak, *Church and Cultures*, 156.

Even though some planets are farther away from the sun, move at different speeds, and have varying characteristics, they remain in the system. People at a distance from the norms of the cultural system are considered deviant; they deviate from the central tendencies of the culture in various ways. There may be more differences in values, some less in beliefs, and even less in understandings and assumptions. The difference between planets and people in their systems is that people can choose to leave. The deviant person can leave the system or remain in it if they choose to do so. People deviating from the norms of society more often choose to stay in it and try to change it to meet their personal needs and preferences.

We differentiate between good and bad members of a society by how well they exemplify its values. Americans walk their dogs, most Central Africans kick their dogs,[11] the Islamic world hates dogs, and China may have just held its last dog meat festival. What behavior is normal is decided by each cultural system. The values and behavior of other systems are considered aberrant. These feelings of normality can and do change over time since cultures are dynamic, but the change is not even throughout the culture, such that the transition to a new norm is often tumultuous.

The deceptive thing about culture is its power to control people in their social environments. Western people do not think this is possible because, as individualists, we believe we control our lives and manage our own decisions. Of course, much of the force culture applies is necessary for the group to survive and perhaps flourish, but here I want to talk about the influence of culture outside God's plan for us that puts a gap between him and us. Our culture makes demands that we, without much thought, obey and think are important because *we* decided they are. But actually, it is our culture that tells us they are important. We actually defend the very things that control us, good or bad, while maintaining a sturdy value on our independence. Certain unbiblical cultural absolutes we cling to for our survival remain what we think are essential values for us even after God has shown us *his* way to contentment and wellbeing.

For example, Western culture tells us it is imperative to exhibit confident self-assertion, control what we can in our environment, and compete when necessary to attain what we need or want. This is individualism. It leaves us on our own to achieve our survival. The approach is hardwired into us by our culture to feel natural and even to be considered

---

11. This is similar to the biblical view of dogs being vicious and dirty scavengers. They are put in a category with wild pigs in Matt 7:6. The ungodly are often referred to as dogs, Phil 3:2; Rev 22:15.

virtuous. The self-made man or woman is celebrated. The intense expression of these values gives the appearance of self-confidence. However, insecurities will surface in unpredictable ways if the cultural bases for these carefully constructed but fragile feelings of achievement, identity, and worth are questioned or threatened. In my experience, that is what discussions about culture in the West tend to do. Most people simply assume it is the only way to do life and consider it shocking to question the system. As different as God's plan is for us in Christ, many Christians do not let go of these means to achieve personal survival. The remnants of these negative cultural values are damaging to their faith and the church. This is the danger of syncretism.

Cultures have huge, though sometimes subtle, differences between them. Though there are universal categories of human behavior that find their way into every cultural system, the expression and meaning of behavior in any category and its motivations are derived entirely from within that particular culture. For example, sorrow can be found in any culture. However, the reasons for it, the occasions that allow it, and the appropriate manner of its expression are only known to the insiders, even if there are some parallels with other cultures. Behaviors such as eating are universal, but what people eat, how they eat, with whom they eat, when they eat, and where they eat are particularities that are unique to each culture.

My years in Central Africa exposed me to differences in these categories, including subtle reasons for why people eat. Relationships are more a part of the reason than hunger. This makes it nearly impossible for traditional Central Africans to eat alone. All behavior has meaning in a particular culture because it comes from its reservoir understandings, beliefs, and values. There is logic; it makes sense to them, but it is also specific to them.

The process is like a tree that bears leaves and fruit from the nutrients it gets from deep in the soil through its roots. With culture, as we have mentioned, the deeper levels of cause for behavior are invisible to the eye. A tree makes a good model for conceptualizing the many aspects and functions of cultural systems. See Figure 4.2.

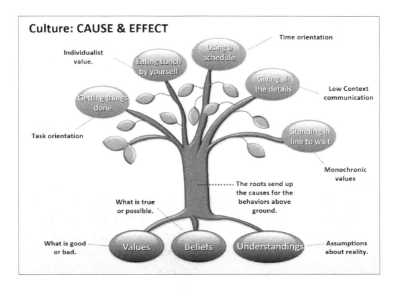

Figure 4.2. Aspects and Functions of Culture.

Cultures, like trees, pass on their DNA to each new generation. But each seed dropped into fertile soil has what it will need to germinate and grow in the elements, just as each human culture passes on the guidelines, rules, and traditions for the survival of its members in the world. Each new human generation has its own perspective on the system passed down and may be very different on the edges, deviating from traditional patterns in behavior but maintaining the essentials that sustain the group to withstand the threats to its existence. Sowell has given a good description of this reproductive aspect of culture:

> Cultures exist to serve the vital, practical requirements of human life—to structure a society so as to perpetuate the species, to pass on the hard-learned knowledge and experience of generations past and centuries past to the young and inexperienced in order to spare the next generation the costly and dangerous process of learning everything all over again from scratch through trial and error—including fatal errors.[12]

The fundamental problem with culture is that the system is human, and human civilizations tend to disintegrate over time as the processes weaken. Just as trees have a longer or shorter life span affected by disease, harsh weather, or the atrophy of old age, cultures also face survival

12. Sowell, "Cultural Diversity," 403.

problems. This happens when the social units in place to transmit cultural information for survival, such as the family, religion, and education, become less functional. These institutions would ordinarily serve to maintain healthy values, beliefs, and understandings from the past that have yielded the essentials for survival and help develop new values as the environment of the culture changes. The breakdown of the process of these institutions in maintaining or reproducing past moral standards and social responsibility in the young causes social disintegration. The institutions can become dysfunctional and destructive in individualist societies. The young are as easily infected by dangerous ideas as functional ones by social or ideological authorities. The next generation is then much less prepared to contribute to the survival of the existing society. Though there is always room for improvement, the young may be led to new "solutions" not yet proven to sustain the society.

The natural environment gives a tree health, or it destroys that health. In the same way, the social environment affects the health of a society. As we have said, social diseases can cause the loss of integrity, ethical standards, and moral bearing. These cause disintegration of the vital tissues and organs of beliefs, values, and understandings of reality. The resulting deformed fruit of dysfunctional behavior ultimately leads to fragmentation and eventual collapse. The disintegration of the social units of family, education, and religion that generally pass on the health of the society often happens when cultures go through stages of what we call "development" that, as we saw in chapter 2, put family and religion in the private or personal sector of life and put education, government, and economics in the public sector to lead the society. These changes actually work against the organic system for survival. As God and his ways are pushed to the margins, the gods of human ideologies take his place.

There are different kinds of trees as there are different cultures, and trees go through growth and change as cultures do. Sometimes a tree must bend to get enough sun, and sometimes a culture must adapt to new technology, economic change, or new modes of protection from enemies or diseases.[13] Mechanisms for maintenance and change essential to survival must be built into social systems, but we humans seldom understand ourselves or our cultures. The frail integrity of the members of the society and their obliviousness to culture and how it works are the

---

13. I have used the model of a tree for a long time, but its use was recently developed in greater detail by Hedinger, Steele, and Wells, "The Culture Tree".

weak links. Societies cease flourishing as virtuous people wane in their influence.

We have shown how the tree model incorporates causes outside the tree for its growth and survival, such as soil nutrients, sun, and rain. These are analogous to God's provisions for the survival and flourishing of humankind. Whenever these provisions are blocked or compromised, the leaves wilt, and the tree dies. God's Word gives us numerous universals concerning the problems of human nature. The most obvious are the problems of ignoring his existence, the need for salvation, or rejecting his will. But before we write up that tract using propositional truths to point this out to a particular group in need, we might start by finding out their cultural definitions of social sins, personal transgressions, and offenses against the gods. These have been passed on in that context for generations in the "seeds of the tree."

The categories of social offenses are there, but what people's conscience tells them is morally or ethically wrong will differ, often to a great degree, from the conception of another group or culture. To start out without this knowledge is to be blindsided eventually by their misunderstanding of your message. Sin is universal, but how people conceive of wrongdoing is culturally defined. Their ideas about social and personal wrongs fit their cultural system for survival. There is no God to sin against in Buddhism. The only result of not meeting social standards of right and wrong in Hinduism is bad karma, and no one else can help you with it. Robert Priest shows the moral conscience of the Aguaruna of Peru to be opposite our Western moral conscience regarding social evils.[14] The universal category of anti-social or immoral behavior still exists, but we will have to start from where they are to take them where they have never been. This is one of the most important aspects of biblical ministry, even in one's own culture. The issue of conscience is one of the areas where the message of Christianity must penetrate the existing worldview and beliefs of the culture. Not understanding the powerful influence of culture on conscience will make conversations about the Gospel with unbelievers irrelevant.

Culture always affects our expression of Christianity when we come to Christ. To trust God is to leave a human system for survival to accept his way in our lives. This is not easy and is a process rather than an event. The question is how thorough the process will be. It depends on

14. Priest, "Experience-Near Theologizing," 186–93.

discipleship and spiritual formation in the body of Christ and on our surrender of the elements in the old system on which we have relied for a long time. While it is essential that our trust in God be expressed in our lives in ways relevant to the people in our culture, it is crucial that we do not hang on to old ways of survival that conflict with God's ways. Our culture is the vehicle for the expression of loyalty and obedience to Christ to be understandable in the world around us. However, it can also be a subtle adversary making many things seem right to us that actually come between God and us—working against our trust in God alone.

Typical legalism is an example of how a cultural frame of reference influences our faith's biblical frame of reference. Western cultures have a relatively high value on avoiding ambiguity. We express this in low context communication that is objective, direct, and detailed. This is augmented by a monochronic lifestyle and a preference for objectivity. We are uncomfortable with unresolved problems, have an urgency or crisis orientation about the future, and prefer rational logic. Our inclination for organization is seen in our highly compartmental way of thinking. Together, these partialities make us prefer succinct, propositional information and systematic truth in the Bible in clear categories. This preference for clarity is sometimes expressed in Christianity by a legalistic approach to the Bible to avoid ambiguity and enhance feelings of certainty and security. In syncretizing cultural values on order and clarity with biblical teaching, some make lists of universal dos and don'ts to define the boundaries of behavior acceptable to God and sanctions for those who step outside the box. Similar to the Oral Torah of the Pharisees in the New Testament, this attitude separates them from the balance of grace and truth that came to us in Jesus Christ.[15]

Prescribed behavior in such a group is thought to be directly from God's Word, but actually, it is ruled by their cultural frame of reference— their attachment to their categorical, organized, black and white view of the world. Biblical interpretation for them would follow the hermeneutic of the plain meaning. They do not know that by "plain," they really mean "what is plain to us," never realizing that their cultural system and subcultural legalism is defining this "only possible" meaning of a passage. Their frame of reference is invisible to them, yet it controls their unsuspecting minds and hearts. As a result, they are universalist in their view of God's ways with people—a one-size-fits-all mentality. God has

15. John 1:17.

laid down all the rules. Everyone's story must be the same. They may feel that Christians must answer at the judgment for every shortcoming defined by their system (which obliterates the grace of God through the sacrifice of Jesus). But it is neat and defined—orderly. It agrees with their objective and logical views from the old system of survival. However, in reality, their emphasis on ritual over relationship is a false Gospel that can reach cultic levels.

When any group sees their own interpretation of reality as the only legitimate one—their own cultural beliefs and values to be the only valid ones—they cannot enter the cultural context of the Bible to see its truths through the eyes of those people. They have no frame of reference open to them for understanding the Bible except their own. In this state of mind, they cannot understand the truth combined with grace[16] and freedom.[17] They have defined God in a way that precludes knowing him as he is—a God of overwhelming grace, love, forgiveness, and longsuffering. No idea of God's grace means no humility before him. All the evidence we have from the New Testament is against this being saving faith. Knowing the value of Christ's death on our behalf is a picture of grace that does not fit the legalist's logical world of quantitative achievement. It is an awkward fact that in legalism, God's approval is conditioned on works.

It is easy to see how our cultural preferences shape our interpretation of God's Word and our experience. In the same way, they distort our understanding of the experience of those outside our group. No culture can be a standard in the evaluation or interpretation of another. Trying to exert ours in the biblical text or on those in our ministry is cultural legalism. Cultures are human systems, and though truth and goodness can be found in them, they remain human and must be subject to scrutiny as to their helpfulness in each area for understanding God's purposes for our lives.

So why does the disregard for the powerful influence of culture persist? The reason is, as we have said, this cultural framework which we trust for our survival and on which we build our lives is invisible to us. We don't know how powerful and unrelenting its influence is, and we, especially individualists, resist being told of that possibility. We unconsciously believe our way is the best and *only* way to interact and cope with the world and our experience. We assume everyone else in the world

---

16. John 1:16–17.

17. John 8:32; Rom 8:20–21; 2 Cor 3:17; Gal 5:13–14; 1 Pet 2:16, etc.

around us interprets their experience and chooses their actions on the same basis as we do. But, of course, nothing could be further from the truth. In a very powerful sense, every culture is its own world.

Except for a few who see the desperate need for awareness of the problem, we are culturally blind. We are much like tone-deaf people, for whom music is music, or those with anosmia who don't notice the smell of garlic, for whom food is food. Some people may not see certain colors that are discernible to others; some hardly feel pain others complain of at each instance. The difference is that those who have these biological deficiencies are much rarer than those of us who do not recognize cultural differences, good, bad, or neutral, in terms of powerful causes of behavior. Cultural difference, when observed, is considered an abnormality, an aberration or deviation from the "normal" cultural frame of reference everyone should and wants to have—their own. The anthropological word for this is ethnocentrism.

More widespread than legalism is syncretism, the mixture of two systems into one as a hybrid cultural or religious frame of reference for understanding the world and interpreting experience. This usually comes about when a person is enculturated in one system and then, through the strong influence of another culture, adopts some outside cultural or religious forms (though they may reinterpret them) and puts them to use in their own system to enhance some level of survival or satisfaction.

These people are still ethnocentric. They are merely adding additional features to their existing system of survival. These beliefs and values usually remain superficial though they may not be superficial in the system from which they came. The original worldview seldom shifts without a highly credible influence from the outside. So strong is our ethnocentrism! Genuine conversion to Christ, on the other hand, is just that, an extensive worldview change. If the worldview is not transformed, the result is simply syncretism.[18] Some people claiming to be born again remain on a popular level of Christianity with a great deal of syncretism in their lives. To use Jesus' analogy, they are trying to put the new wine into the old wineskin.

Cultures change over time. The old patterns and traditions may not all be useful today, but neither are they arbitrary. They are usually early solutions to survival in some aspect of life that have become so ingrained that they are no longer thought of as intentions for survival but rather as

---

18. Van Rheenen, *Communicating Christ*, 89.

just the way we do things. Some, of course, become dysfunctional and need to be changed or fixed. Other dysfunctional ones may be retained to our disadvantage, and instead of helping the society, they hinder it.

Formal cultures are reluctant to change old traditions. But in informal cultures, change is often for the sake of change. Western Christians often flirt with the newest values in the world around them with little thought about their contradiction with God's Word. Before we change some long-standing value in our culture, the question that must be asked is why that tradition is there. What problem for survival did that pattern of behavior solve for people in the past? If we do not know and make changes out of an appetite for novelty or diversity, the old problem, once resolved by the traditional practice, will likely resurface. There is also a tendency in Western societies to ignore or belittle the wisdom of the past and to rely, with a certain arrogance, on the belief that we have the better way of doing things in each generation. Neither is a good motive for change. They are seldom accompanied by the critical thinking needed to accurately evaluate where we have been and what direction we need to take. Because of this, syncretism in the expression of our faith has an easy road ahead of it. It is the individualist's popular, informal, and independent way, but independence and informality lead us down a road that ends somewhere. In our syncretism, we rarely ask where.

The people of a culture need to look back to see how they have survived in the past. No one can say that massive change from the past ways without a thought about the problems for survival resolved or created in society will end well. Nonetheless, cultures are dynamic and change with time. Some changes for meeting new threats to survival are necessary. Other changes are made arbitrarily in informal societies. Sometimes, in Western culture, a belief in God has been seen as merely an expendable tradition that holds back progress and freedom in lifestyle. But becoming post-Christian, where it has happened, has meant every effort is continually given to maintaining society and holding it together. They never looked back, and the days when their cultures flourished are over.

Cultures are human systems of survival, and without God, they fall short. God created humankind to live in social groups with cultural frameworks within his purposes and with his guidance. Only a relationship with God and an understanding of his purposes for humanity can offer the wisdom people need for a culture to flourish. But before we become too optimistic about that, we need to notice that this transformed society or culture is not in the Book. There we see a spiritual form of the

Second Law of Thermodynamics—that humankind and its institutions will continue to degenerate, moving toward a disintegration of order, law, justice, and morality toward the end times of this planet. So we must look to the renewal of individuals through Christ as our way forward rather than to the revival of whole societies.

Some changes are necessary, others enriching, and yet others destructive for a culture. After a social change and the novelty has worn off, our revised values and behavior will seem so normal to us that we do not often notice that it happened. We adopt yoga from Hinduism or meditation from Buddhism because we see its value for stretching our muscles or relaxing our nerves. It is not shocking because our ethnocentrism becomes a filter allowing only things in the new practice that we feel agree with our cultural preferences and expectations to come through to us. We do not accept the new behavior with all the functions it had in its original system. What we consider uncomfortable—things that put our current sources of feelings of security and wellbeing at risk—are, consciously or unconsciously, rejected, while the more seemingly agreeable are subtly, if not avidly, absorbed. The result is some belief or value, some behavior that seems to fit perfectly in our current understanding and way of life, or the one we desire.

Very little thought, if any, is given to the potential outcomes of this or that addition to our culture for the future. We may be throwing off old traditions we think are inadequate or which seem to withhold personal fulfillment or happiness. We adopt some approach or join some group that appears free of the old and happy with a new solution. We do not notice any possible adverse effects in the beginning. We have this amazing ability to modify or reinterpret a new idea or practice until it fits seamlessly into the way we think things ought to be. It happens in all cultures, though less dramatically in traditional cultures. We may see the process in another culture but miss it in our own.

This process and the blindness that comes with it are dangerous. It affects our spiritual survival and wellbeing when it alters our reading of Scripture. People syncretize what they read by unconsciously making it fit what they think provides security or happiness already. They are adding pieces of God's Word to their existing worldview. What is considered threatening to our constructed cultural sense of wellbeing is left out as irrelevant, while what serves our purposes is added to the existing system of mental, emotional, and social survival. Old beliefs about what is true or possible and values about what is important, necessary, or authentic are not necessarily changed by the influence of the new solution. Our behavior then reflects this new mixture of beliefs and values, and in time, the mixture hardens.

So, we are good at filtering out things that do not fit our feeling of the way things ought to be or the way we want things to be and absorbing things that we perceive enhance our existing system, our cultural frame of reference, our personal survival. These filters can keep us at a distance from God by blurring the intent and blunting the sharp edges of his communication to us in his Word. Many then, as "Christians," syncretize their cultural absolutes with biblical absolutes in the same way we might accept some practice or value from another culture and absorb it into our own. As I discuss in later chapters, cultural expectations are not the only filter that distorts our view of God and his Word, but they are overarching in their influence on other filters in place. I illustrate this by putting that filter first in Figure 4.3.

We see God's Word through lenses or filters that often do not allow him to speak for himself.

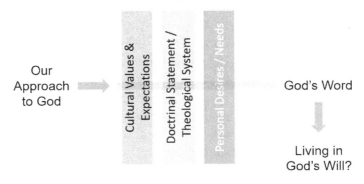

Figure 4.3. Filters that Distort our View of God and his Word.

As Western Christians, the parts of our cultural values and expectations that resist change the most have to do with our individualism and its expressions of independence and internal locus of control. In my generation, our insistence on logic and objectivity and our passion for monochronism play a significant role in our expectations. In younger generations, the freedom and independence of individualism have a more substantial role. These values and understandings uphold yet other cultural values and expectations of this filter. Such is our ethnocentrism. It is like the concrete foundation of a building made of brick. We like change and constantly replace bricks or put in new windows, but this is building maintenance. We seldom do renovations of fundamental values; we rarely reset the foundation. We resist the warning that individualism and freedom cannot exist together for long unless people are virtuous. That virtue must rest on surrendering to the creator God of the universe. Instead, our individualist, self-centered culture asserts itself and strives for personal achievement to avoid dependency, submission, and tradition. These individualist feelings often remain part of who we are after letting God be part of our lives. They go to church with us on Sunday. They filter out his true intentions for us. Once again, the power of culture lurks in the background maintaining a gap between God and Christianity.

People cannot survive in any system without God, and Christians cannot flourish by syncretizing their cultural ways with God's ways. The grave danger of ethnocentrism in either of these cases is the subtle way it gives us a strong sense of security. Our culture has made our survival, however frail, achievable in so many ways and for so long a time[19] that we see it as the only way anyone can survive and be happy. But when we open the Bible, we are faced repeatedly with the alternative, and it is unsettling. We think it cannot possibly mean we should let God take over entirely. It's unthinkable. Feelings of security are of immense importance to everyone, even the strongest, perhaps especially those who appear strongest among us.

This attitude may be the most powerful tool in Satan's arsenal. We not only ignore this need for God, our system feels natural and comfortable to us; it makes sense. Achievement of our emotional, physical, social, and mental survival lies in how skillfully we exploit our culture's advantages. Our pleasure and happiness, and even what we may consider our virtues, lie in being the best at using this cultural frame of reference to our benefit—competing better and achieving more. The individualist is considered clever when they "succeed" in life. All this is unconsciously assumed, so naturally, so innocently, yet it is so opposite of those encounters with God's way in the Bible. Nothing may be more deceptive or dangerous than a false promise of security from a temporary, cultural, and therefore human source. When Christians do not let go of the human

19. Long to us but, in reality, it has been a very short experiment in the mixture of democracy, individualism, and freedom—a flicker in the long dark halls of human civilizations.

ways to feelings of security and survival, they live in contradiction to God's Word. They remain popular Christians.

But why do Christians go on this way? It is because we have such robust cultural assurances that we assume that God sees it that way too, even made it that way, that he wants us to be Christian individualists, that the security we feel from our self-assertiveness and achieved status is his way. We think we meet his conditions by adding him to our world. He can add a layer of protection, enhance our efforts to achieve happiness, be there for us when things go wrong. In a way very natural to us, we can assume that this is the perspective of the biblical authors. Yes, we see a different language and culture in the biblical context, but we assume, unconsciously, that, deep-down, people there are basically the same as we are. They want the same things, have the same needs, and would do the same things we do if they had a chance or had any sense at all.

So, since surrender cannot possibly be the answer, we read our cultural expectations into the text as I mentioned before: our desperate need for logic, order, and specific things to do, our fear of ambiguity, our unconscious individualism, our monochronic, direct, and objective preferences for information, our freedom to make personal choices, our efficient pragmatism, our pursuit of happiness, that sort of thing. We imagine that the people in the Bible felt like we would; that those events meant the same things to them then as they would to us in our own time and place; that this or that text contains a logical order of objective information if we can just find it. How could it be otherwise? Such are the human traps of Western culture, keeping even Christians at a distance from God.

Any culture is an adequate vehicle for God to use to reveal his will to humankind. In fact, a cultural system is necessary for any understanding at all. But no culture should filter that content through its own preferences and expectations. We must let God be God and let him speak for himself using the cultural frame of reference he chooses. Teaching about the influence of our culture on ourselves, our hermeneutics, and our theology should be commonplace in our Christian schools and seminaries so that the pastors and teachers God gives to the church can help us navigate not only the truth of Scripture in its context but also the influence of our culture on the text, as we understand and apply it in our situation.

The Gospel finding its way to Western cultures was not a surprise to God; it was obviously his intention. Every culture has negative and positive effects on the message and on the church. However, he planned for the church, through his Word and with the gifts of pastors and teachers he gives to her, to help us see him as he is and understand the true nature of reality from outside the negative influences of our culture. He expects us to let him be God despite cultural absolutes that conflict.

Church leaders cannot do this very well or help others without understanding how their culture influences them. How can we make God's Word known without examining the human cultural context influencing the message, our teaching of it, and those to whom we are to make it known and understood? Culture has such powerful and hidden control over our personal world that we cannot neglect it without consequences. Nor can we ignore the influence of the culture, whatever culture that might be, of our audience on their minds as they listen to us. We must learn to evaluate and control these influences as leaders, or they will control us. A deep purpose of the church and its leaders is to overcome this cultural blindness in our understanding, teaching, and ministry. Western culture, like all cultures, is a human system for survival, not a biblical one. God's Word must become primary and culture secondary for Christians to flourish in their faith.

CHAPTER 5

THE CULTURAL CONTEXT OF LANGUAGE
Where Is the Meaning?

IT IS A FOREIGN AND ancient land to us, but the Middle Eastern and the Mediterranean societies of over two thousand years ago are the New Testament's social contexts. God chose to use these contexts and languages to reveal himself at that time. To read this revelation through the lens of its own historical/cultural situation becomes expedient since, as we shall see, meaning in communication is assigned to verbal and non-verbal symbols by culture and experience. We must use the values, beliefs, understandings, and conventions of that world, rather than our own, to understand the people, their context, their behavior, and their conversations.

In communication, the intentions of the words are a large part of the message. The social values and daily experience assumed by the speaker to be common among his audience add another significant portion of the meaning to his written or spoken words. Then, how the words are spoken, the inflection used in an oral conversation adds to the meaning of the words, as does the social context and behaviors of those in the situation. Finally, the collective, social identity of the people of that time, as opposed to our individualist, personal identities today, gave them feelings of confidence and self-esteem with insiders, or anxiety and uncertainty in conversations with outsiders that we may not detect in the words alone.[1] These non-verbal cues and attitudes color the vocabulary in rich hues of intended meaning and prevent unintended meaning among the people using it. Since only 10–20 percent of the meaning lies in the actual words used in a conversation,[2] non-verbal, socio-cultural, and historical context are *essential* to the meaning created in the reader or listener of a story or letter.

The unmentioned social values, the history, and the everyday life experiences of these people cause the words to carry emotional and cognitive associations that do not belong to us in our modern-day Western context. So, the words are highly attached to the original context in ways that render their meaning less intelligible when translated into another, unrelated language by the cultural outsider twenty centuries later. Not only the words but also the meanings of the original people's behavior are defined by their social values and expectations, their cultural frame of reference, not ours. The use of language in communication is buried in human culture. This understanding should be Hermeneutics 101 for every would-be pastor and Bible teacher. Communication theory is essential for communicators, and biblical ministry is communication.

Experience common to one group and that common to another group is obviously different. But the same words may be used to refer to each group's diverse experience. You can imagine this in your own culture. I remember sitting in a biology classroom in the tenth grade when the subject of a cow came up. There were several in the class who had never seen a live cow. To those of us who had spent some time around cattle, there was a richer meaning. We shared familiar associations—cows in a pasture, cows walking to the barn at milking time, cows in their stalls being milked and eating hay, cows we could touch and pet, and those of which we had to stay clear. Even the smells of dried alfalfa, silage, and the milking room were part of our associations with the word "cow." Others in the class had a picture or two to draw on from a storybook or reference book. Some in the class may have been in a third group who had seen a cow but only at a petting zoo. Their real experience was very limited, so their associations of meaning with the word "cow," their mental images and attitudes, were quite different from mine. This example is of people from the same culture and language group, even of the same age, and is

1. See Gudykunst, "Anxiety/Uncertainty," 281.
2. Hall, "Hidden Differences," 53.

about a very concrete, objective subject—a cow. But the experience of touching a cow in its natural surroundings was not common to everyone in the group. This limited example points out the foundational rule in communication that associative, emotional meaning is in people. If you get past the language, culture, social, and historical differences, there is still the personal experience of the audience to consider.

Another example of the meaning of words generated by association with our experience was annually demonstrated in my classroom as a teacher. I would ask the students to write down the first thought that came to their minds when I said the word "truck." Here is a short list of the responses: dirty, big, pickup, powerful, freight, intimidating, driver, Ford, hunting, brother, transport, and wheels. Why so much variation when I had the idea of a nostalgic toy dump truck from my childhood in mind? We were from the same culture and language group. Trucks were common to all of us, but each student had various associations from their experience and personal preferences triggered by the word. In addition, they had no common context for the word, so each student imagined their own. When I put the word in a story about a problem with the power lines leading to my home, it made a big difference. I told them of my call to the electric company and their response of sending a man in a *truck* to check on the problem. This time nearly all of us had associations in the category of utility trucks. Why? Because I gave them the context of a commonplace experience which we shared in our lives: the use of utility trucks in fixing electrical power lines. There was one exception, however. A student from Singapore still had an image of a motorbike in mind, though it had a toolbox strapped to the back of it. This was his experience with electrical service vehicles in Singapore. It is clear that meaning is in people. Even using common vocabulary, the meaning for each person is connected to their personal experience and level of familiarity with the context.

We see the difference outside our culture even more clearly. We would not begin to compare the personal meaning of the term "World War II" in the mind of the American in that day who, at home, suffered the shortage of coffee and sugar and had to substitute for all kinds of everyday needs for several years, to the meaning it would have for European Jews who suffered much differently.

What if we were talking to people from a different language group of vastly different human experiences? What if we knew very little of that experience? What if our languages were so different that we did not have adequate words for the ideas they expressed or the cognitive domains needed to interpret and think about those expressions? What if a chronological chasm of two thousand years created huge gaps in knowledge of industrialization, medicine, science, technology, and social media? What if the cultural disparity represented enormous gaps in how social relationships worked, in values, in moral understandings, in the purpose of life and how to achieve it, in how to maintain personal survival? What if the communication was written and we could not see or hear any nonverbal cues or ask questions to clarify our understanding? Yes, these are the questions that arise from the sciences of cultural anthropology and communication theory. A consideration of them is as crucial to our hermeneutics as understanding the difference between literary genres or between a verb in the aorist tense and a participle.

Jesus took familiar elements from the lives of ordinary people in his audience: vineyards, the smoking wicks of oil lamps, the eye of a needle made of bone, the disorientation of excellent wine at the end of the wedding, the emotional impact of losing a special coin, the social impossibility of a father joyfully welcoming home his younger son from a life of sin. There were no cheap perfumes, people's feet were generally dirty, the land was cultivated and planted by hand, millstones and clay jars were common, people depended on patron-client relationships[3] instead of insurance, and life expectancy was very low such that beggars, orphans, and widows were common.[4] It was a world where life was linked to the past instead of the future, privacy was not expected, good was limited and the evil eye plentiful, individual freedom was feared, and submission, duty, tradition, and harmony were the highest social values in the collective society.

This was the real world Jesus entered. He used this social framework and these cultural forms to weave understandings through parables as analogies of what was outside the experience of those people. The common was used to create an understanding of the uncommon. Their language and grammar system was entirely dependent on the meaning and sensations associated with it by the people's experience and the social

---

3. See Malina, *Social World of Jesus*, 143–47.

4. Thirty percent of the New Testament Jewish population who made it to one year old died before the age of six. Sixty percent of the survivors died by age sixteen. Seventy-five percent of the population did not reach the age of twenty-six. Ninety percent were dead by the age of forty-six. Less than three percent made it to the age of sixty. Carney, *Shape of Past*, 88.

values of the day. Jesus succeeded in creating meaning in that context by using their system, being part of it, and knowing it from the inside, and he did so perfectly. He was a participant in his own creation and had an inside understanding of the hearts of those people.

So, when we of an entirely different culture, different period, and different experiences, come to the words of the people of the Bible using an entirely different language that has no one-to-one correlation to theirs,[5] we must be aware of these issues and use a great deal of caution to not distort the original meaning. But what if we have no training in cultural differences and communication theory? What if we assume that all people are basically the same, even if less developed in the sciences and technology? Or what if we think that translation is simply a matter of lexicons and grammar—assume that we understand what the text means by a "cow" or the emotions and meanings in social relationships? If we presume that analogies about unearthly truths, using objects and experiences familiar to them, but not to us, will be just as clear to us today, does it matter? Yes, very much. At the very least, it calls for humility, theological modesty, and a recognition of our dependence on God. In reality, it very much calls for careful attention to the influence of culture and human experience on the communication and events in the text and on our interpretive efforts. To entirely neglect these essential areas of communication allows an unmitigated syncretism of our modern understandings with those of the biblical world, a swapping of their words and emotions for ours without a blink, an unknowing replacement of their experience with that of ours today, and false confidence in this syncretistic, anachronistic mixture in our churches.

The result of not understanding the influence of culture on the Bible teacher, on the people and teachings of the Bible, and on one's audience is always some level of syncretism that can, at best, result in a popular Christianity. I want to remind us that our goal is to pass on the authentic treasure God has entrusted to us. The result is to be the changing of worldviews and regeneration of lives of human beings in their cultural contexts. For that to be the outcome of our efforts, we will have to study culture for its effects on us, on the message we bring to the world, and on those to whom we minister. We must avoid encouraging a popular, syncretistic Christianity which does not hold up outside the church and

5. De Waard and Nida, *From One Language to Another*, 60; Nida and Reyburn, *Meaning Across Cultures*, 7. See also, Smith, *Creating Understanding*, 50–64.

gives the world a false understanding of the Gospel. It comes down to what we hope will be accomplished in the lives of people.

As mentioned in chapter 2, we are often distracted from the intent of a passage in Scripture by our analytical search for linear information in the objective vocabulary and organized grammar. Having used two other languages in ministry, I have painful recollections of the importance of knowing a language well to step into someone else's world with any degree of understanding. Language is crucial to understanding another culture. People think in their language. In cross-cultural work, we must learn to think as they do, see their experience through their eyes, and empathize with them about its impact on their lives. Ultimately the meaning of their vocabulary is in them, shaped by their cultural frame of reference and associations generated by their experience, not in words alone. Without proper decoding, which only that culture supplies, knowing the vocabulary is essential, but it is not enough. I must here remind us that opening the Bible is crossing cultures in just such a way.

Language, its cultural context, and those to whom it belongs must be studied together. None of these elements should be omitted in biblical studies for teaching God's Word. We rightly emphasize relational gifts and relevant communication skills, which have their place in pastoral ministry, but we must not overlook other essential preparation. Our teaching pastors should be immersed in the languages and cultural systems of the Bible. This will keep us aware of the human connection with the meaning of an original word in the biblical situation. It is not only different than our English "equivalent" in a version of the Bible; we will be aware that its meaning is enmeshed in the cultural system and human experience of its context.

Michael Agar, a professor of linguistic anthropology, tells us over and over in his informal ways that, "Language fills the spaces between us with sound; culture forges the human connection through them . . . . You can master grammar and the dictionary, but *without* culture, you won't communicate. With culture you can communicate with . . . a limited vocabulary." Communication is simply more than grammar and vocabulary.[6]

We have to enter the biblical world of thought and try to align the intentions that, in any particular context, lie behind the words for that situation, in that particular culture, for that person, given their personal

---

6. Agar, *Language Shock*, 19–30.

experience. It sounds too complex even to try, but we all do it every day and have been for some time. We communicate in our own cultural context in alignment with the culture, the situation, and hopefully, with the experience of the person with whom we talk. It is what makes the words of a two or three-year-old child humorous. They do not yet know their cultural context, nor do they have the experience to make the same associations the adults in their lives can make. Later in life, however, we know the cultural values in play and have much of the same experience to rely on in the process. It becomes second nature to us to negotiate meaning with one another. The ease of it gives us the idea that a Spanish-English dictionary will be adequate for our vacation in Spain, but alas, unless they deviate from the central tendencies of their culture, they don't seem to understand us or us them. Unfortunately, we often approach the Bible the same way.

Any college course in American or English literature begins with our expectations for various genres in our own Western cultures. It would include parables, proverbs, prose, and poetry that we would understand and enjoy. But it is more difficult for us to study non-Western forms of these vehicles of meaning. It is not that we cannot recognize their forms or vocabulary in another culture and language, but because their subtle meanings come from experience and associations uncommon to us. Not having the same experience becomes a formidable barrier to creating even an approximate meaning in the Western mind. Not only does this variation in experience hinder the process, sometimes there is a very different genre in play, such as the apocalyptic style of the first century Middle East or Haiku poetry of Japan. That is why a useful foreign language course emphasizes differences in the cultural context of that language and the experience of those people that affect meaning.

Once again, these considerations should cause in us some theological modesty as we read the Bible and push us toward a study of the cultural frame of reference, social context, communication style, languages, and the unique experience of the people then and of those we hope to influence with the message of Christ now.

But we must also be aware of our unconscious need to accumulate objective information in a linear format. We may admire the straight shooter in our Western communication style, but people in the Middle East and Asia value the opposite. They admire indirectness that depends heavily on context. Our reversed expectations in the West can cause culture shock. But it is our own culture that is the chief barrier in learning another. Our expectations are so strong, so natural, so "right." How can other people be so "wrong"? In sharing the Gospel in Japan, we find it disturbing that they feel reason, absolutes, and exclusiveness concerning religious topics are disturbing and immature.[7] Our approach adds unforgivable offense to the Gospel. Our propositional truths do not just fall flat before us; they close and bolt the door to communication and relationship. Their preferences, expectations, and purpose for communication are much different than ours. If we ignore their style, it is fatal to relationships and ministry.

In the same way, our Western approach to Middle Eastern stories and accounts will fall short if we seek to accumulate data instead of entering a world of relationships, wisdom, and high-context communication. In this type of communication, a good deal of shared experience, essential to the understanding of the information, as O'Brien and Richards repeat in our ears, "goes without saying."[8] The author depends on his audience to draw on that common experience to load his words with their intended meaning in *that* context. That is why it is called high-context communication. It puts the responsibility for meaning in communication on the listener or reader, which we not only find frustrating in our Western culture, we tend to ignore that this could be the case.

As we have said, the experience assumed by the author and its effect on the words in the Bible are not common to us. We must get to know a good deal about it to successfully navigate the waters of their prose, poetry, and stories, even though we may prefer the objectivity of our own style and quantitative information. Luke knew the context of his audience when he recounted the birth of Jesus and did not draw our attention to things commonplace to them or to the natural outcomes of certain social events. But, everyone who would have read this document at that time would have done so with pale and blank faces, with knots in their stomachs. They would have felt the deep emotions of the social disaster taking place. They would have sensed the socially fatal isolation of the young couple, understood the profound irony of the upset to the exclusive hierarchy, and felt the social jolt of shepherds and pagans replacing family and friends in the events. They understood. Unthinkable things had happened. Only in God's providence could so much expectation reversal and social catastrophe result in the most positive event in

7. See Earhart, *Japanese Experience*. See also Rots, *Shinto*.

8. O'Brien and Richards, *Misreading Scripture*, 12. See also Malina, *New Testament World*, 14.

all history. His ways are, most emphatically, not our ways. In chapter 3, we saw some of his intentions in these events for the people of that time. These have specific and significant ramifications for us today if we can but see them through the haze of our modern cultural interpretation of the events.

Earlier I alluded to concepts from communication theory, saying that people think in their language, and their meaning is in them, not in their words. Don Smith[9] and Michael Agar,[10] among a plethora of authors on intercultural communication in the last thirty years, give us more about how meaning in communication is so filled with cultural and personal coding and decoding that unless we have insight into the culture and experience of the receptor audience, little is achieved in our conversations let alone our best lectures or sermons. Charles Kraft then deals with the extent to which God is "receptor oriented" in his communication to mankind using a Middle-Eastern context.[11] We must realize this in the text as much as we must be receptor-oriented in our communication with each other or those of another culture. Breaking the cultural code is of essential value in intercultural communication and relations. It is of even more importance in reading foreign, ancient documents whose authors and receptors cannot be interviewed today.

In the West, we depend on words in day-to-day conversation to carry their conventional, Western sense. It would be very confusing if we could not. But even among us, this is not entirely what is happening. Every person's experience causes them to associate a personal meaning or attitude with the words used in conversation. The same words that create hilarity for one person may create anxiety in another. Since we share the larger cultural context, we have many values and experiences in common outside these personal areas, and communication works reasonably well for us. We can depend, for the most part, on words to deliver information for us. But we all know what it is to be misunderstood and begin our next sentence with, "Oh, I didn't mean that . . . ."

So, the gap between words in a language and their meaning in people is connected to personal experience, influenced by cultural norms, and inclined toward personal preferences and persuasions. In the end, it is not so objective as we might prefer, even in our own culture. But because

---

9. See Smith, *Creating Understanding*, 50–64.

10. Agar, *Language Shock*, 13–30.

11. Kraft, *Christianity in Culture*, 115–21.

of our Western expectation and dependence on objective meaning and explicit information in words, our hermeneutics must call our attention to where the meaning for communication is in the high context cultures of the Bible.

As Westerners, we are low-context in our style, causing us to prefer directness, objectivity, and details in communication. These cultural expectations for meaning give us the need for a check, an assessment of our tendencies so that we do not attribute our style and expectations to a Japanese friend in a conversation or to the author of the Middle Eastern text. This lack of understanding of the difference in meaning for words between people has an even more serious effect on our spiritual lives. It can affect our relationship with God and keep us at a distance from his intentions for us.

This distance is amply illustrated with the use of the term "father" in the New Testament. It has so many meanings among us tied to our experience but is central to understanding our relationship with God. Though some are blessed to a great degree,[12] none of us has had or been a perfect father, and many have had a bad example of a loving one. Controlling, demanding, critical, cold, selfish, or absent fathers fill that term with associations from which many children do not soon, or ever fully, recover. Children accumulate these experiences in the early, formative years of their lives. They go very deep, so deep that it seems disrespectful, even repulsive, or at least awkward for many to call God "our Father." It certainly brings no comfort or feelings of security. It breeds instead the disquieting feelings of anxiety, apprehension, even fear or dread. Some may even avoid the term in conversations about God or in their prayers.

While our weaknesses as fathers or previous experience should stand highly in contrast to God's loving desires for us, many are caught, paralyzed, some nearly irreparably, in a world that cannot accept or imagine that fathers can be such. These wounded people are not often aware of what blocks the way for them, while others get such consolation and reassurance from the concept of God as our loving, sacrificial, forgiving, and wise Father. It is difficult for them to grasp that he intends only the best for them and his providence is at work for their good and the fulfillment of his grand plan for creation. We must come to terms with these associations with the word "father" that separate us from God.

---

12. C.S. Lewis records that George MacDonald had a nearly perfect relationship with his father and that was the root of his in-depth insight in his ministry. See Lewis, *George MacDonald*, XXIII.

Associations from failed relationship experiences and dysfunctional families deeply affect the meaning of the vocabulary used of the new family in Christ. How much of our vocabulary in church is really saying what we want it to mean or what God wants it to mean? Experience and culture have been at work in our lives, but when they are God's words, we should not let associations from culture and personal experience come between us and their biblical meaning. However, we often, unknowingly do.

Associations can also be discouraging when we confuse "my idea about me" with God's thoughts about us. This often waters down our understanding of his grace and forgiveness. We see these words in the Bible but find them hard to accept about God's approach to us. We feel they must be for someone else because we are too bad, too sinful, for God to think that of us. Yes, we know something about ourselves. We know how bad or selfish we can be. Does this need to change? Yes. Can God forgive such a person? Yes, he can and will. But some of us, though we know that in our heads, often find it difficult to forgive ourselves, and our associations with our own behavior, thinking, and feelings about ourselves get in the way. Our feelings about those who have hurt us may also come between us and God's grace. Forgiveness—accepting it from God, forgiving ourselves, and forgiving others—is a topic in itself. It is all about grace, a word we need in our vocabulary every day. But the personal meaning of it may be distant from many of us today. How many other words have negative associations for us from our experience? How long will we let how our culture and experience have shaped us get in the way of our trusting of God?

The whole idea of being born again is to start over. I do not mean to make it sound easy. I don't think it was for Nicodemus. But previous experiences that negatively influence our thinking should stop when we step into the true realities of God's providence. He is above and beyond all of that. We now must have the words *love* and *grace* and *father* in our vocabulary. It now must be he who gives us the meaning for these words instead of previous experiences in our old life. The old has passed; all things are new.[13] The words we use with his intentions are essential to our relationship with him and with each other. We must let God be God.

Bible teachers must discover negative associations we have with words and concepts in the Bible that are culturally and personally shaped and do not allow the truths of God's Word to be understood. They must

13. 2 Cor 5:17.

help us escape the influence of our cultural and experiential frame of reference, our internal dictionary. They must help us let God speak for himself.

So, culture and experience affect us and the words we use to an enormous degree. We must deal with the Western and personal expectations they produce in us that can block our ability to see what someone else in our own or another culture, but especially in the biblical culture, might expect in the accounting of an event or in the course of a conversation.

Then we must understand what was conventional to the people and authors of the Bible and why. More sensitivity to the original cultural frame of reference can give that truth more intensity, relevancy, and significance in the original situation and, therefore, ours. The implications and applications to our situation can then gain precision and take on more weight to impact us more deeply. We begin to see and hear the actual experience of those in the original audience, know how they understood what they saw and heard, and know an author's intentions more clearly than we could otherwise. We can then contextualize from the original situation to ours today with more confidence.

If the topic of where the meaning of words is to be found is threatening to us, it is because our cultural system gives us a sense of security. One of the ways it does this is its emphasis on the objectivity of what is true or false, just and unjust, what a word means, and what it does not mean. It is one of the reasons politics are so upsetting. We cannot imagine letting down the black and white categories of objectivity and going on with life as if it never happened.

Each of us, as individualists, has been carefully constructing who we are within this cultural system for a lifetime. We have built an understanding of our identity and worth. We understand the world around us, how it works, and how to navigate a course for survival. The system is crucial to us. Certain pillars seem to hold it up, pillars like individualism, objectivity, internal locus of control, and the ability to predict what to expect around the next corner. We do not like anyone tampering with these main supports on which we each have built our life, our vocation, our personal world, and our understanding of God.

It can be upsetting if we are told that meaning in words is not so objective, that there are factors outside the dictionary that fill them with personal or cultural meaning. Rather than simply transferring information using a universal symbolic code like we would prefer, it means that meaning is actually negotiated using several factors. When we talk about

God's words in this way, it is distressing. Students say things like, "We are talking about specific words God chose, and they must have a particular meaning that is the same for everyone." Yes, it is threatening for the western, informational, low-context reader, but as we saw in chapter 3, we are stepping into someone else's world. Our cultural understanding of the nativity events can leave a lot of the original contextual meaning out of the story for us. It is not all in the words. We must keep the words, every one of them is essential, but I want us to see the fuller impact of the truths they teach, given God's use of context to shape the meaning. Remember that if you don't know that culture, you will insert your own. There must always be a cultural context for understanding.

Stepping away from our cultural expectations is not easy, but our security must be in God himself. A life built of cultural understandings and values alone is like a house of cards. We must keep others from bumping the table on which it is constructed. That table is our cultural system as we have come to use it. We have trusted it to support our struggle or used it to our advantage, and it has sustained our determination to survive or succeed all these years. Our efforts at protecting and defending it are desperate. If the table is bumped, our feelings of security in the world we have constructed collapse. God wants us to trust him instead. No one is being asked to reject their culture but to let God speak for himself within that cultural framework, in his own way. My concern is that we get everything he says to us, not just what our culture lets through its filter or twists into its Western categories. When one culture is used as the lens to understand people in another, there can be a great deal of distortion. Is it possible that the system that has provided us human survival could have flaws in helping us live the Christian life? The answer is yes.

Sometimes I wonder what we would be like if, in our education, we were introduced to the need to understand our cultural frame of reference and how it affects the lives of those with whom we live and minister. What if we really knew what people in our ministry were struggling with in their walk with Christ and could speak to that directly in our discipleship and sermons? What if we were taught how those of other cultures see the world and life in it from a different perspective? I am not saying that we should be introduced to other cultures as better, but as different.

We must make a change. We cannot minister to people in a generic sense. Yet, we have little idea how culture affects them or us. We think people are people. But we cannot study the Bible as if the people there were like us. We cannot conquer biblical languages without the cultural framework that creates meaning between the people who used them in their context. We can no longer trust the lexicon's objective information without an inkling that the experience of each person or group shapes the meaning of the words in their mouths and ears. We must not continue in the old way.

We must look ahead. What do we want our ministry to accomplish? Are we serious enough to give time and effort to learn about the effects of culture and experience that affect communication? We have a choice.

CHAPTER 6

THE INTRUSION OF CULTURE
IN KNOWING AND SERVING GOD

I BEGIN HERE WITH THREE preunderstandings: First, all ministry with people is intercultural. We can never overlook the element of culture in everything we do to help people, in our own culture or others, in their relationship with God. Secondly, intercultural ministry begins with the servant knowing him or herself and their own cultural context. We simply fail to understand that our culture " . . . controls behavior in deep and persisting ways, many of which are out of awareness and therefore beyond the conscious control of the individual."[1] Thirdly, there is always the risk of asserting the self and the negative influence of culture in knowing God and being part of his plan. The elements of self and culture that affect us serving God may be listed as follows:

- Culture's positive and negative influences on each person as a system for survival
- The personality, sense of identity, commitments of loyalty, and spiritual maturity of the person
- The personal agenda of each person in terms of their strategy for social, physical, and emotional survival, achieving feelings of self-worth, and attaining a sense of wellbeing and satisfaction.

---

1. Hall, *Silent Language*, 25.

- Each person's collective and personal experience within their culture giving them particular associations for the meaning of various cultural forms, including the words and non-verbal codes of communication.

The subject of Christianity's relationship to culture is not a new one, but we in the West have yet to realize the significance of the interference of culture in our understanding of and relationship to God. Each culture, as a human system, presents this challenge. Meaningful ministry in our own culture and, even more so, ministry in a second culture, is severely limited by blindness to our own cultural frame of reference, our personal agenda for survival, our spiritual immaturity, and our human experience that filters our perception of the world around us and our interaction with it unless we can remedy the matter. But as I mentioned in the introduction, there is a mysterious resistance to looking at our own culture. To do so is an intrusion, a bothersome interference in our lives. A remedy for our dilemma will be hard-won.

"For my thoughts are not your thoughts, neither are your ways my ways," declares Yahweh. "As the heavens are higher than the earth, so my ways are higher than your ways and my thoughts than your thoughts."[2] God reminds us how different he is from us. We are, of course, limited human beings, but one of the things that makes us so different from him is our human cultural system with the values, beliefs, understandings, and assumptions we have from a very limited human vantage point. It became our frame of reference without our permission, and we are unaware of its influence or what we have become under its power.

The human condition and the cultural frame of reference that we trust to understand the world around us create barriers between God and us that we have not been trained to overcome. Every cultural system presents its own challenges for grasping the nature of God and the role he has given to us in his creation. I want to deal here with people in Western cultures—Christians in their own cultural definition of that term.

I will begin with a brief summary of our situation. We live in an informational, logical, scientific world of cause and effect emphasizing the individual and their achievements, the urgency of time, and an internal locus of control. In our insistence on egalitarianism, we emphasize informality in the expression of these values. But we seek to know and approach the omnipotent God of the universe, infinite in wisdom, love,

---

2. Isa 55:8–9.

and grace, revealing himself in an ancient Middle Eastern and sometimes Hellenistic context where people assume an external locus of control and polychronic time orientation in a relational, non-scientific world. Formality, social hierarchy, patrilineal families, collective society, and considerations of honor and shame are the context of their lives. How are we at understanding God's use of this non-Western cultural frame of reference in the Bible? Not particularly good. How are we at understanding our own system and its influence on us? Not particularly good. We are, in fact, relatively ignorant of both. And our misunderstandings have consequences in our lives and ministries. Let me list a few.

Worship: The worship of God in the evangelical West is not altogether based on who God is, but also, to a greater degree than we realize, on what human beings have become in their own eyes. Let me generalize. In our Western cultures, people are low-context, informal, controlling individualists. That may sound a little caustic, but it is the result of having an internal locus of control bent on self-survival, and our culture places us helplessly in its grasp. This positions people at the center of their own world, looking at God on the outside. Because of this, as Christians, we can become preoccupied with calculations of his potential influence, or for some, interference, in *our* plans. Our culture has taught us we must assert ourselves and achieve our wellbeing and not lose control.

We do not worship because we have no other desire than his way or no other significance than what his grace has given us. We are too much "in control" of our lives for that. We worship him so that he might accelerate our trajectory toward *our* ideals, make us feel better about ourselves, or to simply check it off our list. We are looking out for ourselves. We want God's help but at the same time try to appear independent in the eyes of those around us. We have, or try to have, an "independent dependence" on God. We want to make him part of our plan instead of becoming part of his. This makes our worship weak, something other than " . . . in spirit and in truth."[3]

Relationships: Once again, as individualists, we have to be in control of our own lives. God is all about relationships, but just as our individualism disrupts our relationship with God, it disturbs the relationships to which he calls us in the body of Christ and with those around us in the world. It can cause us to try to control our surroundings and the people in our circles to ensure we can have the position, status, and feelings of

---

3. John 4:23–24.

identity and worth we are trying so hard to achieve and maintain in our social world. Our self-assertion can alienate others rather than attract them. We can compete with them rather than put them first. This works against loving one another and unity which are signs of the truth for the world around us.[4] It also contaminates meaningful social relationships with those outside the body of Christ, an essential part of establishing the trust we need with them for sharing our faith in word and deed. Though individualism and achievement values can result in good development and innovation, the need for control and self-assertion over others is their most unbiblical side. It makes empathy next to impossible. Though the cultures of the Bible have their own weaknesses, we are at opposite ends of an individualist-collective continuum with those cultures, making it hard to understand the activities and communication in their world, a consequence of not knowing our own or that social context well enough.

We must also mention how the individualist, who needs to control relationships, must find certain ones and networks within which they can have an assertive role. The biblical world of the Gospels was collective and, though there are exceptions, people did not need to assert themselves. One's membership in the group assured all social and personal needs were met by the system if they remained in good standing. They did not seek for needs to be met outside the group. Following Jesus meant leaving the security of this larger social group for a small, struggling one. The problems at Corinth in the less collective Hellenistic culture show the divisiveness of groups in the church. They dishonored God and destroyed the display of his grace in the church before the world around them.

On the other hand, the individualist must make an effort to find their place in particular social networks since belonging to groups is not automatic in their society. For the less assertive Western person, this search is difficult. The goal is the feeling of self-worth that comes from acceptance and inclusion. Many find that feeling at its peak if they can be associated with those perceived as socially significant. Groups are a problem in the Western church. Being part of a group that is elevated in popularity, power, wealth, or another form of success in the larger group's eyes has become a divisive characteristic keeping the rest of the community away from them. This syncretizes their faith with this cultural need and personal search for social recognition and its advantages. It creates

---

4. John 13:34–35; 17:20–23.

separation from God as it takes his place in their lives for fulfillment and contentment.

To be considered an insider is important to most individualists who, in seeking self-survival, actually need others to affirm their worth by this inclusion. Some, of course, try their whole lives without success, and others seem to know the rules and ropes well enough to enter and exit these groups with more ease. This is the belonging that most individualists seek but, being individualists, tend to use for self-esteem preservation. I am, of course, generalizing. Not all individualists would be this mercenary in their friendships, or certainly not in all of them, and we might expect that, least of all, Christians would be this way. But my observations of social contexts would show this last assumption to be less than accurate. Except for the grace of God, we are typically as blind to the influence of our own culture as anyone else. We are Christian individualists, and that has its dangers.

Seeking and enjoying normal friendships is a gift from God, but needing them to this degree for social recognition and affirmation is not his way. If we intend to let God be God, we must find all the worth we need from our relationship with him and his work on our behalf. If we seek that elsewhere, it not only separates us from God but from other people as well. So, division in the body of Christ is a price to pay for individualism given free rein, and it may be the costliest to the watching world around us. For them, unity in the body is the sign that God sent Jesus.

Explaining God: Western evangelicals also belong to an informational world. They are drawn to the efficiency and detail of information systems in their low-context, monocultural situations. This causes them to seek to explain God in detail, enumerate his attributes, and identify his ways with specificity, order, and logic. And, of course, this information must be systematized. But this approach can reduce God to information about him. He can become a volume on a bookshelf. We tend to see our theologies as the final word on God and spend a great deal of time defending them and rationalizing away any variations. We create an explanation of God's person and works using some verses and neglecting others that seem contrary and then see it as God's explanation of himself. But God is more than information about him, perhaps especially our version of that information—including what seems to fit our system and excluding what does not. He is much more. We tend to shy away from less objective concepts, such as his transcendent mystery because it cannot be harnessed into a searchable database. It resists a detailed explanation. And we do not like to think that there is a lot about God that we simply do not and cannot know. We can control information, but we cannot control mystery.

We have little tolerance for what we cannot quantify. We need a period at the end of the sentence. There are exceptions. Sometimes people exhibit the extreme of wrapping him up in miracles and revelations, signs and sensations everywhere. But it might also be the ultra-objective method of confining all behavior to God's quantitative commands for our theological categories—his sovereign lists of things to do and not to do for approval with no place for transcendence, mystery, or relationship. Or we may go to yet another extreme of putting all under his sovereign control with no responsibilities or choices left for human beings. We must remember that theology is our description of God and his ways, not a relationship with him. Relationships involve choices. He has made his, and we make ours daily. We must never let our theological system become God.

Humility: Because our culture is based on values of egalitarianism, individualism, achievement, materialism, and an internal locus of control, we know a lot about self-assertion but little about humility and, therefore, little of the fear of God. The words honor, loyalty, submission, and duty have little place in our vocabulary. We know nothing of being in the presence of true royalty. When we try to worship, we have no alternative in our system but to bring God down to our level of understanding, make him logical and predictable, and make him fit our theological scheme and our cultural frame of reference. Once he is manageable, there seems no need for humility; in fact, it often becomes a source of pride to have achieved "understanding" of God and his ways, whether through an exhaustive organized theology or discovering the "secrets" of his will that no one else knows.

Prayer: In petitionary prayer, our bent toward efficiency and instant information only a click away causes us frustration when God does not seem to deliver on his promises *as we see them*. Still, we try to explain his influence in our world, calibrating it to fit our cultural and theological system and describing it in ways to keep it as rational and orderly as possible, all the while being haunted by words like grace, faith, and trust. We approach God with an irresistible preference for this order and objectivity, applying our logic to the possible outcomes of our requests of him. It too easily becomes a focus on us and our quantitative expectations of God rather than on God himself and his qualitative providence, his working in the world, his plan for the universe, his will on earth as it is in heaven. We are generally unaware of his frequent answers to prayer that are not an immediate yes or no to what we asked for in terms of what we expect, but a movement in our favor in ways we do not expect.

In our thirst for order, objectivity, and quantitative measures, we often turn prayer into ritual activity instead of allowing it to be a relationship bathed in grace. It can become a list rather than a conversation. If we are not careful, we may think it a spiritual achievement to have a long list or spend more time praying than others, to get up earlier than anyone else to pray, to go to greater lengths with sudden, inspirational spontaneity, unique postures, and particular language. Then enters pride, the most serious of sins, where only humility belongs. So, what are to be the most intimate moments with God become opportunities for inflating oneself with achievement to attain self-worth. Again, these are dangers of Western culture syncretized with biblical Christianity.

Letting God be God: Instead of letting God be God, our informality leads us to talk about the most sacred and majestic things only casually and often with some embarrassment. We fill our worship with entertainment and chit-chat. We might not be so casual if we were really meeting with the God of the universe as Moses or Isaiah did. We become distracted in church by our own interests and pursuits. Our boredom is sometimes reflected in various methods to create more excitement in worship, more novelty in prayer. We need to keep people involved and interested. In the end, we are humans who do not realize we stand in the presence of the living God, Yahweh himself. If we did, we would not need gimmicks. We would never use prayer as a simple transition to end a segment or introduce the next activity on the program. Moses's relationship with God could never be described as having a "quick word of prayer" with God.

And then there is silence. The last thing we want in church is to *be still* and know that he is God.[5] Thirty seconds of quiet is cause for alarm in the average service. What happened? We do not realize that it will take the silencing of all the clamor in our lives to hear God. It goes deeper. Some of us in the West are afraid of silence, sometimes fearful of our own thoughts. We fill our lives with distractions lest we should come face to face with ourselves. Our superficial lives of activity are often void of real

5. Ps 46:10; Zech 2:13.

meaning, and it haunts us that, in the silence, God may be waiting. What will he ask of us?

Until we let God be God, we can never know his will with contentment. When we do, our strength will be found in our trust in him, and quietness will be its blessing.[6] The noise and distractions will no longer be needed. Recreation will remain just that. It will no longer be an escape from self, for self will be in its place. We men can return to living quiet and peaceful lives,[7] and women to the beauty of a gentle and quiet spirit.[8] The noise will die away. We will have the strength to speak with courage and wisdom when needed, but the freedom to remain silent and trust God for our own reputation. When called for, we will defend our home and family, even our country, but do it in the strength God gives, for he is our ultimate protector and salvation. We will stand against our unseen enemy with the full armor of God.[9]

Mystery of God: Western Christians know little of the awe of God's mystery, the sense of non-self in the presence of the singular, all-powerful God on the throne of the universe. It demands a humility foreign to our culture, submission and loyalty that are ready to trust his providence in all things. But humility and submission are hard words for the Western soul. If God *is* approached with fear and awe of His majesty, sovereignty, and mystery, there are consequences for the worshiper. He or she must humble the self. God becomes the center, and the worshiper can no longer talk about me, my achievements, or my status in their approach to him. Popular Christians in the West would be utterly undone in the presence of such a God. Their neat theological system would crumble, their logic fail, their world fall apart because it is built around their Western self. We may prefer the direct approach to God without the mystery, the quick and popular, objective mechanics of the latest forms of worship, the emotional but superficial "feel good now" moment, an informal hanging out with God. It is the immediatism of a "let's do this" individualist mentality that pushes ahead.

Many of us lack the prerequisite of a perspective of God being totally other than mankind. Therefore, our worship can be shallow and more people-centered than God-centered. We are preoccupied with what and

6. Isa 30:15; 32:17.

7. 1 Tim 2:2.

8. 1 Pet 3:4.

9. Eph 6:10–18.

who we are, with what we want to achieve, with what we want to be in the eyes of those around us. But all the while, God is watching, looking on the heart, searching for those who worship in spirit and in truth. He watches and waits, but we are looking the other way. We have trivialized God, lowered him to the category of information that we can organize into a system, memorize, say we believe for the sake of belonging—not to Him, but to the group that says the same things about God, how he works, and what it means to be a Christian.

So, we have recast him in human wraps, a predictable "God" who must meet our expectations. Our culture has intruded into our knowing and serving God. The confusion of cultural absolutes with biblical absolutes has become a new mixture that seems agreeable, a smooth syncretism that hardens into patterns of compromise in our lives. This attitude puts self at the center and is a breach of loyalty to God, one we hardly notice, for there is a way that seems right to the person, but, as the proverb tells us, it leads to death.[10] Its sources are culture and self, not God.

But God is more than what we can know about Him in our busy info-culture. He is other than our culture-shaped minds, our Western, time-bound, materialistic, scientific cognitive domains can comprehend. We will need a new mental compartment. We will have to meet him in a Middle Eastern context where, using that frame of reference, he gives us understandings of his purposes in the universe beyond that culture or ours. He does not give an account of himself—an understanding of everything—but of what he wants us to know, leaving much to our trust of his providence, power, love, and grace. We will have to meet him on his terms.

God's ways in the world are very different from what we might imagine or prefer—very different than we might expect given the definitions we have attached to his being. Because we do not comprehend this difference, *our* ideas of ministry success prevail, our lack of contentment continues; we try to exert more control, but our insecurities haunt us. We find truth in his word; we put it in lists and boxes and feel that now we finally know him. But many of us have yet to learn that the intention of truth is not simply organized information but the molding of a kind of person. It is always inseparable from the power and mystery of his providence and grace. These understandings were as rare to the Middle Eastern cultures he condescended to use as they are to our modern worldview.

---

10. Prov 16:25.

Their religious culture intruded in their approach to God under the new covenant as much as our Western individualist one does for us.

Human culture has no explanation for the otherness of God. Our cultural absolutes attributed to him distort instead of explain. We must be content without knowing a great deal about his providential activities. His purposes in our lives and ministries may not fit our definitions. We may prefer things to be black and white, but he is light in an infinite color spectrum, with colors we have never encountered and for which have no names.

His providence orders events in a way that always results in fulfilling his master plan, but at the same time, he responds to our prayers. He allows mankind to choose his way, even when it results in suffering that he does not intend for his creation. Our lack of submission cannot stop his purposes, but he waits for it all the same, so we may take on an active role in his plan. His request of us is not blind faith but trust in his great, unfathomable Being who controls the universe for his own perfect ends and does so with love and grace and justice toward his creatures. But he is a God we cannot fully comprehend, one who has not told us everything; we must walk by faith. He is not limited to our personal preferences, our Western logic, our modern sense of time. We can often see his workings when we look back, but we may have no notion of them in the present. His care and help do not always look like they could be his, so stereotypical are our expectations and cultural preferences, so rigid our legalism. It is a commitment to this God as God, not our idea of God, that opens doors and moves mountains. There are no alternatives.

We will have to meet him in his world, on his terms, and relate to him in his ways. His majesty and mystery must overwhelm us for them to cause us to see ourselves accurately—from an eternal perspective in the rapidly fading hours of our human experience. The outcome is wisdom in the souls of people delivered by his grace. In their lives, we see a flourishing faith, a reliance on his grace, and a thorough-going trust in his providence. They know the deep-seated peace of contentment and desire an unbroken intimacy with God. They are not perfect, but they know who is and are unreservedly loyal to him. They wonder at the deep mysteries surrounding his creation, and his lavish grace poured out on it. These people are an anomaly in the church in our fast-paced Western world of human achievement and craving for information.

God's Grace: Grace came through Jesus along with truth.[11] This grace would move people from doing to being, from the law to its fulfillment—a relationship of integrity with God through Jesus Christ. Of course, cold obedience was never God's purpose in the Old Testament period, and his grace was not unknown. To make God's intentions for the people under the law clear, Jesus expressed God's purposes in his sermon in Matthew 5–7. It was also an introduction to living under the grace about to be revealed where the behavior that honored God would not be from obedience to the law but a condition of the heart.

Jesus introduces the "new heart" God seeks by saying that, even under the law, it was not so much not to kill as not to be a murderer. Do not commit adultery was to be understood as do not be an adulterous person. [12] We begin to see that it is not just "do not covet" but more "do not be a covetous person." Do not steal was to be understood as do not be a thief in your heart. Of course, we are not to steal, covet, kill, or commit adultery. But not to commit the act while wanting very much to do so in the heart was to misunderstand God and brought the harshest criticisms from Jesus upon the Pharisees.[13] It was to have hearts painted with the hypocrisy of whitewashed sepulchers. "Unless your righteousness surpasses that of the Pharisees and the teachers of the law . . . ,"[14] that is, God was interested in the hearts of people even under the law. So it would continue to be under grace. Unless we become honest in our intentions and concerned about what we are, what we keep ourselves from doing is only part of the intent. It is not that we do not sin, but that we become the kind of people for whom it is not our intention to sin against God and our fellow human beings. When we sin, the forgiveness of God in Christ produces a profound humility motivating us to better live for him. And so, again, we see God emphasizing a qualitative life over a quantitative record bragging that "I have never done that." The to-do list of the oral Torah was longer than God's Law, but Jesus' sermon was not an inspiring message of recognition for the Jews of the time; it was a scathing criticism. But while intentions of the heart were disregarded for works of the flesh, God was at work shaping his grace in Christ.

11. John 1:17.
12. Matt 5:21–30.
13. Matt 23.
14. Matt 5:20.

Our culture is basically contrary to grace. There are so many counterfeit ways to pleasure and fulfillment of desire within reach of Christians and non-Christians alike that, in our passion for immediate gratification, we become entangled with cultural solutions in our pursuit of security and well-being. It is true in every culture. We are too distracted to consider God's grace. We need more, and more often, things that seem to promise fulfillment but fall short. Normal sensitivities are numbed, and the self-centered pursuit becomes irrational, controlling, degrading. In the end, there is no life.[15] Christians, in their culturally influenced pursuit, can even use the church, a theology, their position of leadership, and their Western spin on a Middle Eastern text to this end, but it is not God's way, and it destroys the faith of the followers.[16] But surely a bigger church will bring that contentment; a flashier service will captivate more people; a cleverer and livelier sermon will get recognition, and more control will keep it going in this direction. This is a Western template controlling the text for a selfish end that will never ultimately satisfy. Then, there is grace, and God is waiting to lavish it upon us.

People who understand God's grace are not content with our theologies as finished, our churches as institutionalized, or our Western eyes on a Middle Eastern text. This puts them in smaller numbers, not surrounded by lights, overlooked by most, but unforgettable if we meet one of them and take the time to listen. They are moved by a desire foreign to our culture—a longing for God that might seem distant to us, apart from this world. They have taken the narrow road and stayed on the path. For these people, spiritual awareness of God's grace and religion have parted ways in knowing and walking with God. Of course, religion is the least important and the most dispensable once awareness of grace has taken root. This is why the Old Testament precedes the New Testament. Once we learn to ride the bicycle, the training wheels are no longer necessary. They will become a hindrance if left in place. We must move on into the freedom of God's grace and the understanding of his providence, motivated by our wonder, awestruck by his majesty, secure in his power, guided by his Word, and content in his will and way. Legalism is, at last, done away. Institutionalism is seen as a danger. Every defense is built against, every engine of war leveled at self and pride.

15. Prov 14:12
16. See Matt 18:6.

Religion serves only a small purpose on our journey and is generally comfortless by itself. But it seems to be the only path many know, even for many who call themselves Christians. When we see God in terms of morality without a relationship bathed in grace, religion is slavery. This slavery is frequently motivated by guilt and often leads to legalism. Its restrictions must be left behind for God himself. There is no other comfort to still our anxieties. If ritual behavior does not facilitate loyalty to God, indebtedness for his grace, and trust in his providence, the efforts are wasted. It must be kept to a minimum for fear it will take over our attention and become our god. Very little ritual is necessary at all.

Freedom is found in Christ alone; we must not look for it in religious rituals. Christianity itself will not result in it; it is only a way to it. It does not save. Only God's grace and the merits of Christ's death on our behalf can do that. Fully opening ourselves to them brings salvation in all its splendor, the final solution to every concern for survival. In his grace, we find rest for our souls. No one else's expectations lead to it, no amount of ritual, no level of correct behavior; it is God and each of us alone. Drenched in his grace, forgiven and accepted, before him in the honor given to us by Christ in his sacrifice, we stand before the God of the universe in overwhelming joy through no record of our ritual and works. It sets all other matters in life in their proper perspective and puts ritual in its place. Our old values, beliefs, and assumptions are thoroughly replaced. God is God in the life lived in his grace, and all his ways are perfect.[17]

17. 2 Sam 22:31.

CHAPTER 7

THE FILTER OF CULTURAL EXPECTATIONS

IN FIGURE 4.3, I NOTED three filters that can come between God and Christians. We might shorten them here to cultural expectations, theological systems, and personal needs. It is something of urgency to discuss a filter or lens between us and God himself, but *three* of them, unknown to us, working silently in the background? It is quite disturbing! These filters keep us on a popular level in our faith, disguising the syncretism of our beliefs with our culture. Down the road, there may be a blind-sided collision with the truth for many who think they are Christians because they participate in Christianity. We must confront the distorting effects of these filters on our perception of God; they cannot be ignored. We want to know biblical truth, and though we read it on every page of the Bible, we do not always see it. Our sensitivities are dulled, and our minds are blinded by the filters we use. We must open this encrusted door to the silent, innocuous, and intertwined influences of culture, theology, and self. In chapters 1, 5, and 6, cultural expectations were discussed from various angles, but further clarification will help us.

Rational Western logic, individualism, and monochronism have been mentioned as some of the core cultural values in the West which shape personal expectations that separate us from God. But we cannot express strongly enough how powerful this influence of our worldview is in our outlook on life. C.S. Lewis talks about learning in his early training about "the honor of the intellect and the shame of voluntary inconsistency."[1] Cold logic in reason and research, the persistence of individualism in relationships, internal locus of control in achievement, and monochronic control of our situation bring efficiency and order to life for us. With our self-assertion and results orientations, this value system makes sense, saves time, feels natural, and carries a tinge of moral obligation. After all, this is how life presents itself to us. Using these cognitive domains and values seems right and honest to us—the only way we can understand reality and our experience. We feel confident that these are the understandings everyone has or wants of the world around them. Adding strength to our wholesale adoption of these assumptions is the fact of how much good has been accomplished, how much research carried out, inventions produced, and lives saved using the offspring of these understandings. Anyone can see this, so why would people have or prefer some other way of understanding life?

How could ancient Chinese understandings of *chi*, *wu-wei*, or *feng shui* still influence people considering the scientific and industrial advances today? How can the Japanese still appreciate ambiguity in communication and put so much effort into harmonious relations at the sacrifice of precision and clarity? How can Hindus see events resulting from karma and Native Americans attribute spiritual essence to all of nature? These questions reveal our extreme ethnocentrism. We assume that, deep down, everyone really prefers the same things we do.

How do this reasoning, this passion for ordering information, and the categorization of facts, create a barrier between God and us? It does so by making us feel we can and should use this Western system, this cultural frame of reference, and all that goes with it to understand God in his Word. Our culture tells us that, really, it is the only way to understand anything. Yes, the documents are written differently than if they had been inscribed today, but we can remedy that by applying logical order and structure to bring out the "true" sense. After all, logic must be God's standard and preferred mode of reasoning, even though he allowed the authors to use their own style. Although it is a little vexing to us today, we have a workaround. We can transpose the revelation into our frame of reference. Sometimes it is rather ingenious the way we can pull truths out of the Book, see order and logic in a passage, find meaning for every word in a parable, and dispel the mystery. It sounds like this would bring us closer to God rather than become a barrier. So, what's the problem?

1. Lewis, *Surprised by Joy*, 173.

The point is that God did not give us an orderly, logical, indexed account. But if so, it is because it was not his intent. What damage might we do if we apply our Western rational logic, our objective, monochronic order, our low-context, individualist, guilt-and-innocence frame of reference to the text? What if we put lexical meaning ahead of contextual meaning? If we reassemble content in orderly, labeled stacks within the demands of a theological system? It is as if we cannot help ourselves. We must get this information into a tidy arrangement—a well-packaged, objective, logical, Western system even though God did not find that necessary. And those awkward passages that do not fit our theological system, there must be logical ways to work around them or loopholes that do not allow them to upset our method and arrangement of the information. Some of us have strong feelings about this, even though we would be slow to admit it. How will anyone understand the true message without our system? C.S. Lewis once said, "We might have expected, we may think we should have preferred, an unrefracted light giving us ultimate truth in systematic form—something we could have tabulated and memorized and relied on like the multiplication table."[2]

But he did not. The question is, why not? What did he intend? The answer becomes more evident as we realize how intentionally God used that original culture and those social relationships as the context within which to reveal himself and how much is lost in studying the words alone. Words are forms, as are social structures, institutions, rituals, habits, and symbols that people use to function, live, and communicate to survive. We talked about words in chapter 5, but we must remind ourselves here that the meaning for all these forms is internal to the community. That meaning might be concrete, explicit, implicit, satirical, symbolic, emotional, or ideological. But at any level, that meaning is tied to the values of that group, the cultural frame of reference, the contextual use of that form, and the experience of the people giving them their associations with it.

Bruce Nicholls set forth that all forms in the biblical text are just as inspired by God as the words. He tells us that "God the Holy Spirit overshadowed cultural forms through which he revealed his word in such a manner that these cultural forms conveyed what God intended to be

2. Lewis, *Reflections*, 188.

revealed. God was not at the mercy of human culture. He controlled the use of it for His particular purpose of revelation."[3]

So, God employed the use of Middle Eastern forms of all kinds. The fact that it was a high-context culture means that they put a great deal more emphasis on the information in these forms already evident in the context of their interactions than we do in our low-context culture. When we use our cultural values and forms as the scaffold of the event or conversation so we can understand the details of an exchange in the Bible, it becomes a filter that strains out the necessary contextual information and replaces it with irrelevant and foreign content as the framework for meaning. It causes distortion to the original meaning, to the connotation of that day and context.

This being the case, we need to learn about the cultural forms of the Ancient Middle East to be accurate in our understandings and applications today. Our assumptions of like feelings and perceptions of even familiar forms such as family, marriage, personal identity, virtues, etc., will be out of adjustment. Our expectation that they saw their world and social system as we do ours, with all its forms and values, will create interference blocking our attempt to determine the original meaning and establish appropriate applications in our modern context—the intentions and purposes of God himself for us. We must not forget, however, that without knowing our own culture to a useful degree, we will still not know where God's intentions need to touch our lives differently than we presently allow.

As we saw in chapters 3 and 6, there were differences in social controls in the biblical contexts. For example, while we are more oriented toward the binary thinking of right and wrong in terms of innocence and guilt, they understood social control in terms of honor and shame. When we read the word "honor" in an English translation, we think that the English word is basically the equivalent of the Hebrew or Greek word. So, we know the meaning. But in our logical minds, the idea is much more digital and has to do with recognizing personal achievement, bravery, or celebrity—being honored. By this logic, a person either has or has not been honored. It is not the norm for people to be honored; that is what makes a person singled out for an honor special.

In the biblical social world, however, honor was a quality of character a person inherited, possessed, and passed on, a standing they had in

---

3. Nicholls, "Towards a Theology," 53. See also Nicholls, *Contextualization*, 45.

the ingroup of a collective society as one idealizing the group's traditional values. In the Middle East, it was and still is the measure of one's worth as ascribed by that group. Since a standing of honor was granted by the group, disgrace or shame was only felt by a person if others became aware of their dishonorable behavior. Feelings of personal guilt had no part in this. Judas, for example, would have felt no guilt or shame while pilfering from the money pouch of the disciples unless he was found out. His public identification of Jesus in the Garden of Gethsemane was different. There was no way out of the disgrace it brought and no social remedy. The shameful behavior of someone in the group was remembered in that oral, relational, patrilineal society for generations.[4] Those who socialized with a disgraced person were shamed by association. Jesus' involvement with sinners and forgiving the most shameful people was highly resented by the Jewish leadership.[5] Sin could not be forgiven, and the shame removed between men.[6] There were no social mechanisms to repair the damage. This understanding makes the scene of Jesus forgiving Peter of his denials highly significant to him and the new group to which he belonged and who were aware of his behavior.

Being a male with noble Jewish ancestry (references to Abraham, Aaron, and David are common in the New Testament), having courage, and displaying generosity and wisdom were characteristics of this honor.[7] The norm was for everyone to possess the status of being an honorable member of the ingroup. In tightly-knit collective groups, one's identity, protection, and worth came from that group. Enduring shame in their eyes could be overwhelming for the individual, and it was extremely difficult, and as mentioned above, often impossible, to re-establish lost honor. Shame could be either intentional or unintentional (see chapter 3). In either case, it was considered aberrant, an impurity.[8] These deviated from the central tendency of members with honor.

Outsiders—Samaritans and Gentiles—did not fulfill the very first requirement of the patrilineal ancestral social status. These were not worthy of any honor and did not require the honorable Jewish person's

---

4. Prov 25:8–10 shows the shame possible from revealing another person's confidence in a dispute and the impossibility of restoring it. Disloyalty in a patrilineal, collective, traditional, honor-valuing culture brought the highest degree of shame.

5. Luke 5:29–50.

6. Luke 5:20–21.

7. See Plevnik, "Honor/Shame," 107.

8. See deSilva, *Honor*, 241–315.

involvement in any situation. Imagine for a moment the depth and dimension this value on honor gives to the story of the good Samaritan who was considered an untouchable in the Jewish hierarchy of personal honor and privilege. It was unthinkable that a Samaritan could do anything honorable. To use this outcast as an example of the neighbor in God's perfect Law of love was an impossible and unbearable thought for a proud, high-status, Abrahamic expert of that law. Jesus had again put the very last first and the very first, last.[9]

Once we in the West understand the dimensions of honor and shame through their eyes, it is not hard to see its enormous implications for an event in the text. But if we don't know what it meant to the original author and his readership, we lose much of the contextual meaning when we read the English word. This attempt at a one-to-one correlation in meaning between cultural forms of different cultures, in this case, the vocabulary of the two languages, erases a great deal of significance in the original text. As we saw in chapter 5, the social experience of the original audience caused meaning to be associated with vocabulary—experience to which we are strangers. Our low-context understanding of an event becomes a filter to the serious implications that were clear to those in the original high-context culture. We must use caution with words like honor, love, or believe for these biblical ideas because of the very different western connotations we attach to the English words.

Honor, shame, and high-context communication mentioned here are only three cultural values among some thirty where we, in the modern West, are at odds with the biblical cultures.[10] Modern, evangelical, biblical scholarship is beginning to enumerate these differences. It is enlightening to see the dimensions of meaning these studies reveal. Still, it takes a generation or two for such understandings to reach some of the pulpits and classrooms in our culture.

In addition to the gap the cultural values on honor and shame in the Bible create for us, a set of values connected with individualism in the West creates even more distance by filtering out valuable information from the collective perspective of biblical peoples. Individualism is the perspective of human beings understanding their world and their experience in reference to the self as the pivotal point of the cultural frame of reference. People are concerned primarily about how they are doing,

9. Luke 10:25–37.

10. See Appendix 1 for a comparison of biblical and Western cultures.

how their immediate family is doing, if others are fair to them, if others recognize their progress and achievements. This is a generalization, to be sure, but common enough for recognition of personal achievement to be seen as the key to feelings of self-worth for the vast majority. People outside the nuclear family and best friends are usually of secondary concern unless they can help affirm one's own identity and worth. This is why concern, care, respect, or empathy for others are praiseworthy attitudes or actions. Though they occur, it is not the norm.

Western people interpret their experience and that of others through this individualist lens. This filters out any interpretive options. Independence, privacy, monochronism, competition, and personal ownership are values by which it controls relationships. Others in a neighborhood are of secondary concern, so if someone we know gets a new car or adopts a child, or even gets a divorce, for example, we might have a personal opinion about it, but it is basically "their business" or "not my problem." If one person is not overly controlled by their individualism, chances are his neighbor will be. If you meet someone and start talking, you often do not have a conversation. Within minutes you end up listening to the person talk about him or herself. The individualist's world revolves around the self.

This is not the case in a collective society. Everything you do and how you do it is everybody's business and is measured by the group's norms. Care is taken that no one upsets the harmony of the community or damages its honor. Talk is about one another's family and social events, as this promotes that necessary harmony. This is done in a high-context fashion since everyone already knows a great deal about everyone else and their standing in the collective community. To talk about yourself is of secondary value; it may even be strange since everyone probably knows more about you than you do yourself. A great deal is understood and does not need mentioning. An outsider listening in, especially from a low-context culture, may miss a great deal of information essential to understanding what is being communicated unless he can gather it from the context and experience of those people.

Another value related to individualist societies that filters the meanings of the Bible is optimism and its cause, an assumption of unlimited good. Unlimited good refers to the availability of any resource, benefit, opportunity, recognition, or possession that enables the individual to gain advantage, pleasure, leisure, wealth, position, etc. The West, and particularly the United States, has a strong sense of good as being unlimited.

This causes us to believe that people everywhere have an equal chance to advance themselves. The individual must exert the effort, but all you need to get ahead is available if you look for it, work for it, or compete for it. Some less motivated or deviant individuals may con someone else out of it, but it is there to be swindled. There are always those who would rather get the benefits of the resources in the society, especially in democratic capitalism, without the effort. There are various means to this end, crime being only one of them. The freer the society, the more prolific the means to this end. But theft in our modern Western society, though punishable by law, is against the victim. Someone has stolen his money or his car. But in biblical days in the Middle East, people assumed good was limited. There was only so much to go around, and it was already distributed. A theft was against the group as the burglar has stolen from the society's finite amount of good. As you can imagine, hoarding was a severe sin.

A successful social system in our Western world depends on the longevity of the integrity of the people involved. Combining freedom and individualism in a context of unlimited good can be a volatile mixture if the people are not generally moral. Connected to this value on unlimited good are further values on egalitarianism, social competition, and the pursuit of personal happiness. Without virtuous people, the system is at terrible risk of failure.

These are Western values highly in contrast to the cultures of people we meet in the Bible. In the society of that day, success depended on each individual's honorable character, preservation of harmony, and reinforcement of the traditional social system in place. As with any social system, there were weaknesses to be exploited. The Pharisees in the leadership positions had used the religious and social systems to hoard available resources. To be exposed by Jesus didn't bring warm feelings.[11] While tax collectors were political mercenaries, the Pharisees arrogantly used their religious positions to rob their own people with their oral Torah authority. What could be worse in a religious, collective society convinced of limited good?

People see the world very differently where the understanding is that good is limited, already distributed, that what exists is always insufficient and cannot be increased. It is a zero-sum game that can quickly get out of balance. Since the pie is already divided and distributed, a person will have less if someone else accumulates more than their share. One

11. Mark 7:8–13.

person's win is another person's loss. It was a delicate responsibility to maintain an equilibrium of good, any kind of good, among those in a collective community. The perception of someone hoarding resources would disrupt harmony since people did not have an equal chance to get ahead; there was no legitimate chance at all.

To read our Western social or economic expectations of unlimited good back into the context of the Bible causes serious confusion. The possibility of democratic capitalism did not, in any form, exist for them. Our egalitarianism gives everyone a level playing field for personal progress if they are all playing more or less by the rules and are willing to put in the effort. Among people of the biblical cultures, this was not the case, and feelings were very different. Someone getting ahead was not playing by the rules; they took the resources or opportunities to do so from you or others in the community. What difference does this make to our understanding of New Testament teaching?

An example of limited good in the biblical social context had to do with children. Having children was a critical issue for women. To be barren was a heavy loss to a woman's feelings of meaning and worth in life, a barrier to establishing her honor, her value in the community. Another woman having many children, and especially male children, would create envy. Women were often desperate in their barrenness. The question was always in the air, "why her and not me?" These are the feelings behind the interactions of Sarah and Hagar.[12] Hannah also is extremely troubled by her barrenness. When God gives her the son she asked for, she prays a song that reveals the reversal of her situation in terms of the loss of others.[13] Mary sees God's miraculous work in her that she should have his son as a reversal of the advantages of the proud and rich to the humble being lifted up and the hungry being filled with good things.[14]

We might be somewhat shocked by Mary's words, by her feelings concerning the proud being scattered, the powerful brought down, and the rich sent away empty and, in contrast, lifting up the humble, those without power and wealth. There is an echo of the imprecatory Psalms here. The intense feelings of limited good abused, ardent tribal loyalty, and God's choice of Israel ran deep. Here they come from one we sense to be the gentlest and humblest among women. But when you look back

12. Gen 16:1–6; 21:1–10.

13. 1 Sam 2:4–5.

14. Luke 1:46–55.

over their history and then ahead to the rest of the New Testament, God has, through all the ups and downs of their relationship with him, made the first last and the last first. Good is indeed limited to those to whom God will give it and emptiness to those from whom he will remove it. There is no attempt by biblical authors or Jesus himself to change or correct the cultural understanding of limited good. God uses the existing context to reveal himself with unerring accuracy. If we ignore the culture God uses to frame his message to humankind—if we insert our own in its place—we will have our message instead of his.

There are examples of envy concerning the belief in limited good throughout the Bible. The Old Testament repeats the concern of the people when the wicked prosper, and they are reminded to be patient and wait on the Lord for they will inherit the land while the wicked will go down in misery.[15] They are warned not to envy the wicked,[16] often referred to as the stingy in English translations.[17] In the New Testament, when his disciples get concerned, John the Baptist sees his decreasing in influence as the expected outcome of Jesus' increasing influence.[18] Jesus talks of where our true treasure lies and warns of the outcome of the evil eye of envy.[19] We are not to question the distribution of resources, not envy others, for God is making the last first and the first last.[20]

The social control for keeping this balance of good in the Middle East has been and still is the evil eye. This is the malicious look of envy that could be followed up with mischief or an accusation of dishonor. For the Jewish leaders, it led to the extreme of having Jesus killed.[21] In Central Africa, envy created by an imbalance of good is not an evil eye but envy in action. It might be followed up with witchcraft or the ultimate response, poisoning. Generosity is the golden rule in such a society, and hoarding is an unforgivable sin against the rest of the community bringing irreversible disgrace. We know what our Western feelings would be concerning the corruption of tax collectors as we see them in the Gospels. But do we know what the Middle Eastern feelings would be? Tax collectors were

15. These are themes in the background of Pss 37 and 73.
16. Prov 24:1, 19.
17. Prov 23:6; 28:22.
18. John 3:26, 30.
19. Matt 6:19–24.
20. Matt 20:8–16.
21. Matt 27:18.

traitors to their collective group, collaborators with the Gentile power oppressing their people, gathering the limited resources, and hoarding some while giving the rest to outsiders. In that day and time, forgiveness was not a common sentiment, but in these intolerable cases of social infamy, it was quite impossible. Is it any wonder that Zacchaeus went to such elaborate lengths in an attempt to right his wrongs?[22]

It was the strongest contrast for people of that time that Jesus would put a pharisee at the front of the temple telling God how good he was and a tax collector at a distance in the rear who felt his shame before God very deeply. The most socially shamed people with a good heart were better in God's eyes than those of highest honor in the eyes of the people who had selfish and proud hearts.[23] How did people feel about Jesus' story? Like those who profiteer in a time of war, tax collectors were hated. It was unthinkable that Jesus would speak of them with *any* favor. Only those with ears to hear could take in the truth that when God put the first last and the last first was a matter of their hearts—their pride or their humility—not their social honor or shame. When looking through their eyes, we see the depth of feelings involved in each situation. We also see that just as our culture can be a filter that keeps us from seeing God's purposes, so could theirs.

One last example is in order. In the parable of the vineyard workers in Matthew 20:1–16, the words "is your eye evil because I am generous [to someone else]?" are translated as "are you envious because I am generous?" The passage is clear enough in the essentials, but the early workers feel it a lot more strongly than we Westerners may think. The landowner was not just giving the later workers the same pay and therefore perceived as unfair to the early workers; he took what should have been extra pay from the early workers to give more than deserved to the later workers in a zero-sum game. Who was he to inject such interference into the situation, upsetting the flow of resources, making himself the manager of their good? The owner's response is: "Don't I have the right to do what I want with my own money?" In their minds, in that society of limited good, no, he did not have the right to upset the balance and distribution of resources in this way.

Of course, the parable is not intending to teach us anything about the validity of the cultural understanding of limited good, only how they

22. Luke 19:1–9.

23. Luke 18:9–14. See Matt 5:20.

were using that belief to limit God's purposes and prerogative. Jesus uses that frame of reference because it is the one his audience shares. By doing so, they will get the full impact of God's ways being different than man's ways. God steps outside the human rules. He chooses whomever he wants to work in his vineyard. He advances whom he chooses without regard for social position or seniority in the ranks. He makes the first ones last and the last ones first. Jesus is showing his audience how their culture was getting in the way, filtering out God's message. Generations of Judaism and patrilineal descent from Abraham did not earn one a right to a reward or a position in his court. Many would come to him in the last hour and be admitted to the kingdom on terms altogether different than the hierarchical value of being descendants of Abraham.

The West also has a strong value on an internal locus of control. In the West, people take the initiative to change what they can of their circumstances, better their lot, earn more money, rise above their disadvantages, or, for the more idealistic, to make the world a better place. Many people in the world, including those of the Middle East, do not feel they have the power to make changes in their circumstances. They think instead that many things in life are predestined to happen. Life happens, and people must learn to cope with the difficulties and survive despite adverse circumstances. These things happen outside their control, and there is nothing they can do to stop them or undo them unless the gods should relent or their luck changes. Collective societies also exerted external control over the individual. Traditions must be kept, and religious hierarchy obeyed. People had to cope with the social rules and the Pharisees' religious regulations that laid life out for them day after day.

Paul occasionally spoke to animistic audiences in Asia and dealt with eating the meat offered to the gods in Corinth. The power of God is central in his letters, and those under the influence of the gods who embraced the Gospel experienced deliverance from fear and oppression that Western people do not understand. The power of Christ defeated the forces that had been in control of their lives. These became an example of towering faith amid suffering and a model to all the other believers in their area.[24]

In that day, coming out of the ancient Judaism of your family and collective community and embracing Jesus as the Messiah was risking personal identity and worth. Leaving the animistic gods of your fathers

---

24. 1 Thess 1:4–10.

without fearing they would take revenge was risking your life. These are the daring moves of people caught in the deadlock of an external locus of control, spiritual or social. But even though they suffered severely, they were joyful that Christ broke the chains of their bondage. They knew conversion as repentance, transformation, and freedom. We may not quite get the picture of the power of the Gospel and the Holy Spirit in these peoples' lives. People who had no control were delivered from the controlling power over their lives through no effort of their own. It was the gift of God's grace that went beyond the forgiveness of sin. It turned shame into honor, bondage into freedom.

These are but a few examples of how our Western filter of cultural values and expectations comes between us and the biblical text, putting us at a distance from the author's intentions and understanding the original audience. If we can become aware of this influence on our thinking and understanding of an ancient situation, we will gain a great deal more from the text. We will see more of the original significance of the words and forms in their cultural context and the experience of the people. Seeing their implications for those people, we can make more accurate applications to our lives in today's situations.

This filter of our cultural expectations is one of three core aspects of contextualization. There are three cultures to be considered in biblical ministry: the original culture, our own culture, and the culture of the audience we hope to reach with biblical truths. The message of God is meant to bring change to people in all of these cultures. Not knowing the influence of each of these cultures on the message we want to articulate, on our very thoughts about it, and on the minds of those who hear our message results in something other than the intended substance of that message. The influence of our own culture on the process of understanding God in his Word is simplified in Figure 7.1. There we see summary examples of the components that make up that filter.

We see God's Word through lenses or filters that often
do not allow him to speak for himself.

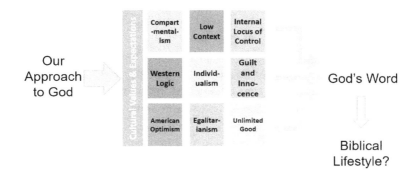

Figure 7.1. Components of the Filter of Western Cultural Values and Expectations.

The biblical authors and their audiences viewed the revelation that came to them through the lens of everyday Ancient Middle Eastern life—the one God intended them to use. It might look something like that in Figure 7.2.

Ancient Middle Eastern people heard and saw God's
message through filters he used intentionally for meaning.

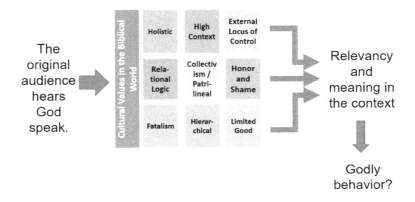

Figure 7.2. Components of the Filter of Cultural Values in the Biblical World.

The two models are in sharp contrast. As an example of the third culture, our audience, we can use Central Africa. Our message to people there would be affected by cultural assumptions, beliefs, and values yet again very different from ours. Theirs may be closer to the biblical cultural perspectives; however, honor and shame as a social control would be augmented by fear of power and magic.

A significant difference between Western values and those of the biblical context contrasted in Figures 7.1 and 7.2, and again with the description of Central African understandings and values, is the issue of hope. Limited good and irreparable shame remove hope in the biblical context, and limited good combined with fear of the power of spirits and the magic of witchcraft damages it in the Central African context. To have hope in these contexts was different than to have hope in our Western context. We find the use of the concept awkward in the New Testament, but that is our context creeping in again. Hope is part of our Gospel message to these kinds of people. It cannot be said too strongly how important attention to culture is in biblical ministry.

CHAPTER 8

THE FILTER OF THEOLOGICAL SYSTEMS

THE BLANK LOOKS ON THE faces of ministry students in the first few lectures/discussions in my class on intercultural ministry gave it away. They had not the slightest inkling of the concept about which I spoke. Even with a liberal arts degree, they were deprived of exposure to culture's influence on behavior and communication. What to do? Though a few came to a realization that they were on the edges of something that made a real difference in our view of life, the Bible, and the people around us, many who left the class wondered what had happened in there. I am left wondering if they caught anything about the connection between Christianity and culture and what the combination means for theology and ministry.

The next filter we need to discuss is one we might never suspect, that of theological systems. These, too, can distort our understanding of God. (See Figure 4.3.) There may be nothing more sacred to the conservative Christian scholar, next to the Bible, than his theology. To touch on that subject with questions can bring out a graceful response, but it often ignites defensiveness. We feel we are defending the truth. But human theologies should be read with caution since there is much we do not know, and the authors are products of their own cultural systems. Studies in culture and intercultural communication intensify the need for caution. We cannot ignore that meaning for forms is connected to culture, both in the original context and in our own. Our theologies can be affected by syncretism with culture, and if so, can contribute to the gap between God and Christianity, the opposite of their intention.

The students in that class did not suspect that they might project their own culture on the text of the Bible or that their favorite theologians may be susceptible to the same human miscalibration. They lived in a clear-cut world: God reveals his purposes using words, people talk and teach using words, and words are words. They would likely say that we have lexicons if we don't know the meaning of a word, grammars if we need to see the relationship of one word to another, hermeneutics to put them together to make sense or prove our theological point, and theologies against which to test our conclusions. All these tools *are* at our disposal.

But the words God inspired the biblical authors to use are from a social context that shapes the meaning of a passage. The scholar today is a product of a different culture. If they miss God's use of the original cultural frame of reference in their research and their order and systemization of the content, they will overlook important aspects of the message. It puts us on thin ice to understand ministry, teach theology to the next generation, or take the message to the next culture.

Even students interested in missionary work did not always see the relevance of intercultural studies. They were wondering why all the fuss? "Missions is about people in other countries hearing the message. God gave us the message; we already know it. We just have to learn how to say it in their language." How does one break the news of the critical influence of culture in the task to these energetic visionaries without destroying their enthusiasm? It does make one grateful that his doctor has not overlooked the essential nature and workings of the human body in his study of medicine. Time, patience, prayer, and wisdom are needed.

It is not a popular topic among individualists. Talking about any influence of our culture, let alone adverse effects seems to be a sort of high treason. In the area of theology, it is considered sacrilege. We fear that new thinking outside the box of traditional theology and, more particularly, our chosen theological framework may not take the text as seriously as we do, as the inspired and inerrant Word of God. And, heaven forbid, it may not take *our system* into consideration. But we overlook the dangers *we* bring to the meaning of the text when we theologize with no thought or understanding of our cultural frame of reference and its influence on us, and with no sensitivity to how the biblical text relies on its own cultural context for meaning.

Our doctrine of inspiration causes us to approach words of the Bible as if they were not in the mouths of real people living their lives in a concrete social context. But God chose to use those people and their frames of reference to speak to humankind. They could have understood him in no other way. But, we often substitute our own cultural frame of reference. Dean Barnlund, in speaking about cross-cultural communication, of which stepping into the biblical world through reading the Bible is an example, tells us of the danger of ignoring the cultural differences in meaning:

> To enter another culture with only the vaguest notion of these underlying dynamics reflects not only provincial naivete but a dangerous form of cultural arrogance. To grasp the way in which other cultures perceive the world, and the assumptions and values that are the foundation of these perceptions is to gain access to the experience of other human beings. Human understanding is by no means guaranteed because conversants share the same dictionary.[1]

Theology is essential. In addition to exploring the glory of God, his work in our lives, and his purposes for creation, theologians of the past have righted many wrongs, exposed many false teachers, and uprooted many violations of God's intentions for the church. There have been many false teachers along the way, as Jesus, Peter, and Paul warned us.[2] From Paul to our day, the true teachers[3] of the church have fought false doctrine and kept the message of God's Word before us. Such was God's intention for every generation. But we must remind ourselves that our theology is not inspired. It has its limitations.

We must be open to considering the human element in theology. The Western theology that my generation studied came from a modern worldview based on highlighting objectivity and rationality that came to us through the enlightenment. It creates a need to quantify and organize information, eliminate variants to our categories, and strive for systematic clarity. We are insecure outside this cultural frame of reference. In our need to avoid uncertainty and ambiguity, Western theology of the day sought a singular, objective, comprehensive explanation of the details

---

1. Barnlund, "Communication," 28–29.

2. Matt 7:15; 24:11; 2 Pet 2; 1 Tim 6:3–16.

3. 1 Tim 1:3–7; 2 Tim 4:1–5.

of who God is and what he does. The resulting systems often became a final word from our vantage point.

But our historical situation and cultural expectations bled through our theological method while we thought we were objective. All theological commentaries are contextual. Ours usually reveal our individualism, internal locus of control, needs for objectivity, order, and logic, optimism and views of unlimited good, low context preferences for communication, and sequential time. Values on achievement and competition also lurk in the background, as do feelings of guilt and innocence, an appetite for information, egalitarian views of humankind, and a universal view of God's ways with humans. The result of this approach is a comprehensive system of a universal, logical nature, with a great deal of abstraction. Our cultural frame of reference, which drives our personal preferences, is satisfied in this way. We then move into a defensive position as anyone does when their cultural system for survival is threatened.

So shaped is our theological system by our cultural preferences that if we export it to the non-western world, its logical, ordered, abstract, informational nature will not meet the concrete needs of those high-context, relational, holistic cultures. Chinese theology or African theology will look a good deal different from our own. The question we raise is if theirs comes from syncretism with their culture. We seldom level that question at our own system. Though all theologies need to be culturally relevant, all must be questioned as to their basis in Scripture and if they have been overly influenced by culture and human preferences.

Though not everything in our theologies is distorted by our cultural frame of reference or oversight of the biblical one, we would like to think that our theology comes only from the Bible, that our epistemology is based solely on revelation from God. But theology is never culture-free, our authors never entirely objective, and we can never know all there is to know about God and what he does and does not do. And, as we mentioned in chapter 5, language, ours and those of the biblical contexts, is never independent of its cultural system. As long as we do not see this, we will remain at a certain distance from God's intentions in our thinking. This does not mean past theologies and modern commentaries have not helped the church; many have been indispensable in their application of biblical truth to our day. But it does remind us of their humanness. The authors are not inspired as biblical authors were, even when they are supporting our theological system.

Since there is much that we cannot know about the infinite God of whom we speak, it makes it difficult to put him within one or another human set of theological boundaries. Still, we manage to find ways to satisfy our preferences. This human weakness calls for a little, as I mentioned in chapter 1, theological modesty. Regarding these limits of theology, Christopher Wright uses the analogy of a cartographer.

> As cartographers will agree, every existing map and any possible map is a distortion to some degree of the reality it portrays. Not every feature of the real landscape can be on a map, so the question again is, what purpose is the map intended to serve? What are the most significant features that the person using this map will need to see clearly? What can then be omitted—not because they don't exist in the geographical reality but because they are not of primary relevance to this particular way of viewing reality?[4]

Those decisions about some of our theological systems are already made or are in the making. Like maps, the Bible can be easily distorted, with the best of intentions, to fulfill the need of the interpreter, to emphasize their preferences as the important aspects the reader needs, to overlook what seems irrelevant, or to leave out what does not agree with his system, his logic, order, objectivity, individualism, etc. The more unconsciously this is done, the more unconstrained it is in the out-of-awareness areas of cultural influence and personal preferences. The author did not come to the text in a vacuum. Like Job's three friends who had only one option in their theology as the reason for suffering[5] and did not allow God to work outside that framework, we too can restrain God if we look at the Bible through a culture-bound theological system.

We must be aware that our cultural absolutes in the command center of our thoughts and preferences will strong-arm us unless we put our foot down. We have no other way to interpret our experience other than our cultural frame of reference. A novelist in our own culture can depend on it. It is not easy to turn it off when we open the Bible. In fact, because we are in foreign territory when we open the scriptures, we lean on it more heavily to help us figure out what is going on and what it means. What are our cultural values and theological systems filtering out for us? What are we adding to the text because, reading between the lines with

4. Wright, *Mission of God*, 68–69.

5. Job 18:21; 20:29; 22:5.

our own cultural lens, we feel it must be the intention? These questions call for maximum caution on the part of all of us. The leaking of these human and cultural preferences into our theology can lead to legalism, syncretism, or mysticism.

One more observation about a culture-bound theological filter at work is what it does to cross-cultural ministry. When we see the teachings of honesty, love, respect, or loyalty given to us in God's word, we can know these are required of every believer everywhere. The teachings are universal, but, as we have said, the behavior necessary to carry out these requirements is simply not the same for every person, every culture. Our theologies and doctrinal statements may plant their application in cement instead of the soil of the next person's heart, the soil of the next cultural system. It must take root in that soil and bear fruit recognizable to those people as love, honesty, respect, loyalty, etc. This is the relevancy of God's Word in every culture.

We must enter into a contextual discussion on these aspects of God's Word for their implications and applications for each context, learning from each other, growing stronger and less categorical in our expected expression. Unfortunately, we sometimes prefer to think we are the only ones who know what behavior fulfills the biblical requirements. This is cultural legalism—requiring *our* cultural form for obedience in a different culture.

So our theology, which should be so helpful, can become a filter only allowing us to see God through the human system we have constructed. Figure 8.1 gives examples of the potential parts of this filter.

We see God's Word through lenses or filters that often
do not allow him to speak for himself.

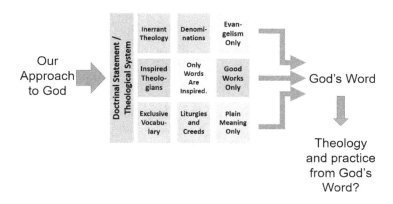

Figure 8.1. Components of the Filter of Doctrinal Statements and Theological Systems.

The information we accumulate about God may give us feelings of security, especially when it seems comprehensive, but we must let God be God. We must return to thinking about God on his terms, be willing to look past our favorite theological positions to allow him room. Yes, I realize there can be danger in these words. But we must return to the God who is above and beyond what we can know about him. And we must return to thinking about him and his ways outside our culture's requirements. In the essentials, we will remain steadfast. But in many cases, though we may not give up a less than essential theological proposition, we will hold it more loosely, not allow it to destroy relationships in the body of Christ. As Christianity, as we have known it in our own culture, faces persecution, we must embrace essentials and pull together as Christians. Unity is a sign of the credibility of our faith in Jesus.[6] Though it has *never* been unimportant, challenging times ahead will call for greater unity than we have considered necessary in our day. We must close this gap between God and Christianity.

Life for each of us takes different turns and unexpected detours. We must be able to see God at work, in his providence, in his own way, and be able to articulate his goodness, power, grace, and sovereignty in

6. John 17:20–23.

all things. We must not let non-essential position statements based on cultural preferences become the final word. Our knowing God requires a relationship including but going beyond information. We cannot let our culture-bound theology limit God.

CHAPTER 9

THE FILTER OF PERSONAL NEEDS

IN THE LAST CHAPTER, WE considered theology as a filter. It may be that for us because of personal needs. There are many variations of true and time-worn doctrines held from personal motives thought to be biblical convictions. The danger is that we all have blind spots where understandings are blocked from our view by loyalties to our chosen teachers, personal experiences shaping our perspective, influences of our ingroup, or our cultural preferences and all that within the circle of salvation. Our theology can be a filter only allowing God to say what it sanctions because of personal reasons.

The last of the three filters that comes into play is our culturally defined, personal desires, needs, and preferences (See Figure 4.3). We all come to God in prayer or read the Bible with needs. God wants us to bring these to him. But, we may have an agenda. It may be an honorable one, or it may be somewhat less principled. When we read the Bible, we want God to speak to us in our need, strengthen our faith, give us the assurance and confidence we seek, draw our attention to our blind spots, remind us of the great grace lavished on us and bring us to our knees. But, sometimes, we expect the Bible to give us what we want it or need it to say, perhaps for the advancement of the self, and we manage to hear it give us that for which we are searching. Armed with what we want the Bible to say, we sense a feeling of confidence that God spoke to us. Some people move on to ministry, building on a special calling or on this or that novel truth that no one else could know without telling them.

The danger is that our needs and motives are not always so well known to us. So, once again, we may not be letting God be God. We may be boxing him into what we want or need him to be or what we expect him to be within our cultural frame of reference. We may miss his intended message when we read the Scriptures selectively with this personal need filter. This affects everything in our lives. We are getting directions for the road that *we* want to take and possibly ignoring the crucial signposts along the way that warn us of danger and seek to turn us back. This approach almost always has an emotional framework. When their expectations are not met, these may feel that God did not speak to their need; he was not there for them. They did not sense his presence. But God is always there, waiting for our trust. He has given us all we need.

This searching for what we want or need is often seen in how we pray and talk about prayer as we see it in the Bible. Prayer is frequently the last resort in times of need instead of an ongoing conversation. At times it can almost be separated from God himself. People say "prayer really works." Often with a surprised tone in their voice. There are hundreds of mentions of prayer working on the internet with no mention of God at all. Our personal needs and desires are filtering out a meaningful relationship with God for a vending machine approach. We may plan elaborate, novel, and even ingenious ways of praying, thinking God will be more inclined to answer. But this is not prescribed for us in the Bible. These attitudes on our part put distance between God and us. They filter out his character and intentions for us and keep us from natural, ongoing intimacy.

Taking prayer out of the privacy of one's own room has dangers. It finds its way into the huckster's public ministry agenda, onto the schedule of the mercenary clergy and even the incredulous politician. It can become a display of spirituality as that of the Pharisees was.[1] But prayer is altogether different from these examples. There is no power in prayer or the one praying. Power is in the hands of the living, creator God who cares deeply, listens with attention, and moves in our lives. But it is a relationship that is bound up in trust. There is no magical formula, no secret key, posture, or method, however novel, that will influence God more in our favor. Prayer is always and only worshiping God, asking his forgiveness, praying for others, and bringing him our needs as Jesus taught us. He is always listening, waiting for us, grace overflowing, with a deep kind

---

1. Matt 6:5–8.

of love, human examples of which can only be a shadow. At the same time, he is the King of the universe, and clichés in our prayers and on church marquees create a gap between us and his majesty.

How should we then pray? Does he answer our pleas? When we pray, and God does not seem to answer, someone nearly always says something like, "Well, God usually responds with yes, no, or wait, and we must be content." There is truth to that statement, except in the word "usually." More often than any of these responses, God answers sincere prayers in ways we do not expect and therefore do not recognize. You would think the phrase, "My ways are not your ways,"[2] would be enough for us, but once again, the filter of our cultural and personal expectations is in full play. We already have in our minds what a "yes" answer looks like in our situation. In response to this habit, we need to recognize that we are very objective people. Should God's response be more subtle, indirect, or even ironic, we often miss it altogether. Many people were praying for the Messiah to come when Jesus was born. God answered. They missed it. And should God's answer be a two or three-year process, we will have lost interest or given up and may be looking the other way when he puts the final piece in place.

We are people of little faith. We give God's providential movement about a week and then try some new approach to prayer that promises a more receptive ear. But it is not that God is not following through on his purposes in creation; human logic and formulas are inadequate. God is beyond human judgment, unbound by any cultural framework, free of the limitations of time and human expectations. His responses to our prayers are more thoroughgoing than our imagination, his understanding of our needs deeper, and his ultimate plan unknown to us. In his providence, he often meets our necessities despite our prayers and responds to needs more desperate than we know as we pray. We will have to let God be God. He has and will continue to act in history and our lives in ways we can only partially understand, but for our ultimate good and beyond our limited view of life and the world. His providence is sure and covered in grace. Our attitude in prayer should reflect our unbending loyalty and our thoroughgoing trust.

God's providence is not in a dictionary where the right topic can be consulted for quick and easy answers for each situation. God is at work continually in his providential care of his children, even when they are

2. Isa 55:8–9.

not praying. But it will demand faith, rather than sight, in his design and strategy for all things working toward *his* ends. Again, we should be desiring to be part of his plan rather than making him part of ours. And we should know *that we do not know* the details of that great movement in history in which he has seen fit to allow us a part. His providential activity may not be perceived in the here and now. Even in the quiet moments of our lives, he is at work bringing about his plan. It may be only in the future that we look back and can trace events that could only have been by the control of his loving and gracious providence in our lives in tandem with our choices. He does not send out a notice or call our attention to his moving in our lives because he expects us to know that he is at work and trust him.

So, God never ignores us. All prayer is answered prayer, and there are far fewer negative responses from God to sincere prayer than we usually assume. A relationship thrives on communication. Trust him. He is there in the silence as well as the clamor of every moment of our lives. He has intentions, and each one of us can be a valuable part of them. Others may never know what he is doing in our lives if that is not his plan. His answers are not always glamorous or exciting; they are not intended to draw attention or bring celebrity status. Prayer is between those praying and God himself. But it sets God in motion. He has ordained to act in response to our prayer and brings peace and contentment for those trusting him.

For some, this matter of an ongoing relationship with God is missing in our petitions. We try instead to hold God to his words but are not trusting him in a relationship. It is, once again, a Western approach. We rationalize that since God said he would give us what we ask for, now he has to do it. We try to force God to pay up according to our specifications and adhere to a legal arrangement, a signed contractual agreement. Our cultural value on rational logic and the preference it gives us for objective indicators filter out his actual response to us. This is the opposite of trusting a person, let alone the infinite God of the universe.

For others, when there is no recognizable evidence of an answer to a prayer, we say the praying person did not have enough faith. By this, we actually mean assurance of God's positive response. But we, who do not know all his purposes, assuming that we know that he will and how he will act on our behalf, have forgotten our place. We have lost the fear of God and locked him inside our theological box, defining how he must respond to prayer when the *secret key*, enough faith, is used. How opposite

Jesus' words about faith the size of a mustard seed. No, the confidence that he talks about and that we need is not in prayer but in the person of God. It is not measured by how strongly we believe he will grant something we ask, but how much we live in the reality of his good providence. We must trust him, not our prayer formula, position, emotional state, or technique. He is God, and our humility, trust, and loyalty to his purposes must be our response.

Personal needs that drive us in prayer or reading God's word may be combined with our own solutions to personal or ministry success. We may have found that a legalistic approach to God's word gives us the black and white view of his ways that we crave. We can know exactly what God always wants in every situation, for every person, because it is always the same. We begin to see it on every page of the Bible, and we cobble together a system that makes all verses lead to a simplistic and objective outcome. All uncertainty and ambiguity are gone. We find relief in a quantitative world where there is an answer for every question. This detached approach is a soothing balm to our nervous system when a relationship with loose ends is too threatening.

Or it may be that we have decided that the mysticism of signs and wonders is our solution and gives us the feelings of God's special attention to us that we require. Once again, we begin to see it on every other page of the Bible. How could anything else be true? But it is a matter of syncretism for most of us, mixing cultural solutions with God's word and prayer. We pray that God would help us feel personal worth in Christ while we do our best to get under the lights, appear more spiritual, achieve an image of someone having everything under control.

We have a cultural, and therefore personal desire as individualists to be in control. Legalism gives us that control and relieves us of unpredictable intrusions of God in our plans. If not legalism, then a water-tight theological system will serve. We need control, and we require it in every verse we read, every doctrine we formulate. When others do not snap to grid with our understandings, we may feel they simply reject the truth. But God will refuse the box we have constructed for him.

Yet, for others of us, every reading of the Scriptures is immersed in desperation for good feelings about ourselves and our circumstances. Our insecurities are overwhelming, and though we are turning to the one source capable of laying them all to rest, we miss that rest every time. For that rest is found, once again, in a relationship, not in information alone. If we look for God to affirm some activity or behavior we know is wrong, a God who loves us will not do that. But he will continue to set his alternative before us—a relationship fulfilling every void with trust. He will give us rest. We do not have to have all the answers to life's twists and turns; he intends that we trust him.

The drive for personal needs and desires filters the real God from the Bible and replaces him with what we want to find there. We must give up ourselves for Christ—give him the reigns. It will take a trust that we may not have yet known in our lives, trust in a relationship wrapped around realizing his plan instead of ours. Relationships are about giving and trusting, not secret hopes of satisfying selfish ends. We will either take or leave a relationship with God, but feigning it is the worst option and creates a gap between God and our real needs.

Some find relief in the informal, friendly, down-to-earth, buddy-buddy presence of Jesus in life, thinking that he likes us the way we are and could not demand more than we typically give. He makes allowances for our thoughtless, boys-will-be-boys way of life. But this shallow approach leaves the fear out of "the fear of the Lord," the deep respect for the creator God of the universe bringing it to its appointed consummation and the part he has for us to play in the great drama of his providence. It is an avoidance of his proper person, his life-changing grace, and the meaningful relationship to which he calls us. Our impertinence will be brought up short unless we recognize his greatness, power, authority, and ultimate justice, all tempered by his grace for those who choose it. Once again, it calls for trust beyond our present experience.

Our personality makes a difference. In God's providence, we have been shaped in ways that can fulfill his desired purpose for us in his plan. But extroverts and introverts come to God with different needs. Melancholy souls and cheerful, animated ones read his Word with different moods and intentions. To know ourselves is important when reading his Word since our approach to his Word controls what our eyes see and our hearts grasp. We should not try to erase how we are; we need only to "renew our minds," reframe our thinking so that what we are becomes his to use as he intends. So it is that our understanding of self and culture's influence on the self with a humble heart is the gateway to a meaningful and purposeful relationship with God through Christ.

Figure 9.1 offers some examples of the details of how this personal needs and desires filter can stand between God and us and distort his purposes in our lives. Again, these needs can cause us to find what we want to find in his Word and demand answers to prayer that meet our expectations.

We see God's Word through lenses or filters that often
do not allow him to speak for himself.

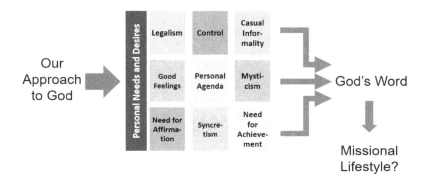

Figure 9.1. Components of the Filter of Personal Needs and Desires.

This filter and others that we allow between God and us blunt the impact of God's very personal approach to us, not in the matter of our salvation necessarily, but as regards our ongoing relationship with him. They dull our delight in him and his way with secondary and often self-ish motives. They also keep a good deal of significance in many biblical passages just out of reach. Satan blinds the minds of unbelievers to the truth of Christ; he also distracts the thinking of believers in these ways. We may find ourselves struggling to breathe, fighting for clean air, even though God offers us freedom from the stranglehold of self.

The filter of our personal needs and desires seeks to control God by how we interpret his Word and pray in his name. We must, instead, allow God to be God when placing needs and wants before him. We must reduce the impact of our expectations and preferences with a passion for his way in our lives. An illustration of this filter of the assertive self transformed into a submissive one for a relationship with him would incorporate the values in Figure 9.2.

We must see God's Word through the lenses or filters
that allow him to speak for himself.

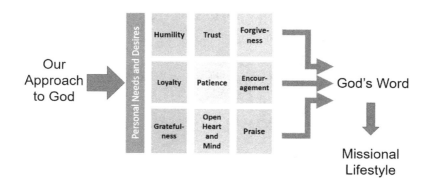

Figure 9.2. The Transformation of the Filter of Personal Needs and Desires.

In this matter of the filter of personal needs and desires, there are also expectations of God's Word that do not match his intentions for his revelation. Some might expect God to answer all our scientific questions or reveal information only for them. They might expect that he intends in his Word to tell them everything about himself, so they must go about discovering the things that are not explicitly given to them to fill in the blanks. They may need a unique code, secret meanings for words, or formulae suited to producing the missing information in the Bible. These expectations keep us at a distance from God. (See Figure 9.3.) He has given us all we need to know to become his faithful people, no more, no less. Now must trust him for what he has not told us about himself or his plan.

We see God's Word through lenses or filters that
often do not allow him to speak for himself.

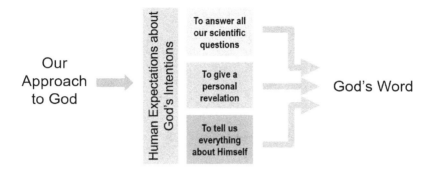

Figure 9.3. The Filter of Personal Expectations of God's Word.

CHAPTER 10

CULTURE AND THE SELF

THOUGH THE CULTURAL INFLUENCES I have been talking about can lead to behavior and attitudes that do not honor God, we often overlook them because they seem so natural. We want to serve and honor God. But the messages from our culture about the need for achievement, recognition, personal happiness, and the necessity of internal locus of control often have the upper hand. These ruling needs and values with their attitudes and the behavior that results from them are seldom mentioned when we share the Gospel with someone. Neither are they the subjects of discipleship.

We begin to have problems with them on day one, and Church ministries rarely speak to them directly. Sermons talk about becoming mature in Christ without connecting that to the many common cultural values that continue to govern our lives. There may be various reasons for this, but common among them is that we all share these values, the attitudes feel normal, and many cultural urgings are invisible to us. They are the only reference points we have known, and though we find ourselves in new territory, we keep going back to the old familiar map and trying to function from that perspective. The signposts along the way in God's Word are unfamiliar. They don't look like we expected them to, and we are afraid to trust them. So, these cultural controls come between God and us, between God and Christianity.

Cultural expectations, concern for self, fear for our reputation, and worry about the success of a ministry or institution can obstruct the way to serving God and his people. They can easily divert efforts and priorities, sending them in the wrong direction, and by our own efforts, we arrive at a dead end. We must correct our course, deactivate the filters, dismantle the barriers, and repair the damage. If there is no change, only a hollow, popular Christianity syncretized with the social values around it will remain evidence of our effort. Thinking people will leave this sort of Christianity having never seen the real thing.

Our conflict is often resolved by syncretizing what the Bible tells us with the culture's solutions for success. This, of course, has its consequences for the church. When Christianity turns inward for survival and loses its compassion for a lost world, and when Christians weaken in their selfless loyalty to God, they will not be a witness to God's grace in that world. They leave no reason in their wake for the lost to consider God's existence and purposes. In the nature of things in a broken world, society will continue to be driven and pitched in the dark, cold waters of godlessness without any credible warnings of disaster; the lighthouses will have not been lit. Our society will move through a post-Christian stage to an anti-Christian response to us who are to be the messengers of hope, who are to bear the Gospel of the grace of God that brings peace. The importance of self-survival and the institutional church will have overcome our mission.

Culture is very much at the source of our problem, numbing us to the significance of many passages in the Bible that have to do with the self. When culture's influence is negative, it is a powerful adversary. We could spend a great deal of time at this point on the positive aspects and the essential nature of our culture for survival. There certainly are many things to be said for it and other cultures as well. We simply cannot survive outside a cultural system. But we are instead going to look at its adverse elements concerning our faith. They are plentiful enough, and their subtlety makes them dangerous for Christians. We will look at culture here as our foe and do so through the application of cultural anthropology.

All cultures have this negative side. After a rise to some sort of organization, all follow a social version of the second law of thermodynamics as traditional solutions for survival breakdown and moral codes disintegrate. Ignoring God, human systems have limited virtue and are never adequate. As mentioned in chapter 4, the solutions for survival each culture offers its members have different effects as the problems they seem to solve come from diverse human perspectives. In a collective culture, the sacrifice of self for group approval and harmony is the daily need for feelings of worth and belonging. Asians must acquiesce, surrender, seek to satisfy expectations, save face, promote harmony, and maintain their place in the group to gain the identity and status the group grants.

On the other hand, we in the West live in cultures built on the foundation of individualism. For us, it becomes a fight every day for or against the self. Our success is in achieving status—creating a personal identity recognized by the group resulting in feelings of self-worth and personal security. We are on the offensive right upfront and must achieve this success for the self. This results in an earned status. Money, importance, power, intellectual prowess, and even looks, along with the skill to control people and circumstances to that end, are among the tools recognized to achieve these feelings of worth and the coveted identity of an achiever.

Failure to attain this identity and worth at some level can be devastating for the individual. There are no substitutes for these methods of survival in either Western or non-Western cultures. People have only the cultural ways given to them, and there is no escape from the constant pressure. Failure to attain the needed worth and identity means a failure to survive both socially and personally. The results are isolation and questions about meaning in life that breed emotional depression or antisocial behavior. Since God intended these terminal values for humankind to be satisfied in himself, removing or disallowing his influence leaves a vacuum that only human skills can work at filling. But human effort using the disintegrating instrumental values of human culture leaves little hope for long-term personal or societal survival. Humanity ignores God at great personal and social costs.

Individualism and its accompanying values of internal locus of control and personal achievement throw their whole weight behind our quest as Western people. Our survival is a powerful motive, and we employ every strategy, strain every nerve, use every possible means our culture gives us to attain it. It becomes a lifestyle of trying to succeed and win at every turn. This pursuit of achievement, as demanding as it sounds, actually becomes normal to us. We learn patterns and habits of what seems to work to reduce the stress and provide, however fragile, feelings of wellbeing and worth. When we become Christians, we need to be discipled out of these cultural patterns, for they can maintain a stranglehold on our trust in God and freedom in Christ. No one is exempt. We will remain under the spell of these methods of personal survival and, by extension, institutional survival until we finally allow God to be God in our lives and ministries.

After many years of this deep-rooted pattern in our lives, trusting God wholly for our wellbeing is a daunting step and is usually met with anxious resistance and fear. But outside a relationship of trust and loyalty with God, there is no lasting remedy. I am reminded of the scene in *The Lion, the Witch, and the Wardrobe* where Mr. Beaver remarks to Lucy that Aslan, the great lion, is not safe, but he is good. Later, in *The Silver Chair*, Jill is thirsty, but the lion stands between her and the stream where she might drink. He gives no outward promise of safety, but she needs the water to survive, and there is no other stream.[1] Trusting God comes hard for the Western Christian up against personal and social survival in an individualist culture. There has not been a thorough revision of our worldview, which leads to the syncretism we mentioned earlier. God has been added on with the hope he does not interfere too much. Dealing with this conflict of loyalties should be at the very heart of conversion. It is then we must decide to break the cycle of this syncretism. Culture's methods and values for survival must be exchanged for God's way.

Though every culture has its challenges, this is very difficult for individualists. Without God, we were left alone to make something of ourselves, and it is natural to feel the drive to continue down this road. Before we met Christ, we may have been deceived by the rich or powerful celebrities of our culture. We may have tried to imitate them and are still stuck in this pattern. We must now see that their seeming success is superficial and temporary. They are not worthy of our envy.[2] Their station in this life is not God's plan for us.

Instead, we must humbly realize how meager our resources are, that we really have nothing to win God's favor, that the goal is entirely out of reach for the self-made individualist with all his achievement and control. Our human culture cannot in any way achieve God's purposes for us. We must bow before God and God alone. All has already been secured for us in Christ. It is dying to self of which Jesus often spoke that remains. All is ready for life in his lavish grace and love.

The influence of culture is subtle but powerful on its members. To abandon our culture's solutions when we become Christians doesn't feel natural. Of course, we would not want, nor is it wise, to think that it is

---

1. Lewis, *Lion*, 86, and *Silver Chair*, 21.

2. Ps 37:1–11.

necessary or possible to forsake all our cultural values and beliefs. However, this being the case and being unable to separate the good from the bad, we tend to bend them all to fit the new environment of our Christian lives, not realizing that some lead us away from God. With our ethnocentrism in full swing, we have trouble separating biblical absolutes from cultural absolutes and live syncretized Christian lives. No one has told us about this influence of culture on our natural inclinations. It is a central weakness of our evangelism and discipleship efforts, the cost we have not counted.

Everyone needs feelings of worth and identity, but if we bring cultural patterns into the church and compete with others for their attainment, we will continue to get affirmation and identity from our efforts instead of from God himself. But as Jesus said of such people, " . . . they have received their reward in full."[3] We are competing with God over what is good for us as much as competing with others in the body of Christ to achieve our agenda. And we are good competitors, the best in the West. Such is our addiction to achievement for feelings of security while neglecting its only true source.

Western values and understandings are calibrated for survival without God. Internal locus of control, rational logic, task and time orientation, and a universalist view of social control are used to this end. As we read the Bible, these values can betray us, and we may see no conflict between them and God's ways. We miss the inconsistency, the outright denial of God's providence regarding our wellbeing. Our allegiance is in word only; the realities of an all-inclusive trust in God elude us. This is the power of unrestrained culture in the life of the Christian, the long arm of syncretism.

As good as some of the aspects of our culture might be if harnessed for God, our thirst is so great and the patterns so deep, we keep drinking at the fountain of culture for daily needs. So, we live compartmentalized Christian lives and continue to use the avenues to satisfaction and wellbeing that are familiar to us and switch to God only when needed. We are like children who want to play in the water, but as C.S. Lewis says, we continue to make mud pies in the ghettos because we do not know what a free vacation to an ocean beach means.[4] The two cognitive domains are separated, sealed off from each other. We teach others about freedom in

---

3. Matt 6:2, 5.
4. Lewis, *Weight of Glory*, 26.

Christ, while we, maybe at that very moment, are competing with others in our ritual behavior, or to have the best answers to spiritual questions, or to know the "secret keys to the Christian life," for the feelings of affirmation this brings.

It is not easy. We have been learning this cultural approach inside and outside the home since we were children. In our late teens, we became experts at it and were enjoying its full flourishing in our thirties and forties. Whether we are successful or not, we know how the system works, and we maintain the effort even though trusting God for personal wellbeing is at the center of the Gospel. Yes, we have been handed a truncated Gospel. In their enthusiasm to bring us to Christ, those who evangelized us talked about the issue of sin before God and the need for forgiveness. But they did not relate it to the dangers of the old, habitual, human, cultural system. How could they? They were not aware of it themselves. Yet freedom from individualism and the need for achievement are part of the Gospel. We can only talk about conversion and obedience to God with relevancy for people by recognizing the influences of culture on them. And to do that, we will have to pay attention to those influences on us.

So, our greatest challenge is an inability to allow for God's providence which severely limits our perspective of his plan for the world. God's providence puts the self in second place—a difficult adjustment for the Western individualist. In chapter 2, I commented that his care and help in our lives do not always look like they could be his, so stereotypical are our expectations and cultural preferences, so rigid our legalism. We can allow ourselves to be blinded to his work in our lives by our selfish ambition and its outcome, the need for control. If we can stop it, we often do not allow God to work in our lives. It would upset our agenda and, perhaps, our theological system.

In our favor, I must emphasize that this cultural training did not come with our consent, but that dulls our awareness of it. It is now deeply embedded and violently resists any tampering. We want God's help on *our* side in our struggle to survive. But, we define God's purposes in such a way that puts us at the center. His function is to help us achieve *our* goals. We ask him for his help but are often disappointed when he does not seem to come through on our terms. We make him part of *our* plan rather than desire to become part of his. There is so much at stake, and God might upset our plan if he calls the shots. Therefore, God is not allowed to be God, but to be the God we have defined, the God we need him to be.

It is amazing how he continues to work in our lives despite us. We do not often notice until long after the event that he has been at work often regardless of our attempt at control. It is distressing that the proud self can still rise to such levels of opposition, overlooking his hand in our lives. As with the Pharisees, even our ritual behavior can become a tool to resist God's guidance.[5] I am generalizing, of course. Some Christians are more sensitive and self-aware. But others, caught in the cultural snare of an internal locus of control, continue to play the game by its social rules and find their own fragile security. Letting God lead is simply contrary to our typical human drive for control. The two ways are mutually exclusive.[6]

A level of success in this pursuit of the self-made person is often accompanied by a sense of pride. But not everyone is as skillful in the ways our culture has given us to achieve this personal worth, and those who *are* skilled live in fear of losing what they have gained. It might be lost with old age, a financial disaster, or a debilitating accident or illness—things outside their human, finite control. Everyone has insecurities to deal with in the Western system. The same is true of any cultural system, but for different reasons.

Cheap attitudes about those with less skill in disguising their insecurities add to one's own constructed self-image even among Christians. But desperation bubbles just below the surface for most individualists, and much effort is expended to close a watertight bulkhead over it and give the appearance of calmness around it. This is often accomplished by using more power to control the situation and people, or its sister, legalism. Others compete with less severity, sometimes with a winsomeness that suffocates the competition to their desired display of a secure self. Some of these strategies are not very private. People who never gush at home may do nothing but gush at church. The victim card may be played, false humility put on show, or the know-it-all smile beamed in all directions, seeking to signal confidence. But these are signs indicating that all is not well, that there is a lack of trust in God's providence. Humility has been left behind. There is a gap between God and this Christianity.

In the classroom, I have often given students an inventory to measure their need to control. The majority are always surprised to see how high they come out on the scale. When you combine an internal locus of

5. Mark 7:8–13.
6. Matt 6:24.

control with the Western bent for competition and self-satisfaction, that internal locus becomes quite measurable in outward ways. We become driven people. We must prove to ourselves and those around us that we amount to something. Most of us are unaware of this deep conditioning as we are of most of our culture's influence. We think we are controlling our surroundings, but they are controlling us. You are noting, undoubtedly, the absence of God in all this, even for Christians.

If our achievements are to be noticed by others and result in feelings of affirmation and approval, we need an audience. There is nowhere a more easily convinced audience for this than Christian circles provide—the very place we should find help and freedom from this need in Christ. How unfortunate if this sacred ground of culture and self is never plowed from the pulpit. Ministry in the West must understand and respect this powerful influence on our motives and behavior. This is the hill that must be taken if the battle for maturity in Christ in our lives is to be turned in his favor.

It is a costly thing for an individualist to come to Christ. God is telling us we must give up the fight. Accepting his grace takes humility which is no more readily found in Western culture today than it was in the Jewish situation at the time of the birth of Jesus. Though meaning, worth, and identity are found in God's love and providence, many have a resilient tendency to syncretize their new faith with the old ways of their culture and continue to struggle with it. So strong is the western value on individualism and its need for control. But the Gospel message is not only about forgiveness; it is also about freedom[7] from the old social and religious systems that controlled our lives. It is the ongoing ministry of the church to deal with this cultural conditioning we all share. This freedom is not intended to make us celebrities, and the way ahead will not be without its difficulties. But if we are willing, Christ, who went before us, will share that path with us. How disappointing to be such self-seekers, but how enlightening to discover we have been tricked. We have become addicted to the drugs offered by our culture that seem to dull the ache, a temporary fix for the need, but then learn that there is rehabilitation in Christ.

In summary, here are a few reminders that I have found helpful in the battle against the influence of cultural values: Remember that God does not stop desiring to work in and through us; we stop him. Remember,

7. John 8:31–36.

God's providence in our lives does not always look like it comes from him. Remember that we do not often notice his workings in the present, but recalling past events of his providence gives strength. Remember that his love and desire for us are stronger than ours for him, and our weakness reveals his strength. Remember, his love is not a romantic notion and is active in our lives without our romantic notions. The biblical idea of "loving" God is made up of loyalty and allegiance, a commitment in a relationship with him. Remember that walking with God is a matter of inward loyalty more than outward achievement. Remember that what our culture, other people, our experience, or even our conscience tell us may or may not be accurate, but what God says is always true. Remember, we must trust God's directions more than our notions; he knows the way. Remember that we cannot take society's evaluation of us at face value; we are measured by God's standard. Remember, the assurance of right things happening in the long run only comes if we allow the creator God of the universe to be in control. Remember, no amount of failure can cut us off from God's love and forgiveness if we are willing to admit our failure and get back in the saddle.

These reminders change our magnetism to the self and to the affirmation of the crowd. Most of Jesus' teachings about honoring God were along these lines instead of calling out specific sins. The exception was the Pharisees, whose hearts were proud. Jesus sought humility in people. It makes all the reminders possible. It is what God saw in David's heart.[8]

In tandem with our selfish need to control our circumstances is the problem of our emotions controlling us. They can come between God and us. Emotions are often fed by cultural expectations and are connected to all our values. Since values cause behaviors, all we do is based on them. We behave in particular ways because we see it as important, fun, good, necessary, reasonable, called for in the line of duty, friendship, love, mercy, etc. Of course, the value may be on selfish pleasure as well. We may also choose not to do other things because they are bad, unimportant, worthless, wrong, selfish, cause unneeded suffering, etc. Once again, the value could as easily be on the fear of the loss of selfish pleasure. All these values we have for certain lines of action are attached to attitudes or feelings and influenced to one degree or another by our culture, experience, personal preferences, and God's Word.

---

8. 1 Sam 13:13–14; Acts 13:22.

Emotions often do not correlate with reality. Given a situation, we may not feel a proper level of gravity or doubt, joy or sorrow. Feelings will often be too strong, too weak, too temporary, or go on too long to fit the situation. This does not mean that feelings are of no value at all. Our trust in God brings overwhelming gratefulness and spontaneous praise for his grace and providence and for the blessings, people, and events that he uses in our lives. The contentment and peace from our faith are powerful rewards. Love can be accompanied by deep happiness and confidence in his providence and mitigate the great sorrow of loss. Loyalty and commitment can be felt deeply as motives for action.

Feelings can be beautiful and enjoyable but will not make bad things good for us. Equally, if they are negative, they do not make good things bad. There must be discernment because temporary happiness can be deceptive and addictive and lead us astray from wisdom. Bad feelings such as false guilt can cause us to reject the very things God holds out to us. Though Satan would like to use the pressure of sentiments created by cultural values, social expectations, and past experiences against us, they cannot hurt us or our relationship with God unless we let them. Knowledge of God's Word, undiluted trust in his providence,[9] and remembering his faithfulness to us in the past are clearer paths to good decisions, whether accompanied by feelings or not. It is knowing the difference between inclination and duty, between desire and need.

We must never underestimate the power of culture. There is no room for compromise. Blinding the minds of unbelievers, culture is also among Satan's tools to weaken the church and every believer. These are human systems and as much at his disposal as they are at ours. We depend highly on them, and that can be used against us. The unconscious worldview assumptions our culture develops in us are difficult to locate and identify, giving them even more power over us than we imagine. Expect our enemy to blackmail us with them at every turn. But we are not alone in the battle. God is with us, and he is patient. He will be at work in us, giving us every opportunity and reason to trust him.[10] We must not keep him waiting.

9. Proverbs 3:5–6.
10. Rom 8:28; Phil 2:13; 4:13.

CHAPTER 11

CULTURE AND THE CHURCH

ONE OF THE PROBLEMS IN an individualist culture is the difficulty people have doing things together. Concern for self and social apprehensions dampen the empathy needed for smooth relations. This affects the church, making it difficult to achieve the oneness that Jesus said was so essential for the credibility of our message.[1] This results in an effort to manage the local church as an institution, one very much like the social institutions around her, in ways that meet the expectations of members for group inclusion, working and worshiping together, and owning and running a corporation together with people they have not chosen to be in their group.

Institutions are created in our context with cultural values that tell us what is expedient, efficient, and beneficial for the organization to accomplish a mission. These are not unhealthy values in themselves, but because they are from our culture, they carry cultural expectations that are not always helpful for the church. The people in attendance have their own expectations, needs, and preferences shaped by this culture that may pressure the church to go in one direction or another. These institutional, cultural, and personal expectations need to be assessed if we are to be both relevant and effective in our missional purposes. We must determine where they come from and whether or to what degree meeting them is a proper function of the church or healthy to her purpose.

1. John 17:20–23.

Since we are numb to the effects of our own culture on us, we will look at an example from another culture to put the need for cultural awareness in Christian organizations in higher contrast. While doing "business as mission" in Central Africa, a sewing shop was one of the businesses created. The staff was made up of a director, two or three professionals, and usually two apprentices at a time. On the outside, it looked like any business might if transplanted from our situation to the context of that country. But inside the institution, it was very different. The structure and organization, cash flow, inventory on hand, and business principles fit the Central African culture, which offered many challenges for a small business. Poverty, tribalism, and an assumption of limited good changed the landscape to such an extent that we had to face these conditions for the enterprise to work at all. This affected how it organized itself and handled clients, how the workers were paid, how the books were kept, and how it could maintain enough stock on hand to be efficient.

We saw the effects of limited good in chapter 7. In this example, we see the additional impact of social systems. The three main categories of social organization are individualism, collectivism, and tribalism. People in any of these systems have no idea how to live or survive socially in one of the other systems. They also know very little about their own system because it is the only one they have experienced. They have been in it all their lives, and it is not only natural to them; it is the only right way to manage relationships. That's right; we know very little about our own individualism, and this gives it free rein in our lives and social groups. Social groups among individualists are very different than groups in a collective or tribal situation. It is, instead, a grouping of individualists that people from the other types of cultures would not recognize as a group at all. Even the difficulties of working together seem natural to us. We have developed coping mechanisms to make it manageable—though they may be the very things that make people around us wish they were not in our group.

Tribalism involves collective society in measurable units with fierce loyalties to one's own and only superficial social obligations to others. The obligations to one's own tribe require unrestrained discrimination that can kill a small business before it gets off the ground. How can you expect people of your tribe to pay the same price as those of other tribes? It's insulting. And since good is limited, people are poor, and "what belongs to you belongs to us," sharing the resources is expected, whether a free product or some of the stock on hand. The same social values meant that we could not allow a staff member of the microeconomics enterprise to grant a loan to someone of his own tribe. It would be unthinkable to consider someone of your own tribe a risk in the loan business. Refusal would be highly offensive.

We see how social systems and cultural values can obstruct the attaining of the mission of the organization. Imagine what these values do to the missional purpose of the local church in that context! Culture has to be consulted but never allowed to control the organization. Without cultural awareness, the western missionary would fail miserably in business as mission and church planting endeavors.

Institutions must embody some cultural values if they are to survive and be relevant in their society. Who is to say if those rules are beneficial for the church and its mission just because they seem to work outside the church? Are we weighing these values against biblical principles? When we know what works in our culture, we seldom ask the question. We like to feel we use some discretion, but basically, being the pragmatic people we are, we do what works.

We may not notice if we are confusing biblical absolutes with cultural absolutes. But, in the process, the truth we work to extend, the contented wellbeing in Christ we hope to instill, the oneness in Christ we want to create, the very worship of God as God can fade in the endless details and demands of running the church to meet cultural expectations. When the demands of the institution become a weight or drain on personnel and financial resources, it loses its focus. The mission of the church becomes subject to the survival of the organization, the success of its leader, or the ease of its members. More and more resources are needed, more strain is put on leaders and the people supporting the growth and maintenance of the institution. Leadership must be sensitive to culture's power and influence—those who can scrutinize the outside influences, keep them on a tight rein, and allow the church to flourish in its organic purposes.

It is the natural disposition of institutions to always be at risk of, and have a natural inclination toward, self-preservation over their stated mission. The more institutionalized along cultural lines in our situation, the more the church's focus is turned inward rather than outward, for that is the foundational value of the culture in which we find ourselves. Churches are made up of imperfect people with their virtues and vices, their inspired commitment, and their necessity, in Western individualist cultures, for preoccupation with self for success and survival. Without God and his mission at the center and continually reinforced, the institution will go its natural way toward syncretism and disintegration. It will lose the wholesome nature of the early church in the book of Acts—its emphasis on God's mission in the world. The members begin to see themselves and their organization as his plan and lose sight of the big picture—his actual plan and mission in the world—that should be at the center of their ministry.

If the social context within which the church finds itself shapes the institutional culture by which it operates, determining how the organization behaves despite the mission statement, it calls for alertness to the effects. There must be a plan for overall commitment to the mission that protects it. Leaders outside the church have seen the connection for some time now, "Either you will manage your culture, or it will manage you."[2] Institutional culture will mirror the social culture. The search for identity and affirmation so prevalent in the culture outside the church will leak in. People may find it an easy place to gain the approval of others rather than finding their secure identity in Christ. The desire to be known as a singer, preacher, giver, or spiritual person is that culture-driven need at work in the very last place it should show up. People may feel they need the church more than God.

The appetite for trendy themes and activities may be mistaken for cultural relevance and can become an addiction. The culture-driven need for novelty and change has leaked in. People begin to enjoy the activities; being part of the church has become fun, and it may have little to do with God. We may be encouraging a popular Christianity instead of a biblical Christianity—people loving and needing the church more than God. Cultural relevance has to do with our message and behavior being understood and touching the real needs of our community, not necessarily our culture's agreement with them. It is not that we should not enjoy church. There should be wholesome, and mutual encouragement, an identity in Christ we share, and a community in worship, prayer, and learning that strengthens us for our witness in the world. Our unity in these ways should become part of our message, and few things could be more relevant in our individualist culture. What is our plan to decide what is necessary and what is not? Normality and popularity are not good standards for necessity.

The church should keep our attention on the movement of God in history, the big picture of his plan, the world from his perspective, his

2. Connors and Smith, *Change the Culture*, 7.

priority in our lives, the contented wellbeing to be found only in him. The institution itself must be secondary to this movement of unity around God's purposes. It is the vehicle. Its purpose should be the engine that motivates and moves *any* institutional affairs and details, if we indeed must have them, in a controlled yet relevant direction that honors God. Culture must be our servant in this, never our master.

When cultural values have the upper hand, Christian institutions can become enmeshed in stressful interpersonal conflict full of competitiveness, self-assertion, politics, and the need for control. These are natural outcomes of our culture's solutions for personal survival. We emphasize outward show rather than inward reality, emotional highs rather than spiritual strength, distractions and activity rather than quietness and wisdom. It emphasizes doing rather than being. And then, with little attention to the interference of culture, this church begets others like it. Syncretism with our culture's expectations will never turn out well for the church. Paul and John were writing letters of correction for this already in the first century.[3]

We need to ask what has changed the essence of the early church from its simplicity and authenticity in the book of Acts to today's struggle for professional attractiveness in ministry, successful identities, and positions of importance? What has Christianity become in our day as we head toward a post-Christian context? Why the ranks of burned-out pastors, teachers, and missionaries? Has our mission become secondary to the demands of our culture and needs of the institution, however that may be disguised? Has survival become the goal?

The salt has lost its savor, the light its penetration. As we have been busy with our "success," the world around us has degenerated in social structure and moral values resulting in a dysfunctional environment that exacerbates the deterioration. Why do we think we are above the decline of the seven churches toward the end of the first century, or again, in the middle ages, just because we have more extensive, high-tech ministries? The church has always struggled with the culture of its context, and we are no exception. Awareness is our friend and only God our protector.

But let us not disregard the proper need for cultural relevancy in our churches mentioned earlier. Knowing our culture's human solutions for survival and how Christians continue to struggle with them in their faith can make our ministries highly relevant to the needs. The goals of resting

3. 1 and 2 Cor and Rev 2 and 3.

in Christ and trusting God's providence can come into sight above the syncretism of our times if we target these adverse effects of our culture. A relevant life and message for Christ can become possible within that same culture—a contextual expression of our faith and loyalty, a meaningful and helpful ministry to others.

Our strategy must become a matter of form and function. We need to analyze the forms we choose and their functions in worship, ministry, and relationships in Christ. Forms are what we use to express meaning. They are methods, rituals, procedures, and symbols. Verbal and nonverbal communication is full of forms such as words, gestures, pitch, tones, context, and artifacts. Rituals are complex forms that mean and communicate something. The forms are cultural and have that meaning only in the culture of their use. In church and worship, the forms must be relevant; they must make sense to the people using them. If the meaning is not clear, people assign their own meaning to them.

But forms also have a function, and it must be biblical. The function of a form is what it does. A word in communication is used to create meaning in a message. The function of a form in worship might be to turn our thoughts towards God's greatness. If we do not consider the forms in this way, we may become committed to them rather than their functions. Or we may assign them a new function that is somehow to our advantage, but perhaps not so biblical, very likely syncretized with cultural needs and preferences.

A word of caution, however, commitment to the forms of Christianity does not result in a meaningful relationship with God. Post-Christian cultures can still be committed to many Christian forms. Only a commitment to the biblical essentials of our faith in God through Christ results in a relationship. That commitment must then be expressed in culturally relevant forms faithful to God's Word in meaning *and* function to emphasize loyalty, trust, and worship concerning God and good works in our lives that honor him.

Every form used by the church must be analyzed as to its necessity, its biblical foundation and function, and its cultural relevancy for expressing the meaning and performing the function intended. If it is not, we will tend to do what our culture demands or expects. Forms in the church are physical things like buildings, pulpits, pews, lights and sound systems, musical instruments, or physical arrangements. They may also be behavioral forms such as used in sermons, communion, postures for the reading of Scripture or for prayer, baptism, head coverings, or taking offerings. They may be less concrete such as terminology, programs, what is done for transitions in a worship service, structures and leadership positions, educational degrees required, the use of money, the expression of formality or informality, etc. It is easy to notice that such a list was not necessary for the early churches. It makes one ask if what we have added makes our church better or more biblical than early churches in Acts might have been. How many of our forms come from modern Western values? Unnecessary forms can add distance between us and God's intentions. Forms outside biblical principles always do.

Since forms mean something and do something, each needs to go through a process of contextualization resulting in a thoughtful and intentional response to it. Why do we use the form? What does the form mean to us? To outsiders? Does the meaning accord with God's Word? Does its function meet biblical expectations and produce God-honoring results? The same thought should be given to traditional forms we want to stop using.

Without critical evaluation of all its forms, the church will go the way of all social institutions, eventually being too concerned about its own existence and survival in the surrounding culture. There will be a tendency to fall in love with the forms or the results they achieve and forget the biblical meanings and relevant functions they are to have in the church and community around us. The world is watching Christianity and leaning away from it. The United States is quickly becoming a post-Christian context.[4] A pile of Bibles was burned just forty minutes from my home a few months ago. Useless, legalistic, or superficial forms and requirements are rejected by thinking people, and more and more youth are disconnecting from the church.[5] We must evaluate our activity and choices and stay on mission. We have to know if the church is influencing our culture or our culture is influencing the church.

All religions have outward forms of ritual behavior. Whether they are the forms for prayer and ablution, fasting, the shahada, pilgrimage, and dietary rules of Islam, or the river bathing, *puja*, images, *ahimsa*, karma, and yoga of Hinduism, religion is full of forms that promise to set

---

4. "Decline of Christianity," Pew Research Center, accessed October 2, 2020, https://www.pewforum.org/2019/10/17/in-u-s-decline-of-christianity-continues-at-rapid-pace.

5. "America's Changing Religious Landscape," Pew Research Center, accessed October 2, 2020, https://www.pewforum.org/2015/05/12/americas-changing-religious-landscape.

people right with the supernatural. But Christianity is *not* a religion. It is a relationship.

Relationships need far fewer forms than we think. Christianity is an understanding of the true nature of reality and a grace relationship with God that is expressed most accurately in natural behavior. It always favors loyalty, allegiance, love, and empathy in natural behavior over forms of ritual behavior and decisively calls for relationship over religion. The church comprises people who know God personally, a "body" of those who share the same relationship with God through Christ, a relationship of grace, peace, and hope for all, calling us to his mission. Authentic Christianity is not just another religion under investigation in a textbook on world religions, as many authors portray it. Unfortunately, if we fall in love with ritual or tradition, put our faith in forms instead of in Christ alone, our activity too can fit the category of a religion and the church that of a social institution. The appearance is very plain to the outsider. Commitment to ritual behavior is a barrier between us and a genuine relationship with God.

Relationships require honoring and respecting the other person, loyalty, communication, and *agape*. Consider a passage from the Old Testament and one from the New Testament. In 1 Samuel 16:6–7, we read,

> When they arrived, Samuel saw Eliab (form) and thought, 'Surely the Lord's anointed stands here before the Lord.' But the Lord said to Samuel, 'Do not consider his appearance or his height, (forms) for I have rejected him. The Lord does not look at the things (forms) people look at. People look at the outward appearance (form), but the Lord looks at the heart'" (not the forms). Parentheses mine.

Then in Matthew 6:5–7, we read,

> And when you pray, do not be like the hypocrites, for they love to pray standing in the synagogues and on the street corners (forms) to be seen by others (form). Truly I tell you, they have received their reward (form) in full. But when you pray, go into your room, close the door (no forms for others to see) and pray to your Father, who is unseen (no forms). Then your Father, who sees what is done in secret (no forms to show), will reward you. And when you pray, do not keep on babbling like pagans (form), for they think they will be heard because of their many words (forms). Do not be like them (full of forms), for your

Father knows what you need before you ask him (no need for forms). Parentheses mine.

One last thought on God's use of forms: In chapter 3, we saw the total absence of expected forms of royalty and social recognition at the birth of Jesus. If we consider Paul's words in 1 Corinthians 1:20–31, we see that God does not use the forms we or our culture might expect. He tells us that God avoided the forms of social status that Jews and gentiles expected in verses 22 and 26. Then, in general, he chose the foolish, weak, lowly, and despised things—forms having no value or even negative value in the society, to accomplish his purposes in Christ.

Forms can be good or bad, ritual or natural, but we have to know the difference, and good forms can be used for evil purposes. The Pharisees used the forms for "acts of righteousness" such as giving to the poor, prayer, and fasting to fulfill their own selfish desire for praise, but they did not have generosity and truth in their hearts. These forms are only good when they are natural behavior from a pure heart. Jesus led the Samaritan woman at the well away from forms and geographical locations when he told her that God was seeking those who worshiped him in spirit and truth.

So, the questions are then, why are we using each form? What forms does the faithful church really need, and what forms are unnecessary and may cause confusion? What forms add relevant meaning to our message? We must ask what the forms really mean in our culture. What cultural expectations are we fulfilling with our forms in the church that give the wrong impression about salvation being a relationship with God? In the passage mentioned above, Paul was concerned about forms of eloquence and social influence being the framework of their faith instead of the Gospel itself. We must ask ourselves if we are attracting people to the church instead of to Christ. Are we encouraging cultural values or biblical values with our choice of forms?

Sprinkling Bible verses over a form does not make it serve our purposes. We need to really know if it serves us or if we serve it. We must assess each form by a critical evaluation of its function outside the church, its common meanings to us in our culture, and then the biblical support for this meaning or function as useful in the church. After these considerations, we must ask whether our use of it fulfills our missional purpose in the church and in our community.[6] Unless we objectively analyze each

---

6. Hiebert, *Anthropological Reflections*, 75–92.

form, it may subjectively meet only our cultural expectations. It may be an example of the syncretism we are trying to avoid.

So, we see that all forms are cultural. All cultures are human. Forms transmit meaning and perform functions for people in their cultural context. They can only transmit this meaning and have this function by virtue of the cultural frame of reference within which they operate. This means that borrowing any of them that we do not see in the early church is reason for caution. But also that valuing early church forms beyond their original meaning and function is just as dangerous. Forms may be important and useful in the culture from which they come but carry the wrong meaning or have the wrong function for the church today. In addition, they can morph from useful ones into those which end up cannibalizing the church from the inside. The addiction to forms of celebrity and recognition that we may see as essential to success deadens the trumpet of biblical values. Eloquence is not necessarily the same as wisdom. Sometimes the savvy to influence people muffles the voice of conscience. These forms are subtle. Samuel was naturally attracted to Eliab.

Unfortunately, it has become the case for many that for today's church to be "successful," it must, of necessity, deny there is any negative influence from culture, that cultural attraction is the way forward. If it results in growth, it must be right. But syncretism will not result in an authentic message. Love's open arms are not there to accept anything. They are to accept any*one* and lead them to the truth. It takes tough love to speak the truth when it is counter-cultural. And if it is not incarnated first, words are of little value.

Though there is some cause in simple ignorance, this feeling is often why Christians may react against any discussion of syncretism. They find talk about the influence of culture unnecessary, even dangerous to their purposes, or, at least, irrelevant. But we cannot be too careful. We must be aware of the harmful effects of the uncritical use of cultural forms. We must keep the mission of the church before us and weigh everything we use to accomplish it quite carefully, constantly asking ourselves about the meaning, purpose, and usefulness of our forms.

We must not see the church's survival as something outside God's control but instead lean on his providence. The church must remain an organic movement with as little framework as possible and only what forms are needed to accomplish its mission.

CHAPTER 12

ENCULTURATION AND CONVERSION
From the Bottom Up

A SEVERE DIFFICULTY FOR THE church in the West has been the influence of the renaissance and the reasoning over relationship emphasis that it left behind that interferes with the Gospel message itself. Our Western view of the Gospel has become one of propositional statements to be considered cognitively and logically. Apologetics have a place. There are certainly a number of facts to consider, but our message must result in the humility of a commitment of trust and loyalty to a person and his work for salvation. The Middle Eastern person did not hear propositional logic from the lips of Jesus. Loyalty in a relationship and following him was likened to leaving one's own family to be joined to a person in marriage. It is only demonstrated by stepping into the new relationship—action based on trust. Words and logic alone are inadequate. Trust was what Jesus asked for, just as God was looking for it in the Garden of Eden.[1] It was what Jesus was expecting in the boat when, after seeing the facts of the feeding of the four thousand, the disciples were worried that they only had one loaf between them for the day.[2] Not that there are no uncertainties or ambiguities in life, for that would remove the need

1. Gen 3.
2. Mark 8:1–21.

for trust altogether. But few of us in our culture are acquainted with this trust. We dislike ambiguity to such an extent that we base our lives on objective reasoning. We use information and logic to deal with it and resolve our problems. How are we to avoid the influence of our Western culture today on becoming God's children and, later, in our Christian lives? God's way for us involves a regeneration, a starting over. Let's look into one of the private conversations with Jesus and get an idea of the real nature of conversion.

One of the most commonly known passages in the New Testament is about Nicodemus in John 3. Out of this has come the evangelical plea that "you must be born again." Being born again is now a worn-out phrase that has lost its original significance in popular Christianity and is abused by our culture as it becomes post-Christian. Many instances of this terminology give a negative impression of what Christians call getting "saved." People say they are born again when there is little or no evidence that they are humbly grateful for God's grace or allowing his way in their lives. They show little acknowledgment of him in the affairs of life and hardly a hint of actually trusting his providence in the world. It is little wonder that the world does not respect the common claim to be born again. If popular Christianity cannot convince unbelievers of the realities of God, it will become evidence for them that God did not send Jesus or that there must not be a God at all.[3]

Where has Christianity gone off the rails? Many Christians seem to be in love with Christianity instead of in a relationship with God. The answer is in those two little words, *born again*. The significance of these words is found in the most common event of human birth and becoming a member of one's own culture. We call it enculturation or socialization. It is the natural learning of the cultural system needed for survival and success in life as our society defines it. It is assuming that frame of reference through which we will see all of life. We saw our cultural system at work as we read the Bible in chapter 2. In chapter 3, we saw an example of how it affects our understanding of the text in the birth narrative of Jesus. In chapter 4, we delineated its parts and functions. Culture affects everything we do, no matter how independent we feel as individualists. Everyone is deeply affected by it: me, you, people in the biblical world, people you hope to influence for Christ. To understand conversion through Jesus' words, we must look at natural enculturation.

3. Matt 7:16–18 with John 17:20–23.

We acquire a particular culture through an enculturation process of absorbing and learning the values, beliefs, and understandings of reality shared by those around us. The understandings here are foundational to all the values and beliefs that will be built on them. The cultural system as a whole is instilled in us by our nurturing family, the community around us, and the institutions a culture provides for the purpose. Our experiences in the system shape our personal preferences and strategies for life. Sometimes the transfer of the system to the young in a society is more functional than other times. And there are always those who deviate from it to some degree by deliberate choice to reject it or parts of it as the only solution for survival. This is more common in informal cultures in the West. Of course, the cultural system itself can become less functional for the survival of its members over time.

So, Nicodemus comes to Jesus under cover of night.[4] He states his realization, succinctly, that Jesus must be from God, but it is a predicament for him as a Pharisee and member of the ruling council. Without a word of small talk, Jesus tells him he must be *born again* to understand these spiritual realities. That is to say, his present understandings and assumptions about reality are inadequate. His beliefs and the values built on them causing behavior for survival on a day-to-day basis are wholly deficient for understanding this movement of God's hand in the spiritual universe and knowing and living for God in that new situation. He learned the original system by being born into it and growing up within its boundaries and definitions, influenced by his parents, experience, and his context's social, ideological, and religious authorities. He is different than other Pharisees, to be sure. But he does not yet understand the reality of who Jesus is. He is asking the right questions, but he does not have the spiritual framework to understand Jesus' response.

Jesus is saying that just as Nicodemus was shaped by his original enculturation and experience, giving him a cultural frame of reference for all of life, he must be reshaped by an altogether different perspective of the nature of reality and the values and beliefs that will come out of this new understanding. The old wineskins will not serve him. Jesus is saying that syncretism is not the answer. He will need to start over. The long-awaited Messiah had come, and it was not at all like his enculturation had taught to imagine. A process must now begin with a whole new frame of reference, a new way of seeing everything. He must start again

4. John 3:1–21.

and, as a child puts his world together, he must shape new beliefs about what is true or possible, new values on what is reasonable, important, and necessary, based on a new understanding of the realities around him.

Nicodemus must experience regeneration. He does not understand. The system that provided for personal, social, and mental survival and religious understanding up to this point is the only one he knows. He is a thoughtful person, but it is still unsettling. He had learned and memorized extensive portions of the Torah, but Jesus was asking for something different than just learning information. What Jesus is saying will put all Nicodemus knew of the Torah, the Prophets, and the Writings into a whole new perspective.

The discussion was undoubtedly threatening to his old feelings of wellbeing. We do not know when he gave his trust to Jesus, but it took some time. He later insists on fair treatment for Jesus in John 7. Though his group has labeled Jesus a Samaritan, un untouchable, he has made an impression on Nicodemus. Then, in John 19:38–42, his behavior gives him away to his elite group as he helps prepare the body of Jesus for burial. For a Pharisee, this is indeed *action* proving his new faith and loyalty.[5] It was a process, a growing realization of the true center of reality. He was counting the cost and changing course. It is interesting to note that coming from the top tier of society with formal socialization and religious correctness was, in this realization of Jesus as the Messiah, no different than coming from the bottom of society and a life of sin as did the Samaritan woman at the well. The notable exception is that it took Nicodemus longer to get over his careful socialization and "perfect" life, longer to step into the new world. She was an untouchable to the orthodox Jew; Nicodemus was one of the orthodox Jews making such social rules. The great encouragement of Nicodemus' story or that of the woman at the well is that if the Gospel of Jesus changed them, it can change anyone. They were born again; the old life was over.

Liking some of the benefits of the way of Jesus but not understanding the essential need for starting over will result in a syncretism of the old system with the new one. True conversion begins with the worldview—those assumptions or understandings about the nature of reality our culture gives to us. These can go unquestioned all of our lives and unconsciously control our outlook and behavior as we go along mindless of the spiritual universe. An encounter with the authentic message

5. Num 19:11; Lev 21:1.

of Jesus seems to have one of three results: it either bounces off the hardened shell of our existing worldview, or pierces it deeply, penetrating it to the core, or is not understood and what is heard—usually what our culture trains us to expect—becomes merely a syncretism of the old with the new. Being truly born again does not mean that we will jettison our human culture entirely. But our perspective, our frame of reference for everything in our lives, our purpose in life will be different. We will still be recognized by others as one of those sharing their culture, yet as one with an entirely different focus than simply the survival and success it promises.

There is no ambiguity about being born again. It will result in life-changing effects that go well beyond a cognitive response. The words of Jesus reach deep into how we became people in our social system, our culture. What are the essentials of the Gospel message for humankind? Though the path will be different for each person, it must begin with recognizing God as the creator God of all and the one who knows us in our hearts. Without awareness of who God is, there is no possibility of Jesus being any more than a moral teacher of the past. The proud cannot be saved. There is no sin to be forgiven, no meaningful relationship to gain, no purpose to life beyond the present moment of achievement or depression unless God is behind it all. If an individual comes to that understanding, it changes everything. It is a worldview-level understanding of the work of Christ that pushes one to go further. It leaves no other options open. What is true or possible has changed. With that, the values of what is truly important and necessary upon which we must act are now the essential motivations in this new understanding, and a correlated behavior will follow.

We must know God, but our old system for survival is blocking the way. Satan blinds our minds with the only solution we have for social and mental wellbeing and survival. It really matters to us. It has served us all our lives, and now it is called into question by a "religious" idea that cannot be proven? Our individualist pride is swollen, our ignorance is used against us, and we too easily reject the new way. Everyone is affected.[6] But to be born again, we must approach God on his terms, through the grace he offers us in the death of Christ on our behalf. If Jesus is not God, then his death is of little matter. But, if he is, everything about his death and his resurrection matter every day. This becomes the

---

6. Rom 3:23.

new framework through which we interpret our experience and make our decisions. Accepting his grace in forgiveness as we have it in John 3:16 and Ephesians 2:8–9 allows us to become his children as promised in John 1:12–13. The realization of God himself and his grace toward us in Christ is the door to a new life based on a new understanding of reality. New beliefs about what is true or possible are before us in his Word and replace those our culture gave us in our enculturation. We are starting over.

It is a difficult step of faith, and that is why we call coming to Christ a conversion. It is repentance, a turning around, a transformation. It is only the beginning to be sure, but the first step must be deciding who is in charge of the survival of the self. Who is in control and maintenance for the ship? Our culture assumes no other way of survival than its dictates. In our new faith, no amount of resistance to this pervasive influence can be weakened, for though our spiritual survival is assured, the enemy is subtle, convincing, and relentless. We had been years in the programming, and the task had been completed. But when we meet Christ, all of that must be set aside, we have been born again to start over, and we must trust him only.

This change will, it must then, result in natural behavior that gives evidence to our new "enculturation" in Christ. It reveals a different kind of person from others in the culture, from the foundation of the worldview, through beliefs and values, to the resulting behavior, we are different from the bottom up. Our original enculturation resulted in us being German, American, or Mexican, but rebirth makes us German children of God, American children of God, or Mexican children of God. The old wineskin of culture cannot accommodate the new understandings, beliefs, and values God gives us. To mix the old solutions for survival with the new ones is contamination that renders the new ones inoperable. But we are starting fresh with a new wineskin.

Just as Nicodemus or the Woman at the well, we must humbly acknowledge God in all we do and say and think.[7] Our new frame of reference is bounded by his love, grace, and providence. It fills the void left by dysfunctional socialization, which is the case of the woman at the well. People with a wholesome or respectable socialization, like Nicodemus, will find it harder to see the need for this rebirth. But in either case, we are

---

7. Prov 3:5–6.

regenerated and are now part of God's plan to regenerate all those willing to come to him in this way. We are born again.

The implications of this comparison of our original enculturation and an authentic, biblical conversion are far-reaching. Our original models of culture[8] talked about values, beliefs, and worldview assumptions. Now the content of each category has been replaced. Though in John 3, it is all wrapped up in the words "born again," there is a clear pattern of new enculturation in the New Testament. Our natural enculturation and this spiritual enculturation are parallel. Jesus used analogies concerning the kingdom of heaven that reflect the natural enculturation process when he talked about becoming like little children,[9] using new wineskins,[10] and knowing regenerated people by their fruit.[11] New Testament writers constantly reinforced the difference between the true reality of God's rule and the world's view of reality in terms of not loving the world or being friends with its ideologies. It talks about renewing the mind, seeing the world from God's viewpoint, and no longer being of it though in it.[12] To be without Christ is to be dead.[13] To know him is to be alive in a new world, born again.[14]

Knowing how our own culture works, we learn something about what Jesus meant in his conversation with Nicodemus. If we neglect an understanding of culture, understanding ourselves as people living in and controlled by the human values of social systems, we will miss some of the considerations that Jesus, who created people to live in social systems, used to explain even the most basic yet central truths of the Gospel. Nicodemus did not understand what Jesus meant by being born again, and it was a temporary barrier between the Son of God and him.

For many today it continues to be a gap between God and Christianity. We must understand ourselves and those around us better if we are to penetrate their worldview with the truth of God's Word. The church in her ministries must pay attention to the influence of culture on who we are, how we see the world around us, and why we do what we do. These

---

8. See Figures 4.1 and 4.2.

9. Matt 18:3.

10. Matt 9:17.

11. Matt 7:16.

12. 1 John 2:15–17; Rom 12:2; Jas 4:4; 1 John 4:4–6; John 17:13–18.

13. Eph 2:1 and 4.

14. 1 Cor 15:22; Eph 2:4–5; Col 2:13–15; 3:1–3.

understandings are essential to every believer. It makes being born again make sense. It makes a new wineskin essential. We need to recognize the old wineskin and avoid its use for the new wine.

CHAPTER 13

THE BATTLE WITH SYNCRETISM, LEGALISM, AND MYSTICISM

IN THE LAST CHAPTER, WE mentioned wineskins. Trying to refill old ones with the new wine is a reference to syncretism. For Judaism, this was mixing the law of Moses and the legalism of the Oral Torah with the forgiveness and freedom of the Gospel coming to them in Jesus. The old categories of values for survival that culture gives us cannot be added to the new solution of Jesus' teachings in any culture. We in the West cannot mix self-centered individualism and internal locus of control with the humility it takes to accept God's grace. Rational logic does not blend with faith in Jesus' atonement and trust in God's providence. Scientific laws do not allow the mysteries of the God of the universe. One will give way to the other in these volatile combinations.[1] The old wineskin still has use for holding water, but the expansion of the new wine in fermentation, to keep with the analogy, will not only ruin the old, previously stretched skins, but the new wine will be lost in the process. Just so, the authentic message of Christ added to our old system will not result in a relationship with God. It will instead be a syncretism offering false hope. It makes people think they already have what Christianity offers, but they have been inoculated against the true meaning of being born again. Satan has won the battle. The new wine diluted with cultural absolutes or human preferences becomes worthless, a superficial coating

1. Matt 6:24; Luke 16:13–14.

over the old worldview. It loses its expansive power to change lives. We must never entrust the old skins with anything more than the water of neutral cultural values. We still need water, but the new wine in a new skin changes everything else. The message of Christ cannot be made into popular Christianity without leaving a considerable gap between it and God. This is the result of syncretism.

We generally attribute syncretism to animistic peoples who adopt some forms of an organized religious system, what we call orthodox or high religion, and add them to their animistic worldview. They do this for added benefits, spiritual or otherwise. But of course, syncretism is found in many more situations than this. Understandings and behaviors in place for survival before influences for change came along often stay in place. For example, people of generational poverty are not changed when money is injected into their situation. Not having experience using money for survival often causes them more harm than good, and they are worse off afterward. Neither does wealth removed suddenly change the mentality conditioned by a highly luxurious lifestyle. It is impossible to survive such changes without deeper changes in one's understanding, values, and beliefs.

Syncretism is one survival system invading or contaminating another without understanding the extensive influence the original one still has and, therefore, with no desire to diminish its influence. It is, in fact, widespread among all groups, though mostly invisible to any of them and employed without any notice of the contradictory nature of some of these new ideas with old ones to which the people still hold.

There can be grave danger in syncretism depending on how it is used and the importance of mixed or modified content. In some ways, syncretism helps us find a better way to do something, adds some activity or attitude advantageous to our survival in our own cultural system. But it is often dangerous because it modifies traditional solutions for survival with little critical thought. People wanting change would do well to question the root of their dissatisfaction.

It is easy to see how animists might add Jesus to their gods or ancestor spirits and go to church or get baptized as ways to appease this sort of ultimate ancestor. They may feel lucky to have stumbled upon this vital addition to their existing worldview or be grateful to the missionaries who brought this good news of how to appease a great ancestor they had neglected, one who wants to help them survive in their animistic world of powerful magic and unrelenting fear. But we don't often notice when we allow for syncretism in our current, Western culture. Our cultural appetite for change causes us to constantly try out new ideas and concepts. We modify or reinterpret them to fit our existing cultural desires and expectations, the old wineskin, maintaining one system.

With so much syncretism around us, we need to ask what went wrong with the choice of the new wineskin that so many remain on a superficial level of engagement with God. With no natural behavior showing genuine faith, we cannot be certain of their salvation. They may not be sure either. Why is it that people do not realize how badly their wineskin is leaking?

Part of the answer to this question has to do with conscience. There is a difference between cultural conscience and biblical conscience; however, they are always combined into a culturally-conditioned Christian conscience[2] for the converted. This is because the meaning for behavior that obeys God's Word is found only in the cultural system of its origin. The question is whether it will be a biblical conscience expressed in relevant and appropriate cultural forms or a cultural, human conscience sprinkled with biblical teachings.

This conditioning of the conscience takes place in the socialization of children in their early years. They are putting together a frame of reference for understanding their experience that will serve them the rest of their lives. Social or idealistic authorities in their lives make deep impressions on them in this stage. Adding biblical truth to the human perspectives and preferences in the child's experience results in a hybrid conscience.

If, for example, the influence is legalistic, and the child does not rebel against it, the restrictions will shape a conscience that becomes a prison of legalistic rules and false guilt to shape their life. And, as the adult elephant believes the stake in the ground that held him fast when he was small is still his limitation, adults can remain under these early restrictions of legalism. They may never feel free later in life to bask in God's grace and the good things he gives us. Their conscience is not just culturally conditioned but twisted by legalistic preferences in their authoritative social surroundings. There is a gap between them and God's grace.

To avoid legalism and shape a biblical conscience, explanations of God's moral code should not eliminate teachings of freedom in Christ

2. See Conn, *Eternal Word*, 183–90.

bounded by love and humility. These are necessary for childrearing. Children must enter adult life knowing the wisdom of God's grace and gifts to humankind. So, "train up a child in the way he should go,"[3] but never underestimate the power of society and sin to meddle with God's purposes. None escapes entirely.

Because we are human, this culturally conditioned Christian conscience rests on a continuum between the extremes of the rigidity of legalism and the flexibility of syncretism unless it arrives at an appropriate cultural and biblical expression of the person's faith. It includes God's moral code without legalism and freedom in Christ without syncretism. Legalism establishes rules where the Bible is silent or general about specifics in obedience. Syncretism allows cultural values contrary to the Bible to define Christian behavior. We are faced with the relativism of syncretism or the irrelevancy of legalism. Both are opposed to a biblical expression of faith with God-honoring behavior. The issue makes it very important to know how much our culture and socialization influence our faith.

Biblical faith expresses itself in a contextually relevant way in a humble, trusting of God's providence in all things. There is freedom for the faithful Christian concerning the good things he has created within the boundaries of love, humility, and loyalty given to us in his Word. Those boundaries are fewer but more far-reaching than we generally allow. Human additions to God's design for the Christian life can interfere with a biblical conscience and create troublesome human boundaries smothering our relationship with God. This limits his blessings and leads to false guilt. The result of living within God's freedom for us should be a discernment of God-honoring behavior and what is beneficial for all in a situation. Paul talks about our freedom in Christ and entreats us to delight in God's grace and the good things he has given us to enjoy but be careful of being an offense to those of weaker faith.[4] Peter talks about freedom for Christians within the same boundaries.[5] Comments from Paul and Peter here make some Western Christians uncomfortable, but the boundaries are clear, and the teaching is covered in God's grace. It calls for walking in love and wisdom.

---

3. Prov 22:6.

4. 1 Cor 10:23—11:1; Titus 1:15.

5. 1 Pet 2:16–17.

The imbalance of too much emphasis on cultural values (syncretism) or adding human requirements to God's word (legalism) on the Christian conscience are conditions that keep us from God's intentions for us. The over-correction of either results in the other. Both are opposed to a culturally relevant expression of biblical truth and work to create a gap between God and Christianity. Our ministry to people should address these extremes. Social research can help us in this battle.

We can measure the influence of legalism or syncretism in the lives of Christians both quantitatively and qualitatively. A clear idea of what we are looking for, the control of intervening variables, good questions, and careful collection and analysis of the data can inform us why we, or those we are trying to help, do what we do and how we feel about it. Information of this nature allows for focus in ministry on the essential issues and problems. Instead of only moderating the symptoms, we can bring the actual issues alongside God's Word for evaluation. The necessity to appraise our own culturally conditioned Christian conscience and help other Christians with theirs is urgent. Our goal is to be biblical Christians. Biblical convictions must be relevant in our own culture, but the cultural values used in expressing these convictions must be assessed.

Christians in other parts of the world see the Bible through their cultural lenses as well. They, too, have culturally conditioned Christian consciences. They will feel guilt or shame for different reasons than we do. In addition to the dangers of our culture over-influencing our faith or human rules for godliness, there is the danger of taking our culturally conditioned conscience, even a biblical one, to these other cultures and infusing the Gospel with it in ministry to those people. We are then creating distance between members of the host culture and God. The process of taking one's own culturally relevant Christian conscience to another context where it becomes part of the biblical message is called cultural legalism, and it creates a foreign expression of Christianity in that culture. Its opposite, allowing the Gospel to be syncretized with the host culture, is cultural relativism.

The answer to these extremes is a contextual approach that respects God's truth, the host culture, the potential contamination of the message with the irrelevancy of one's own cultural applications, and the potential syncretism of the message with the host culture. Culture is the vehicle for ministry in every case, but the contextualization of the original message in each culture must be the controlling factor. People of all cultures, including our own, must let God be God within their context.

So, there are several possible outcomes of sharing the Gospel: a culturally appropriate expression of Christianity in a particular culture or the alternatives of legalistic, syncretistic, or foreign expressions of Christianity.

It is challenging to have an entirely neutral or pure perspective on the Gospel or our biblical teaching in another culture. We have heard and understood the message in our own cultural context, where it has been interpreted under the influence of the needs and demands of that culture. Our understandings are natural to us, and our applications seem normal. In addition, our neglect to contextualize it carefully in our own situation can leave us vulnerable to shades of legalism or syncretism in our applications. When we take this product to another culture, we often add human or foreign conditions for godliness to the message. All the more so if we have not studied the receptor culture and only have our own as a guide. This is no longer just ethnocentrism but a sort of cultural arrogance that is more common than we think and can only be alleviated if the sojourner becomes a learner.

The receptor culture has a tough job to avoid syncretizing their own cultural beliefs and values with the biblical message. But to receive a message contaminated by another culture is too much to undo. They have no idea where one message stops and the other begins. They confuse Western culture, their own culture, and the biblical direction for their lives. They, too, will end up with a culturally-conditioned Christian conscience, only it may have two cultural conditioners, the messenger's and their own. Once this confused mixture hardens, it becomes very difficult to deal with the effects. Going back to undo it is usually impossible for the missionary.

The solution is to help the people of the host culture decide for themselves what the application and expression of their faith should look like in their context. We must be prepared to facilitate that process in the early days. If the messenger does not give them a good example to this end, it is more common that the host people, offended by the cultural legalism of the Christianity the missionaries brought, eventually move away from it to create their own form of Christianity.[6] Without the help and teaching of mature Christians, this is usually quite syncretistic. They, too, run the risk of legalism or syncretism if they do not learn to contextualize the message carefully in their own situation.

6. See Ayegboyin and Ishola, *African Indigenous Churches*, 12, 24–26.

In these cases, our own cultural frame of reference and lack of attention to contextualization interferes with closing the gap between other people and God. We must become aware of how much our culture is affecting our ministry. Ignorance of our ethnocentrism or arrogance about our cultural expression will not do.

The examples are endless. Christian American married couples' public behavior, quite acceptable in its own situation, is quite embarrassing, and some of our favorite individualist, capitalistic financial principles are sinful for Christians in Central African villages. Korean doctoral students coming to the States asked me what version of the Bible Americans use. They were uneasy, embarrassed, and even offended by behavior between couples and the commotion in our churches. In our Western ethnocentrism, we naturally think our way is the only way to be faithful to God's Word. We need to understand more about culture and social procedure, both ours and theirs before we approach such culture-laden topics in a host culture. Their practice may be quite biblical in their situation.

It is a problem for Christians working around the world. When we see a social difference in another culture, we are not good at evaluating it. The reason is that we usually move from our observation to our evaluation of it without finding out what the behavior means to the people of that context. We skip the interpretation step. We do not ask, "What does it mean to them?" As a result, we see syncretism everywhere in other cultures while missing it in our own.

We all must be careful and constantly evaluate how our culture influences our faith, our conscience, and our understanding and application of God's Word. There is no once-for-all calibration of biblical faith and human culture that results in a final, well-balanced, contextualized, Western or American expression of Christianity, a final rooting out of all syncretism. Even though biblical absolutes are constant, culture is not; it is dynamic. If we were more aware of our culture's influence on us, we would be more sensitive to changes as they come along and evaluate them from a more helpful perspective. As it is, Western Christians typically accept change uncritically in our informal value system as normal, interesting, or attractive, assuming it is culturally neutral. We may not see its connection to potentially unhealthy values in our culture.

As culture changes, we must evaluate if we are speaking biblically and relevantly to these changes. Too much cultural influence leads to syncretism. Not enough cultural relevance leads to legalism. Knowing the difference between syncretism, legalism, and relevant applications of God's Word in our culture and in those we hope to impact with the Gospel helps close the gap between God and Christianity in our world.

A third potential outcome in our search for an expression of our faith relevant to our needs is what I call mysticism. This is not the mysticism used of the spiritual attitudes current with the church fathers or later dark ages, but a modern subjective spirituality. We see these mystical forms of Kabbala in Judaism and Sufism in Islam. Though not a religion like them, Christianity has its own spiritual approaches to God that combine a wishful human system with Christianity while changing many traditional values and rituals. It finds God's will in the most unusual places using the most curious methods and is very happy with the results. Some of its forms are what we might call white magic—the enchantment of secret discoveries through rituals and signs. It is opposed to legalism, though it usually creates its own, and it is not concerned about syncretism, using or deviating freely from cultural norms. Like postmodernism, it makes objective truth subjective, so it can mean what the adherents want or need it to mean in their favor—meanings their sub-culture highly values. For the practitioner of mysticism, wealth and health, need for control, and feelings over reason achieve the primary objectives of recognition, inclusion in a group, meaning, and feelings of self-worth.

The polarization of legalism and mysticism in Christian circles is extreme. In mysticism, discerning God's will is "discovering" it and is confused with emotions and signs. Though we are slow to admit it, this is a modern kind of "Christian paganism,"[7] not altogether unlike the divination and seeking of omens of which God warned his people in the Old Testament.[8] The over-reaction to this, and protection against it, is a position of legalism where God's will is totally objective, universal for everyone, and measurable on a binary scale.

Neither extreme is supported by God's Word. Knowing God outside these excesses leads one to be grateful for his grace, respectful of his otherness, loyal to his kingdom, and confident and content in his providence and love. It is true to God's Word and our needs, both objective and personal while being relevant in its own cultural context. As such, we can trust his revelation and allow him to speak for himself instead of locking

---

7. See Waltke, *Finding*, 11–12.

8. Lev 19:26b; Deut 18:10b; 2 Kgs 17:17b.

him into our definitions. We can allow God to be God in our lives and let other Christians do the same.

The choice to move toward legalism or mysticism may depend on whether people seek God himself or something from God. Legalism gives the people a sense of security. Mysticism makes people feel special. Both extremes meet prominent needs among individualists. Legalists and mystics never condone the opposite extreme, and many believers are in range of one or the other instead of holding a firm understanding of a biblical faith that is relevant to these needs.

This bipolar situation is complex. Legalism is information about God and his will for us forced into objective cognitive categories with rigid boundaries. It is safe, predictable, and impartial. That might sound appealing, but it adds regulations and leaves grace nearly out of the system. The Christian is on his own, seeking God's approval. It promotes addiction to words and definitions, propositional analysis, information, and objectivity. It is brought on for most by feelings of insecurity with ambiguity, uncertainty, and change. God's will must be known for all and for all times. In its extreme form, this requirement for conformity to the list of rules created by the legalist can become cultic. The relationship with God is one of a slave to his master.

Mysticism has to do with personal experience and its emotional interpretation. It is risky, unpredictable, and subjective. It rests on feelings of assurance, laying out fleeces, and opening the Bible to random passages for the answers we seek. It cultivates an addiction to experience, emotional extremes, hidden meanings, and magic. God's "hidden" will can be discovered if the person knows the secret ways of finding it. But there is anguish during the long days that go by without a word from God. As King Solomon, who tried so many things, might say, it is a "chasing after the wind."[9] God has given us all we need to know his love and will for us in his Word. It is there regardless of feelings, and we need no signs to confirm it.

Legalism and mysticism are on a continuum of polar opposites, as is legalism with syncretism. Though some Christians tend toward one or the other of these extremes, objective truth and personal experience of grace are valid needs when met in a scriptural way. Both are necessary, but either without the other is toxic. The emphasis on one over the other causes the church to become dysfunctional. There is a gap. The people

9. Eccl 1:17–17; 2:10–11.

forfeit a relationship with God that leads to personal freedom through a deep-seated, habitual awareness of his truth, wisdom, providence, and unrelenting grace. They are not letting God be God.

Mysticism is a third element leading to dysfunctional approaches in Christianity. Toxic legalism, subjective mysticism, or duplicitous syncretism are contaminated expressions of "faith" that lead to spiritually impaired members and an ineffective church. They are contrary to appropriate cultural relevance, biblical truth, and freedom in Christ. I refer to Christians who are part of these systems, who substitute cultural and personal motives and goals for those of the Bible, as *popular Christians*. When people claim Christianity, but their syncretism replaces essentials of God's Word with elements of other religions or adds the messages of gods and prophets to what God has revealed, I refer to them as *folk Christians*. Popular Christians generally ignore syncretism while folk Christians welcome it. What comes between Christians and God in these ways does not go unnoticed by outsiders and widens the gap between God and them when our purpose is to bring them to God.

Our goal is not to be perfect Christians since that category does not exist in this life, but rather *biblical Christians*. This is a realistic category that refers to people who are loyal to Christ as God. They trust his work on their behalf and his providence in all things. They know by his grace they are forgiven every day and loved by him. Their worth and identity are tied to this. They desire God's will more than their own. Their intentions are to be resting, trusting, missional people, seeking to be servants in his ultimate plan. It is not that they do not fall short in their daily lives, but they keep short accounts with God and others, and they are more grateful for his grace each time they experience it. Syncretism is still an issue for biblical Christians since all Christians must continue to deal with it in their changing cultures. But for these, the benefits of distinguishing biblical absolutes from cultural absolutes are well known, and the process is more natural, even habitual. They know both their freedom in Christ as well as its boundaries. They will not be found wandering the dark halls of legalism. They will be cautious of cultural syncretism and avoid the lure of mysticism. The categories of Christians are illustrated in Figure 13.1.

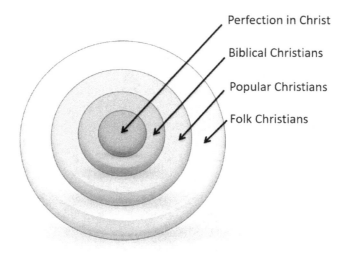

Perfection in Christ

Biblical Christians

Popular Christians

Folk Christians

Figure 13.1. Categories of Christians.

As mentioned in the early pages of this chapter, syncretism is the uncritical mixture of cultural absolutes with biblical absolutes that can come between God and us. Cultural absolutes are values, beliefs, assumptions, and activities that the cultural group or subgroup determines are necessary for full and normal participation in the society, essential for survival, and lead to humankind's fulfillment, happiness, and pleasure. In an individualist society, these would be values like self-assertiveness, initiative in problem-solving, efficiency, personal achievement, physical attractiveness, financial success, entrepreneurial know-how, personal freedom, control of one's circumstances, etc.

The value of these absolutes is taken for granted. Behavior triggered by them defines the person and their status in the group. They are so deeply assumed, so sacred to human success and survival in our Western culture, that they go unquestioned. We would not overtly and thoughtfully welcome the negative aspects of these cultural values into the church. But then, we are not often thinking about them. We might be critical of some excesses, but cultural values, different ones for different people, are still motivations behind a good deal of natural and ritual behavior within and outside the church, searching for identity, meaning, and worth. Not everything in the culture is injurious to our faith, but we fail to see that some values are destructive to a relationship of uncontaminated loyalty to God.

The old cultural solutions for feelings of security, social advantages, and personal pleasures are hard to abandon. Social pressures are also a cause of this kind of selective application of the biblical understandings. In Central Africa, how can Christian people deny their ancestors the respect called for by the extended family and whole tribe? In our Western culture, how can Christians be sure to survive socially, academically, or financially? We have found our identity, worth, and wellbeing up to now in the old system. And besides, we really enjoy a good many things that faith in God might wipe out if we let it go too far. This is not always done quite so objectively as I describe it here. Most of the time, we are not aware that the cultural absolutes are still in place. The fact that they are "absolutes" means they would be expected to stay the same anyway.

So, we are blind to our ethnocentric syncretism in our Western churches planted, nurtured, and administered in this value system. We tend to overlook or even use these Western values in their ministries. Very few members notice it because it looks natural. Some values in every culture fit biblically and encourage the church. For example, non-Western cultures usually have a strong value on hospitality, while Western individualism has a strong internal locus of control. We applaud the go-getters in various ministries, those who step up in the face of desperate needs, those who accept risk and sacrifice in the cause of Christ. But in Western cultures, we must also be concerned with motives. Activity in our culture is used to gain affirmation and reputation. It can too easily become this in the Western church.

It is difficult for people always to discern if it is for self or for God that they expend their energies. We have to constantly check our hearts. The same values necessary for promoting self in the old system may now be driving the ministry of the Gospel. So needful is the good side of these cultural values to stimulate service for Christ that to question them seems counter-productive, even shocking. But that is what God is asking us to do. Though the context may refer to different kinds of behavior than we deal with, the New Testament is full of passages telling us to check our hearts, renew our thinking, leave the old ambitions for self behind, test our actions, and turn from personal pride to humility.[10] Before we toss these references aside as not referring to our situation, we must remember that syncretism is a subtle enemy. Avoiding the discussion of cultural values in the church may condone what the church exists to combat, the

10. See Rom 12:1–2; 2 Cor 13:5; Gal 6:3–5; Eph 4:22–24; Phil 2:3–4; 3:13–14; Col 3:2; Jas 3:13–18, etc.

promotion of self instead of loyalty to God. Understatements that it is not surprising, that it is normal in our culture, that people are just being themselves, do not accord with the verses mentioned. Normality and even legality are not the measures given to us. The standard is found in God's Word.

How is it that humility is left behind when it is the primary attribute for the Christian life? It is because it is highly counter-cultural to the absolutes of individualism. Self-assertion is the tool of choice to carve one's identity from the social block of culture. Humility is only possible when one realizes the measure of God's grace in their life, when security, identity, and worth are found in a relationship in Christ.

Loyalties to self and grandeur are lethal to biblical attitudes and negatively affect faithfulness to God and his people. However, the church may tend to hold on to detrimental values on church growth, use of money, display of talent, the celebrity status of certain people, and social cliques to meet the expectations of their members. These retard or smother spiritual development in the lives of the people. Church ministries often avoid addressing these damaging values stemming from our powerful individualism: the cultural absolute of all is fair in love of self and war for success, the "black hole" of Western culture.

These forms do not look questionable at first, so we must simply be in the habit of testing every form and value we want to select for our lives and the furtherance of our mission in the church. Usefulness or attractiveness are not reasons enough for selection. We must ask if the cultural meaning, function, and message of each cultural form is neutral enough not to lead us away from God but toward him.

Syncretism, legalism, and mysticism form a triangle of continuums that oppose appropriate cultural relevance, biblical truth, and freedom in Christ. See Figure 13.2.

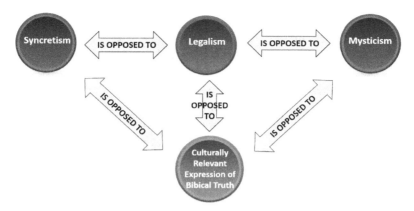

Figure 13.2. The triangle of Continua Contrary to Biblical Truth.

People of genuine faith generally go through a process of shedding personal syncretism to go on to maturity in Christ. Everyone is different in this regard but can be seen to fit generally at any one time in a category like those mentioned in Figure 13.3. This process is made up of a movement from no relationship with God to a highly syncretized one, which syncretism diminishes with growth, or upward movement, as in a pyramid, toward the pinnacle. At the same time, people are growing in Christ, and out of syncretism, there is a development from ritual behavior to natural behavior in expressing their faith. Ritual behavior has to do with intentional activity as prescribed by Christianity. This involves things like getting baptized, going to church, giving to the offering, volunteering time to projects, and even structured prayer at the early stages. It is being at the right places at the right time. It uses the correct expressions, the courtesy expected, and suitable topics of conversation with those at the gathering. It can be real or very superficial. There is great danger for the legalist in this. For them, all "Christian" behavior is ritual and can serve selfish ends of personal achievement, competition for status, and personal satisfaction. Some, of course, are making the mistake of thinking that we are still under law instead of grace.

Natural behavior is that activity outside the church and other places or gatherings that call for Christian ritual behavior. It is activity in the marketplace on Monday, on the freeway, in the neighborhood, and, importantly, in the home. Instead of remaining intentional as it begins, it must become, as it is labeled, natural or informal. Anyone can perform ritual behavior. Biblical and syncretistic Christians alike join in ritual behavior at church or places of volunteer service. Popular Christians may make it to the mission field, but only biblical Christians, though not perfect, have a natural way of serving God, of living in his presence and being part of his plan, of living in conversation with him anywhere and everywhere. A helpful distinction would be seeing the difference between Jesus at the Jordan river being baptized by John or breaking the bread and passing the wine at the last supper, compared to the Jesus we know, as C.S. Lewis would say, "… of the workshop, the roads, the crowds, the clamorous demands and surly oppositions, the lack of all privacy, the interruptions."[11] He was always the same.

When Jesus talks about knowing people by their fruit,[12] he is talking about natural behavior, not ritual behavior. Judas was at the last supper, but that does not predict anything about his natural inclinations. Of course, there is a beginning to this kind of walk with Christ where we naturally seek to honor him in word and deed. It begins with obedience to the things we know we ought to do, very intentionally. It's like learning to play the piano. It starts with learning the keys and practicing scales. Like learning a language, you start with the rules of grammar and learning vocabulary. But one day, the person is expressing him or herself in music or French very naturally, without thinking through the basics with each move or word.

It is more about becoming something than just doing something: becoming fluent in French, becoming a pianist. This, for the Christian, comes through discipleship and teaching as well as through practice. It is the central function of the church to help us learn to ride that bicycle, learn to walk with God through Christ in an everyday, everywhere, natural manner. It is becoming fluent in thought and behavior that honors God.

Ritual behavior does not tell you anything about a person's heart. Unfortunately, however, it is usually the behavior used to judge a person's commitment to God. So, it is essential not to focus discipleship on behavior except in the most basic ways. Discipleship ministry must be at the deeper levels of values, beliefs, and worldview assumptions, creating new motives for behavior. If a person is not converted at the worldview level, if their understanding of reality is not changed, the result is syncretism.[13]

11. Lewis, *Four Loves*, 7.

12. Matt 7:15–23.

13. First stated by Van Rheenen, *Communicating Christ*, 89.

True conversion has to do with what a person comes to know and accept about the true nature of reality—the stepping into God's purposes for our life. The recognition that Jesus really is God's way to himself, the *only* way, the realization of the depth of God's grace, the change of loyalty from self to trusting of God's providence in life; this is change at the deepest level. It is worldview conversion. It may be a longer or shorter journey, but it must go to the root of the understanding of reality and the allegiance of the soul. The journey is not measured by the distance but by the intentions and progress. Some people who are closer to the biblical Christian category may not be making further progress. Some who are much further away may be closer in their intentions and have traveled further in their progress toward the objective. General stages in the process out of syncretism are given in Figure 13.3.

The pyramid seeks to show the stages and the narrowing of each category in the upward movement toward maturity.[14] Though many recognize the need for change in their lives at level one, fewer reach each ascending category toward becoming biblical Christians. The interference of cultural norms, concerns for self, personal preferences, and social pressure work on people at each stage, making it harder to attain the next level. Those who start off well and make it to level three often stop there. I believe what we call Christianity is made up mostly of popular Christians. If the Apostle Paul wrote a letter to us today, he would probably tell us to examine ourselves and to stay on track ascending the pyramid [15] until we "become mature, attaining to the whole measure of the fullness of Christ."[16]

14. Eph 4:11–16.

15. See 1 Cor 11:28; 1 Tim 4:16.

16. Eph 4:12–14.

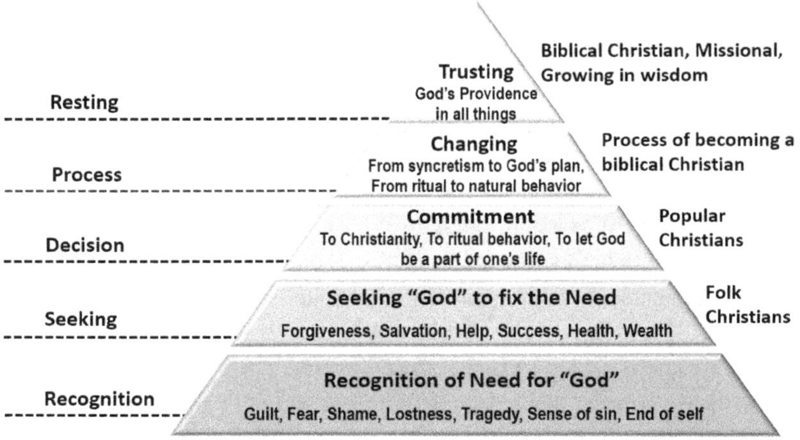

Figure 13.3. Hierarchy of Growth Out of Syncretism.

CHAPTER 14

THE UNCHANGING NEED
FOR HUMAN SURVIVAL

GOD'S PLAN AND OUR PLAN for our survival in this life can be quite different. Each culture has its strategy for the continuation of its existence against the challenges of the world around it. Asian cultures are relatively formal. Respect for tradition and only indirect talk about the future, control of social situations, and a Confucian emphasis on self-control and wisdom are often their natural means in the endeavor for each to fulfill their part in the continuance and flourishing of their people. These ways characterize Christians in their situation. They demonstrate long-term patience, personal reflection, quiet respect, and a need for traditional forms of expressing their faith.

Western informality, on the other hand, gives Christians in our situation a resilient value on change, new approaches, quick fixes, and novel and popular ways to achieve goals. Innovation, improvement, and development are the strong themes of our culture that we believe show authenticity and credibility. It is considered inefficient and even ineffective to be behind the times. It reveals a savvy sort of competence to be on the cutting edge of change. Submission and loyalty feel static and unnatural; wisdom and duty seem outdated. The vocabulary is lost on us in our self-absorbed individualism, expressing itself in casual self-confidence. Our internal locus of control has us constantly looking for a new behavior or a new way of talking about God or our faith that might give us an edge on our expression of Christian values.

The latest popular trend in our culture often strikes us as the ingredient we have been missing in the church and gives a perception of relevancy and authenticity to the expression of our faith. Our credibility depends on our readiness to accept the new trend with enthusiasm. At first, emotions run high. But people in Western cultures are in love with their informality and change. They are easily bored. The new concept, so popular at the time, becomes mundane, and it is not long before we are looking for another way to express our identity in the Christian life. In the end, we are choosing cultural ways to express our faith and should be on our guard. Given our concern for recognition and reputation in individualism, our motives may be suspect. We might also want to look more closely at the lives of those setting the popular trends in our culture before we imitate them.

Not all traditions are valuable or continue to be relevant in our day. And not all trends in our culture are negative. But our inclination to continually move away from tradition may distract us from core issues. Jesus' words, "in spirit and in truth," talk about the person inside us. They identify the person in God's eyes and have nothing to do with tradition or innovation, popular styles, vocabulary, or economic and social ties. It demands wisdom to distinguish between healthy tradition and innovative change, between cultural relevancy and cultural syncretism—discernment we have taken little time to cultivate

It is interesting to note that the cultures of the biblical text were opposite to this need for change. While we desire to move away from tradition as old and outdated, first-century Jewish culture held on to it with fanaticism.[1] Their honor was at risk if they sought change; our credibility is a risk if we don't. Their approach did not welcome the new wine of Jesus and his teaching. Their theology of selective prophecy and traditional honor sifted him out. Our Western culture does not value his teachings as still relevant in our day. Surrender, loyalty, and obligation do not seem to fit our fierce independence as individualists. In our self-reliant seeking of cultural relevancy, however, we may miss traditional truth. It is a word of caution for Christians.

But God's way is different. There is a place between these two extremes of Western independence and early Jewish tradition on their mutually exclusive continuum. God is not playing a game with us concerning our relevant and contented wellbeing in him by hiding the solution in the

---

1. McVann, "Change," 19–21.

newest trend or burying it in the oldest cultural traditions. All we need is before us in his Word and has been there for a long time. A humble attitude of trust in him and his grace and providence in our lives opens the way to the freedom he promised over two thousand years ago. Traditions may block it, and popular trends may miss it. But it is still there. Either may distract and encourage legalism or syncretism unless there is wisdom.

Cultural expectations may be different, but new is not better concerning God's truth. Relevant application to our lives today is necessary, but dogged attention to the old truths is vital. There is no glamor promised when you choose God's way and are loyal to him. There never has been. You may never become healthy or wealthy. You will not, hopefully, become a "Christian celebrity." You may never become well-known and influential in the institutional realm of Christianity, but these are not the objectives. We must choose him and his way for *his* purposes, not ours. Our culture's values are of little import in the matter. What is absolutely promised here and now is the wellbeing of our souls, peace and contentment in trusting his grace and providence, and his unconditional love. This promise does not change with time though we may use new words to talk about it. We must seek his kingdom first. All the rest of this life is in his hands. It was for those who first heard Jesus' message, and it is for us now.[2]

We spoke of cultures as systems of survival in chapter 4. In early secular research, Abraham Maslow's Holistic-Dynamic Theory showed a hierarchy of human needs and drives. His conclusion was that the organism is dominated and its behavior organized only by unsatisfied needs.[3] These needs have to do with survival, they never change, and each culture gives its members what are, to them, normal ways to satisfy these necessities.

A few years earlier, Bronislaw Malinowski did something similar in defining human behavior as a response to seven basic human needs that he referred to as the "permanent vital sequence." He tells us that these needs are seen as motivations for behavior. This behavior is a culturally appropriate response satisfying biological and psychological needs. These needs are seen as impulses to act.[4] These unsatisfied needs and impulses

2. In Matt 6, verses 9–13 are an example of the principle in verse 33.

3. Maslow, *Motivation*, 35–51.

4. Malinowski, *A Scientific Theory*, 137–44. See also Malinowski, "Man's Culture," 182–96.

to act are the motivators for survival, but the action selected in response is a culturally relevant choice among alternatives based on secondary motives. Sometimes the alternatives are limited, and people often say that they had no choice but to take some course of action, but that is actually quite rare. We make pragmatic choices between options based on good or bad motives, ethical preferences, efficiency, potential collateral damage, tolerable outcomes, and the like. So, there are needs, choices of response to these needs based on secondary motives and the resulting behavior. The urgent thing is that none of the categories be left empty of functional solutions. Empty compartments in the pyramid make life dysfunctional. A rendition of Maslow's hierarchy is seen in Figure 14.1.

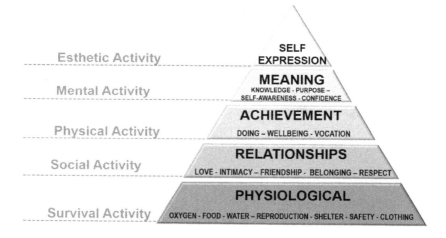

Figure 14.1. Maslow's Hierarchy of Needs for Human Survival.

Neither Maslow nor Malinowski mentioned the need to know and honor God. To them, this would have been the generic category of religion, part of the mental activity level, and would only be relevant if it served the individual's mental and emotional survival somehow. However, it is a flaw in these models, as every human eventually feels the need to resolve questions about the supernatural. It cannot remain an empty category in our culturally shaped lives.

The answers to these worldview questions may be basic or complex, but the need to understand the nature of reality and respond to the idea of the supernatural is never optional. People must know how to stay right with it or to be free from any obligations. It is not an unusual response in Western cultures to see a defensive reaction to God and Christianity and an effort to prove that God does not exist while tolerating religions more incongruous to the social values. Non-Western cultures tend to be less reactive to Christianity while having their own alternatives, often syncretizing Jesus into their different systems or allowing all religions to lead to their own kind of salvation. The notable exceptions would be the monotheisms of Judaism, Islam, Zoroastrianism, and the atheism of Buddhism.

The push for survival in Maslow's tiers of need and motives for maximum personal satisfaction cause behavioral choices relevant to the requirement and, hopefully, socially appropriate in the context. These personal motivations might be guilt, desire, greed, or desperation, but they may also be allegiances to ideals or attachments to people or a social movement. People choose one behavior over another for the satisfaction of needs based on differences in personal motives. See Figure 14.2.

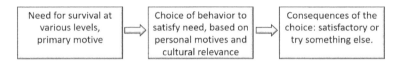

Figure 14.2. The Role of Personal Motives to Meet Needs for Survival.

The behavior is always a choice. Choices in Western culture might be realized by selfish ambition, self-assertion, controlling, or manipulating others for personal success. In non-western cultures, the options would more likely be handled by empathy, indirectness, the need to defend one's honor, or elaborate generosity to establish harmony and promote belonging to the group.

The cultural system is as disinterested in the person as nature is to a person lost in the desert. It's up to the person to navigate the alternatives and make something work for them. People can help other people if they have resources in the particular category of the pyramid in question, but as the system degenerates, those resources are weakened. The system is unforgiving if the person fails to find a solution. An example would be a person's failure in Western culture to achieve social survival—the inability to manage or navigate the social system or find their identity or sense of well-being in the group. These people have a void in the social activity category of the pyramid causing various forms of withdrawal from social situations and disequilibrium in the other areas of need. They are considered failures by the dominant group in individualist societies. Their culture gives them no inner resources to cope with this inability to establish social status and relationships. This, in turn, may result in anti-social thinking and aberrant behavior. The culturally acceptable solutions are not working for the person, and they assert solutions of their own. In a collective society, these people are without hope and often commit suicide.

God is outside human culture, but we can allow the system to stand in our way, causing a gap between God and us. People who know God are his usual way of bringing others to himself. Though conversion happens within and depends upon the cultural frame of reference, it is, at the same time, dependent on God from outside the system. The core element of salvation, the death and resurrection of Christ, took place within the system using its frame of reference; however, its significance and consequences are from outside the system and in no way limited to the system. An authentic encounter with God through Christ results in personal worth, identity, and purpose for each person. Turning to him and trusting him impacts every level of the hierarchy of needs. Though expressed in cultural ways, these solutions to felt needs come from the outside.

But human society is not typically friendly to this outside "interference," especially in individualist cultures of self-achievement. Social forces work against it to discredit Christianity or even remove God from their midst. As this opposition progresses, it leaves people on their own to survive without God's purposes and moral boundaries in their lives. They are left with only the human alternatives for survival at every level and must create their own reasons for life to make sense. Human destiny and the meaning and purpose of life remain hollow spaces in the pyramid for which human systems have no resolution. The consequences of these voids, though subtle at first, will become enormous over time, creating problems and putting society at risk.

It seems natural to act in response to the needs for survival in ways our culture gives us. But there is always danger in human ways without God. These human ways become norms. Each culture is different, but in an individualist society, self-advancement is central, and self-assertion becomes the norm as the society leaves each to look out for him or herself. The ideal of the self-made man or woman becomes highly valued. This value brings the unwelcome consequences of weak loyalties in relationships necessary for family, community, and society as a whole.

Typically, when the search for satisfaction of personal needs in a culture crosses the traditional limit of social tolerance, offenders are labeled unreasonable, antisocial, and self-destructive and may be sanctioned by society. But individualists are not fans of tradition. These limits keep changing, especially in informal groups where they are blurred by human preferences that enshrine personal freedom and relativize moral and ethical boundaries in the pursuit of happiness. Little thought is given to the origin of many traditions that have been the solutions to survival of previous generations, many of them based on God's truth. When these are dismantled, the risk to survival they alleviated returns. So, new choices for survival are constantly before us, and without God, we have no criteria by which to evaluate them, no standard of measure, no reliable patterns to follow.

Culture, then, creates a gap between God and us as an alternate system. Some in the society who know the social limits of self-survival activity and exhibit behaviors characterized by healthier personal motives delay the community from disintegration. But if these more positive personal motives do not include God, they still lack an ultimate dimension and, in the long run, will not be enough to suspend the degeneration that causes societies to break down.

We need to remind ourselves again here that these motives for self-advancement come with us into the church. We can see God's Word tells us otherwise, but the natural habits that the culture encourages and nurtures go deep, and we have fewer living examples to the contrary. It is the most challenging area for which to trust God, but we must let go. If we do not intentionally choose to trust God for self-survival in the human hierarchy of needs and welcome the non-self-centered behaviors that choice allows, the church will mirror the surrounding culture more and more. Unfortunately, that does not shock us enough since "that's the way people are." But it is not God's way. The church must call our attention to the cultural absolutes ruling our individualist lives, or we will continue to make choices in their favor, even thinking they help us in our faith.

If we genuinely choose to allow God to be the center of the ultimate nature of reality, it has particular consequences for us individualists and our ministries. All our other choices for survival, as much as humanly possible, become secondary and often must be rejected in light of this commitment. If we choose God, but he is not the center of our world, if self is still the primary advisor of choices, we remain at a distance from God and each other. We may make it look like we are close to him through our ritual behavior, but we remain popular Christians, and our natural behavior tells all.

What we accomplish in life or what we forfeit is a result of these human needs, and whether we choose God or cultural and personal solutions to deal with them. The conundrum is that we often mentally or emotionally choose God as the answer and yet do not shake free from the control of syncretism; so powerful is culture, and so little is the teaching on how to understand and deal with it. This syncretistic commitment is to the church or Christianity instead of a trusting loyalty to God himself. No matter how many Bible verses a person sprinkles over syncretism to justify it or how much ritual behavior is used to camouflage it, it is still syncretism. How shocking to think it may be enabled by others in the church, school, or mission agency. Nicodemus, the woman at the well, Peter, Andrew, James, John, or the rich young man were all following their own survival plans, but Jesus set the alternative before each of them.[5] The choice he gave them was to be all in for him. There was no middle way. It was the narrow gate or the wide gate. Unless we begin to deal with these cultural counterfeits from the pulpit, people will only want God on their terms. They will not see the need to undo all the hard-earned achievements they depend on for their wellbeing. Their loyalty is first to managing their survival and only secondly to God and others.

5. John 3:1–21; 4:1–30; Matt 4:18–22; 19:16–24.

CHAPTER 15

THE WORDS WE USE

IN AN INDIVIDUALIST CULTURE, WE yield to the self and its needs. In a collective culture, people acquiesce to the group and its demands. These central values of cultures become a battleground for people when they become Christians. So intense are the expectations of our Western culture that they conflict with our desires to love, worship, glorify, fear, and obey God in spirit and in truth. They are also contrary to our need to love one another. Until we surrender to God, culture gives us the only solutions to our mental, emotional, social, and physical survival. These are not easily cast aside. Though ritual behavior in the new areas is relatively easy to display in church, daily life, where natural behavior reveals our true loyalties, often remains less than ideal. The old human solutions are natural, habitual. It comes down to who or what we are trusting for our survival.

Sometimes the solution to this conflict for individualists is to make all of the actions called for by our faith into rituals commanded by God. We can go through the motions and feel we have met the requirement. This satisfies the compartmental, black and white efficiency our culture demands. Submission to God already touches on the tender place of our love for individual independence. We do not warm to authority telling us what to do, and we do not like obligations. If we can satisfy ritual requirements and be done with them, we can get back to the things our culture gives us that make us feel good about ourselves and bring the personal satisfaction we need.

Any action asked of us by Christ is not to become an empty ritual but should be characteristic of a willing heart and a natural lifestyle. For this to be the case, we must trust God for all the solutions that culture used to provide. Some of our confusion about the life God wants for us is in the meaning of the words used to talk about these issues. It is the difference between what God meant by them in the original context and what we mean by them today in our situation.

Lexicons and theological dictionaries provide excellent and essential research on the origin and usage of words in the Bible. In chapter five, we introduced the human side of word meanings. In this chapter, we will discuss the human meanings we have given to two biblical words, love and believe. Today, these words might be misused in our lives and ministries, making a significant difference in God's intended meaning. While the conventional meaning for a word can be found in a dictionary, its usage is framed by the cultural values of its context, and its power or weight lies in the associations it provokes in others, associations that come from personal experience in a particular situation. So, the meaning of words goes beyond vocabulary and grammar. It is buried in the lives of the people of a particular cultural situation, in a particular time and place.

When I speak in French or a Central African trade language, I choose vocabulary that seems equivalent to what I think and desire to express. In the beginning, that's the problem. I am expressing American thoughts using words in another language that I believe express ideas shaped by my American experience. When I first used those words in my expressions, I liked to think the person on the other side of the conversation was getting the same thoughts I was trying to shape with their words. But that cannot be the case because I did not share their experience making the associations for meaning with those words in their minds. I needed time and immersion in those cultures to begin to create my intended meaning in their minds and used entirely different expressions in my latter days than I did in my beginning days.

When it comes to the Bible, pastors and teachers must close this gap for us. We must enter the Middle Eastern cultural frame of reference and see the meaning of the text from inside their worldview and social experience. There is an ethical demand in this for those of us who would teach others God's Word. This being the case, we want to look at a couple of key words, not in terms of their lexical meaning or etymology, but in terms of their human meaning in the biblical culture and then in our modern Western context.

When we move words from one culture to another in translation, we are not moving the "weight" that the influence of the culture and personal experience has given these words in their particular situation. As a result, we readers of the translation, not knowing theirs, use our own social and experiential framework to make sense of the biblical account. When we look up words from our English Bible, we use an English dictionary limited to our cultural frame of reference. The words there will cause associations for us from *our* experience, not that of the biblical author or character. But God was using *their* social frame of reference and *their* experience for meaning. We need to be aware and cautious of our culture's influence on the meaning of his words.

Social values surrounding the concept of honor and shame and its effects on the people in the story of the birth of Jesus were exposed in chapter 3. The complex associations in the hearts of Mary and Joseph are not part of our social context or our experience. The angel told each of them not to be afraid,[1] and we have record of the joy the prophesied event gave to Mary,[2] but we have no other insights into the personal meaning the words and events had for them unless we know something of the social context. We cannot even assume we know the same fear or joy in our experience. We saw in that chapter how we have filled that original social context and words with meaning from our own social and experiential viewpoint. We realize how difficult it is for us to have empathy for Mary of Joseph. We simply have no experience to draw on to feel the same things they and those around them felt.

The original meaning comes from social and religious values swirling around the events. God uses this context and its outcomes to say something about his intentions concerning the birth of Jesus. So, the social situation and circumstances are telling us more than the words alone, in their dictionary meaning, could tell us. Values on honor and shame, purity and impurity, and patrilineal social relations gave sense to the interactions and events. These are only a few of their many cultural values and understandings very different from those of our own Western culture. Our worth does not come from honor or ascribed status but from personal achievement. We see similar differences in traditional

---

1. Luke 1:30; Matt 1:20.

2. Luke 1:46–55.

Japanese or Native American cultures—cultures very foreign to us if we have not noticed.

So words have a dictionary meaning, a cultural or social meaning, and a personal meaning. A translated word cannot mean the same thing to the original speakers as its English "equivalent" means to us unless we calibrate our interpretation to their social context and experience. Modern translations solve this problem by using current vocabulary and sentence structure so that older terms and usages do not add difficulty to our understanding. We need to add to that process the consideration of these human cultural differences. Word for word translations may need to give way to phrases to maintain the original meaning in many cases.

God's words to us are of immeasurable importance and potential, "sharper than a two-edged sword," final, and eternal. The terminology he uses is of crucial consequence for our knowing him. Misunderstanding can cause a gap between God and Christianity—keep him at a distance when we are trying to come closer to him. Nevertheless, the words we choose in our culturally controlled language to think about him and his revealed will, to describe his actions and desires for us, often fall short of his intent.

The personal meaning of words is often displayed in conversations in our own culture, as we saw in examples in chapter 5. Our connotations are somewhat different from those of the next person because of associations we all make with vocabulary based on our personal values as individualists, our experiences, and the emotions and attitudes that come with them. If this happens in our own culture with contemporary people using the same language, it is easy to appreciate that there are many words in the Bible for which we have little or no personal meaning in our day, in our culture, words for which our dictionaries are inadequate.

When we borrow words from the Bible in our Christian circles to talk about God or our relationship with him, we fill them with our meaning and may cause confusion or ambiguity. Words like love, believe, glorify, honor, fear, and worship make an impression but may have only a vague or popular meaning for the users. Originally from a different language and cultural frame of reference, these words were in the mouths of people whose experience was very different from ours. Our English "equivalents" are already tied to our culture and their meanings to our experience.

God's revelation crossing language and cultural barriers was not a surprise to him. His intention is that we understand it for our lives today. But if the words used by God are filled with meaning colored by our culture and times with associations from our experience, we may misunderstand God's intentions for our relationship with him to some extent. The answer is looking at the Bible through the eyes, the culture, and experience of the people of those times and places so these words can retain their intended meaning. This will call for cultural exegesis and communication theory to be part of the study of the text for pastors and teachers.

The word love is an obvious example. It may be one of the most central words in Christianity. There are words for different kinds of love in the New Testament, all of them commonly translated as "love" in English, but here we want to look only at *agape*.[3] We know that there is a difference in this word used in the New Testament and our Western word in English, but we have little experience with that biblical meaning as individualists and fall back on our familiar meanings in our culture. Individualism is the opposite of the kind of loyalty to others the biblical word expresses.

The biblical concept of unity resulting from love is quite exceptional in our society of competition and personal achievement. Used as it was in the Middle Eastern cultural frame of reference, the word carried the meaning of commitment, loyalty, and duty proven by action on behalf of others. We can immediately see the weightiness of its use, whether of that commitment to the wrong things: love of darkness, love of the world, or its reference to the unconditional commitment and loyalty of God to those who know him or of ours to him or to our fellow human beings.[4] In the Bible, it was the expectation that any honorable Jew had for any other honorable Jew as a descendant of Abraham, and especially for sons and daughters of David. God had chosen Israel. He loved Israel.[5] This called for the allegiance of every Jew and gave him his identity and initial honor in the eyes of his group. The meaning of love was framed for them by patrilineal obligations, tribal loyalties, and duty to the supreme

3. For a complete delineation of the various words used and how they differed from each other in meaning and usage, consult Brown, *New Testament Theology,* 538–51.

4. This contrast is demonstrated in 1 John 2:15 for example. John 3:19 is an example of the verb used again negatively. Its positive use for Christians loving each other is seen in John 13:34–35. The commitment and loyalty of the noun expressed in action is seen in Jesus' words in John 14:15. An example of God as the source of this love, his love for us, and our response of love for each other are uses found in 1 John 4:7–21.

5. Hos 11:1–4.

God through obedience to the law of the Torah. Serious Jews would have added undying service and humble obedience to their dedication and loyalty in light of God's greatness, his mystery, and his power.

There was no notion of warm feelings in this use of the word in the Old or the New Testaments. Emotions surrounding this commitment for a Jew of that time would have been feelings of the privilege of duty, the weight of honor, the pride of intense allegiance to God and his chosen people. The assurance of God's covenant with Israel enhanced these emotions and led to further feelings of security and wellbeing. God's love for us is in his complete and unalterable loyalty to his promises for our welfare now and hereafter, so our wellbeing is not based on warm feelings. It is much stronger than that.

In contrast to the Jewish concepts, our English word, noun and verb, generally means to feel affection for or attraction to someone, sometimes confused with desire and even the need to possess someone or something. If we want to talk about loyalty, commitment, giving ourselves to someone, or allegiance, we need to use those words instead. Though we would like our word to mean some of these more substantial qualities, our ideals generally do not hold up in our situation where people are supposed to make something of themselves and find their own personal happiness. Though Webster gives it a fourth-level meaning of "unselfish loyal and benevolent concern for the good of another,"[6] even this less common usage is generally associated with feelings whether it is for a family member or God himself. Examples contrary to this are quite exceptional. We draw attention to their rarity in books and movies.

The use of the word by Christians has its dangers. There are always risks in human love in our Western sense that we sometimes project on love from or for God as we see it in the Bible. Deep emotional involvement, when betrayed, brings emotional pain and depression. But *agape* from God is not like this. If we do not feel God's love, it is not betrayal. We are projecting our feelings onto him. God's love is on a different plane than ours, and emotions have little to do with it. His love for us cannot change. It is unconditional and unalterable. It is not that there were no feelings about God or others in society at that time. They were simply not the point of *agape* in the Gospels, and we must remember that God chose to use that cultural frame of reference for his message to humankind when he used their words.

6. *Merriam-Webster.com Dictionary*, s.v. "love," accessed March 11, 2021, https://www.merriam-webster.com/dictionary/love.

We must also note that the Jewish expression of this love in their social context in the New Testament period is not the model for the demonstration of *agape*. Rather, the biblical teaching, using their word with the meaning it had for them, is our guide. Jesus' teaching of loving your neighbor in that hierarchical, patrilineal, exclusive society was quite different than his audience imagined. They were blocked by their social values in different ways than we are. They were not projecting an idea of affection on the word, but there was no application as loyalty, respect, or honor *except* with other Jews of good standing. The story of the good Samaritan: an untouchable helping a Jew for no benefit to himself, was a highly counter-cultural example of love in the first century among the Jews.[7] We are not acquainted with the fierce tribal loyalty and have no experience of the laws of purity and honor that were rigid boundaries for the Jew of that day. There was zero tolerance for failure to hold to these laws without extreme social sanctions. Jesus' words were explosive in their situation, but they are hard on us as well. Our difficulties with such an incident stem from our individualism. In our society, our every-man-for-himself mentality often discourages engagement with those who have legitimate needs. Though it is central to everything in Christianity that we love God and love each other,[8] *agape* love is still quite exceptional among us. Our culture, just as theirs, creates a gap between God's intentions and our understanding.

Western ideas of the English word love for *agape* add something to the text that is not there, and when we try to put it there, it renders the text inoperable in our lives. It causes false guilt and disorientation. As good as they may be, we cannot depend on emotions for guidance or truth. They do not fuel solid commitment and are not good indicators of assurance. Some who do not feel love for God, or not consistently, may doubt their salvation. Others find it hard to believe God loves them because of a detached father in their lives who showed no affection. These concepts block our way to maturity in Christ instead of marking it out for us. And yet, much of the worship service in many local churches is intended to build up these emotions. We have this *feeling* that commitment follows emotions, not the other way around. Is it any wonder that commitment for American Christians is often quite shallow, and church

7. Luke 10:25–29.
8. 1 John 3:16–18; 4:7–12; Matt 22:36–40.

leaders have to go after it again and again? Commitment built on emotions is usually as short-lived as the emotions themselves.

Our misunderstanding is also what makes it difficult for us to use the words "love God" in the same sentence with "the fear of the Lord." For us, the feelings that go with the two perspectives are opposite. But if we love him in the biblical sense, to be loyal, committed, steadfast in our allegiance, then to *fear* the Lord complements this with constant mindfulness of his attributes, careful awareness of his presence, unrelenting trust in his powerful providence in all things, and deep respect for his otherness, his transcendence.

In this sense, we can understand why Jesus would say that to love God is the greatest commandment. The word love in our Western emotional connotation cannot work in this context. Love commanded is not love if we use "feeling affection" for him as the meaning. But the term loyalty does fit the command, and it works, even though, or maybe especially when, we do not know much about the big picture of his plan in the world. Trust and obedience are the necessary outcomes of this kind of loyalty, resulting in contented wellbeing. This is what God wants for each of us. We can feel an attraction to God, but it is voluntary. It cannot be commanded. Once trust and loyalty are established, feelings of gratitude for his grace follow, and recognition of and respect for his greatness—the fear of God—are natural.

Trust is related to *agape* through the loyalty central to both concepts. Trusting the unknown is not a value in our pragmatic culture. Though we try many things out to see if they work, we trust what we *know* works. We must trust God's providence without doubting to enjoy the security and wellbeing he provides. Loving him is about service and loyalty because we trust who and what he is, not because of what we feel or what we want. It is heightened by a fear of God, respect that allows for his will, providence, and otherness. It is unequivocal trust in what we cannot entirely or logically understand. It is a sense of wellbeing, completeness, and contentment in knowing and trusting him, who knows all about us and is still faithful in his relationship, his *agape*, with us. It is the reality and result of the powerful presence of God's love, grace, and providence in our lives every day. This is what God wants us to experience in our relationship with him.

So, the Middle Eastern mind has its own frame of reference that adds color and texture to the words used that is different than our Western translations can duplicate with what a dictionary might give us as equivalent terms. The word for God's love and grace in the Old Testament is another example of a word with no exact English translation. The many attempts to translate it: goodness, unfailing love, steadfast love, and loving-kindness, to list a few, are a witness to our deficiency of exact vocabulary in English. This is true for another key word in the Gospels, the word believe. Languages do not translate using a one-to-one correlation between words.

Typical usage of "believe" among English speakers is an example of usage outside the biblical idea and distracts us from that meaning. I have often asked my students at a Christian college why they never say, "I believe in gravity," or "I believe in the Eiffel Tower," or "I believe that Abraham Lincoln was the 16th president of the United States." The answer usually is "because they are scientific, geographical, or historical facts." But as Christians, we continually use statements like, "I believe in God," "I believe that Jesus died for my sin," or "I believe in creation." We mean that we believe that these things are true, but we need to think about how we say that. When we use the word *believe* in our culture, we are relegating these critical facts to the domain of what we have chosen to accept, among other options. We would never do that to the concept of gravity. One does not believe in gravity; gravity is simply reality. But the same is true of God. He simply is and always has been. It is even the name he chose for himself, I am.

Cultures have ways of organizing reality. We have what are called cognitive domains in our minds. They are like folders into which we file or save information for its organization and quick retrieval. Things like gravity, the earth's rotation around the sun, the necessity of air and water to sustain life, or the second law of thermodynamics go into a folder of information related to scientific facts or natural laws. Things like not spitting on other people, respecting your neighbor's lawn, obeying stop signs, and not stealing in the grocery store fit into a folder of social norms. Of course, these are only norms in your own culture.

Unfortunately, things like the importance of the Bible, God's attention to prayer, the value of Jesus' death on our behalf, and God's will for our lives, since we call them beliefs, fit for many Christians into the cognitive domain of religious beliefs. As such, they may not affect our everyday lives very much. Our culture has encouraged this so there could be harmony between the members of various belief systems in our society. It is politically incorrect to call them facts. People are to see their beliefs as personal and private choices that fit their preferences in one way or another. Our culture teaches us, despite the bedrock statements of exclusivity in several, that religion is religion. We are told that none is the real explanation of reality. Satan's barrage of counterfeit religions has caused the confusion for which he hoped.

We are generally taught in the public domain to think religions are ancient inventions to help people who did not understand the scientific basis of the universe and its laws. They tell us all the conflicting claims cannot be true, so in fact, none of them are true. We are not supposed to say it, but we put them in a large category of "none of them are true unless I think they are true," and we call this cognitive domain "religion." People just choose to *believe* in one or another of them as they need or prefer. Obviously, this approach does not work with exclusive religions like Judaism or Islam, and, unfortunately, Christianity is thrown into this mix as if it were just another religion. Each of these systems claims to be the only valid explanation of reality, God's activity in it, and his will for humankind. If any one of these systems is true, *all* other religions, exclusive or not, would be human systems of no ultimate significance. But political correctness does not allow us to say such things, and we can always find people in every religion who do not take its claims that seriously. Just as there are popular and folk Christians, there are popular and folk believers in Islam and Judaism.

Along with other people in our society, many Christians put Christianity in this same folder with Islam and Judaism as monotheistic religions. But once we put Christianity into the mix of religions anywhere, we have crossed a line into the cognitive domain of religions in general. We would never mix natural laws with tarot cards in the same mental compartment, but in this case, except for Judaism, we readily mix God's explanation of reality with human accounts. It is far more common than we think. Scholars put Christianity in reference and textbooks on world religions giving the clear idea that it is one religion among many. Christian scholars may do this to show the stark contrast of Christianity with the religions, but care must be taken to avoid the appearance of inclusion in the category. This is often behind our vocabulary when we say, "we believe in Jesus." We are separating ourselves from people who don't believe in his words or work on behalf of humankind, those who believe something else—some human, religious explanation of reality.

But all religions, excepting again for Judaism, are built on a system of ritual and human works, based on someone's visions from beyond that are connected with some idea of the divine or ultimate destiny to be gained. Christianity is not this at all. It is not a *religion*. It is a *relationship* established with God through his grace in Jesus that he initiated. When Jesus says he is "the way, the truth, and the life,"[9] it is either true or a lie. If it is true, then all else is true from creation on in the Bible. It is the true explanation of reality . . . as real as the existence of gravity. As long as we continue to say we believe it to be true among other people who believe something else to be true, we are causing confusion—confusion encouraged by the blinding work of Satan through the plethora of human religions. The biblical sense of the word believe was meaningful, but our English word is too weak to represent this attitude concerning ultimate reality. Just as we would never use it of scientific laws we *know* to be accurate, we should use other words to refer to biblical truths.

We think we are taking our vocabulary straight from the Bible, where we are told to *believe* in God and *believe* in Jesus Christ throughout the New Testament. So what is the difficulty? It is the difference between the cultural meaning of the term then and what we mean by it in today's Western, individualistic culture. In the Middle Eastern context of that time, the word we translate "believe" carried components of trust and activity characteristic of that belief. It is the point James makes of Abraham's faith.[10] It was a genuine trust of God because he *acted* on it. If we follow the stories of the conversion of Nicodemus,[11] or the woman at the well,[12] or that of Zacchaeus,[13] or the turning away of the rich young man,[14] we see the actuality of belief rested in the action or inaction of the person in question.

To believe something in that situation was more than cognitive acceptance of information to be filed under a topic in our highly compartmental and informational way of seeing the world. It is being used holistically and relationally in a holistic and relational culture. It carried a commitment to the more universal ramifications of this or that being true in that kind of culture—one that did not put beliefs in a separate mental compartment from everyday behavior as Western people tend to do today. In general, it was dishonorable in the Jewish culture to say

9. John 14:6.
10. Jas 2:21–22.
11. John 3; 7; 19.
12. John 4:28–29.
13. Luke 19:1–10.
14. Matt 19:16–22.

something was true and not have it make a difference in one's actions and outlook on life. The centurion believed in who Jesus was and, therefore, what he could do. His belief revealed his trust and humility and caused him to disallow Jesus to come to his home.[15] Jesus is astonished at this Gentile, and his words about him were a scathing rebuke of the Jews of his day.

Tradition was also a strong deterrent to the casual use of the word believe in the New Testament. The intensity of their cultural understanding of reality being controlled by the existence of God as *One* and of his law being the ultimate explanation of that is seen in a paragraph by Mark McVann:

> In the Bible, then, communicativeness is effective, valued, and prized if it endorses and explicates the worldview and ethos held by the culture in general, i.e., if it upholds and defends the tradition. It is inadequate, untrustworthy, or contemptible if it challenges, denies, or repudiates the culture's core values. ... Anything less is nonsense or anathema.[16]

In this context, controlled by honor and shame, people were careful to not use a word of commitment lightly, especially if it upset the social order and traditional beliefs. People do not forget this kind of shame, making it very difficult, if not impossible, to regain honor in their eyes. Tribal loyalties were fierce among the tribes of the Mediterranean and Arabian[17] worlds of biblical days. The Jewish nation was just such a tribe, if more refined in other ways. To believe someone was to attribute to them worthiness of intense loyalty, even zealous defense. Malina gives us a rich picture of this loyalty among Jews of that time:

> Relative to persons, faith is reliability in interpersonal relations; it thus takes on the value of enduring personal loyalty, of personal faithfulness. The nouns "faith," "belief," "fidelity," "faithfulness," as well as the verbs "to have faith" and "to believe," refer to the social glue that binds one person to another. This bond is the social, externally manifested, emotionally rooted behavior of loyalty, commitment, and solidarity.[18]

---

15. Matt 8:5–13.

16. McVann, "Communicativeness," 29.

17. Anderson, *The Qur'an*, 62, 71, 80, 94–95.

18. Malina, "Faith/Faithfulness," 72.

Being Children of Abraham gave them personhood; Samaritans and gentiles were not worthy of attention. Later, Paul would struggle to get even converted Jews to accept Gentiles into the church.[19] The individualism of our own culture gives us the struggle of personal, selfish pride and all that goes with it. For the Jew of that time, miss-applied laws of purity and fierce loyalty to the group drove men to act in many ways contrary to God's will for them regarding outsiders.[20] For Jesus, one without Jewish heritage and even a Samaritan in the eyes of Jewish leaders,[21] entering the scene and claiming to be God and asking people to leave their birthright to follow him was beyond an extreme request; it was outrageous, senseless, and injudicious. Jesus upset everything as a counter-cultural influence in their midst.

For someone to say they believed in Jesus was to put everything on the line they had ever known as a Jew. They did not use the word lightly concerning him. In this word was a humility and submission for them beyond what we know in our individualist culture when we use the term. It was not just shameful; it was the ultimate shame in the eyes of the proud Jewish hearts of those around them. Our English word does not contain the idea of humility, yet no other attitude is more important to salvation. To honestly believe in him as savior is to believe he is God. To believe he is God is to admit you are not; in fact, it is to realize you are nothing but sinful against him and in desperate need of his grace. We have used the word believe without these ideas of accompanying action, humility, and the resulting loyalty. Once again, our English word is too weak, or perhaps we must say it means something else. Our culture does not understand the breadth or depth of the Middle Eastern meaning of the term in the New Testament. It might be better to use another word or phrase other than "belief" to talk about the reality of our relationship with God.

This biblical integrity of acting on what you say was not to be confused with equivocation, where someone would say something that was not actually the case to save their honor or to keep from offending someone else's honor. Or they might say they are going to do one thing

---

19. Acts 15:1–35; Gal 1:11—2:10.

20. Jesus' references to God's attention to Gentiles in the Old Testament made his Jewish audience furious in Luke 4:25–30. Peter's entrance into the home of Cornelius was the shattering of long-standing tradition and oral Torah teaching in Acts 10:27–29.

21. John 8.

and then do another.[22] This was a cultural or speech convention that was understood by all and not confused with statements of belief pointing to the truth of a matter which were taken quite seriously.

In today's informational, categorical, compartmental thinking style, we in the West use the word believe about things that may or may not change our outlook on life, especially spiritual concepts. Connections with ideas or concepts that control our day-to-day lives are usually not connected to the vocabulary of "believe" or "belief." After some comments on good fruit only coming from good trees and bad fruit from bad trees in Luke 6:43–49, Jesus shows a kind of exasperation at the inconsistency of followers who called him Lord, a statement of belief in his status, but did not do what he said. He later was surprised; the text is usually translated as "astonished" or "amazed" when the Gentile centurion showed the genuineness of his belief. He *knew* his servant would be healed.[23] Note the humility in this expression of belief in the passage. We will come back to it later.

It is a peculiar idea in the West that a person can believe something without the behavior it demands—know something without living in response to that knowledge. Biblical faith must be followed by natural behavior that substantiates it. For example, your understanding of the reality of gravity causes you to use the stairs or elevator down the hall even though jumping out the third-story window would be much quicker and closer to your parked car. We must ask ourselves what our belief—our understanding of God—changes in our natural behavior.

This lack of correlation between the vocabularies of biblical languages and modern English, or simple misuse of words, is no surprise to God. He gave teachers and pastors to the church to keep us on the right track of his intentions.[24] Words of a language are only moderately a matter of dictionaries. They take on texture and are freighted with meaning in the cultural life experience of their speakers. The simplicity of using the English word "believe" to refer to the extensive meaning of this concept in that high-context culture creates a gap between the Western person and God. Our teaching elders can bring us to this understanding.

An important ingredient of both "love" and "believe" must be highlighted. I have mentioned humility several times in this chapter regarding

22. See Neyrey, "Equivocation," 63–68.

23. Luke 7:1–10.

24. Eph 4:11–16.

true belief. In fact, I have mentioned it some sixty times in this book. It is something of greater importance than we normally notice. We Evangelicals are known by our statement of being "saved by grace" as we see it, for example, in Ephesians chapter 2. But we have this habit of taking the teaching of some truths out of the context of the rest of the New Testament. As accurate as this statement is, and it is true in the most ultimate sense, it cannot be separated from all that is said about the nature of the saving faith that accompanies that grace. That faith is simply not possible without humility. Humility is its foundation. It is the same with central teachings like that of "love your neighbor as yourself."[25] Love is not at all possible without humility. To admit Jesus is God and really mean it, one has to humble one's self. Because of what the word faith means, we can say that it is impossible to be saved without humility.[26] It is the denying of self that Jesus told us was essential to following him.[27] With humility comes submission, and these are hard concepts for the Western individualist, however easily the word faith might roll off our lips.

Humility is not a marketable virtue in the West. The self-assertive individualist looks down on it as a lack of potential and professionalism. It would not be said so bluntly, but they see it as the mark of a fool. Even Christians can become defensive against it. But it must be a virtue found among us and a theme in our churches. Its absence is all too obvious and false displays too common. Our use of the word believe must be laden with humility, action, and loyalty if true to the biblical vocabulary.

At the end of this chapter on words and the differences we can have for meanings given our experience and emotions attached to them, there is one last thought I want us to consider. In popular Christianity, people throw around these "words of the trade" without much thought to their meaning but more to their appropriateness in the context for maintaining their place in the group that uses them or to project an image for which they want to be known. This popular usage erases sensitivity to the depth of the significance and enormity of the dimensions of these words of God in the mouths of Jesus and the authors of the New Testament. We need to be thoughtful and sensitive users of such terms as we have mentioned here. We must not let the informality expected of us by our culture set the tone of our comments about God and his attributes and ways.

25. Matt 22:34–40.
26. Heb 11:6.
27. Matt 16:24–26.

As we have said, there is something of value in counterfeit religions though they lead people away from God. In the case of Shinto in Japan, it is the person's reverence for supernatural beings. For the Shinto person, these are the kami, and they inhabit all of nature. It is, first of all, a difficult subject to talk about at all. The Kami are so far above them that the utmost respect is required. They speak of them very carefully, respectfully, and very indirectly. Most communication about them and their activity is non-verbal in the form of ritual; they find words wholly inadequate, even "a form of human arrogance." Flippancy and informality are extremely ill-advised, disrespectful, sacrilegious.[28] We, however, often lack even a modicum of respect. It is not our Western way in relationships. We have few English words that can serve us. We should use what we have carefully. We do not need, like those of Shinto, to be afraid of talking about God, and we can confidently enter his presence.[29] But to do so without the highest respect is to ignore other parts of the Bible and to forget the fear of the Lord. We must know the meaning of the words we use and not speak mindlessly. We cannot talk about the Gospel like a used car salesman trying to unload a car too long on the lot, nor can we approach the subject of God as if the Bible were written with the popular meanings of our Western English and the people on its pages just like us.

So, "love" and "believe" are central words, and so are the "trust" of God and "humility" they require. They must be meaningful words in our vocabularies or replaced with meaningful words. Trust is essential to all we have said, yet it seems to have paltry results in our lives. These concepts must be at work in our lives to be authentic. Do we "trust God's goodness enough to make continual signs of it unnecessary?"[30] Do we trust him enough to not let our theology limit his works and ways in the world and our lives to the expectations we have laid out for him? Do we believe enough in his greatness to accept that there is a great deal we do not know? Do we trust him enough to allow mystery in his being and plan for the universe? We need to realize that "Simply because God has a plan does not mean he necessarily has any intention of sharing it with [us]."[31] God did not tell Job why he experienced such suffering, but he trusted God's goodness and providence, which was enough for him.

---

28. Yamakage, *Essence of Shinto*, 29–31, 39–42.

29. Heb 4:16; 10:19.

30. See Curtis and Brugaletta, *Discovering*, 191.

31. Waltke, *Finding*, 15.

God did tell Paul why he would not remove the thorn in his flesh, and he told Paul to be satisfied. He said that his grace was sufficient and that his power was made known in Paul's weakness.[32] Do we trust God to use weakness and suffering in our lives for his purposes? If we believe in the realities of God's person and work in the world, in his revelation of that to us in his Word, if we trust him for what we cannot know, cannot change, there will be natural evidence of it in our lives. He is more faithful than the laws of the universe he has made. Let's not talk of him as if he were not.

32. 2 Cor 12:7–10.

CHAPTER 16

GOD'S WILL AND CULTURE'S CONTROL IN OUR LIVES

IT IS NOT SURPRISING THAT we think about God's will for us within a Western framework of values and beliefs. Culture affects everything we do and how we think about it all the time. There is no let-up of this influence unless we intentionally break the spell, which is not easily done. We simply do not know much about our culture's control of our lives. And when we open God's Word, we see it through Western eyes and values. How does this affect our understanding of God and his ways in our lives? How do we see his plan and our part in it?

Once again, the fundamental value of Western cultures is our individualism. It is part of who we are, and only through intentional effort do we realize its influence and suspend its control. We are also reminded that, attached to individualism, the values of internal locus of control, optimism, and achievement shape who we are. This value cluster has particular effects on how we see God's will and ways in our lives, for we see them through this cultural and personal filter. Our egalitarianism and universalism further cause us to think that God's plan for each of us will be known by everyone in the same ways and that we all have equal parts to play in it. Since we were children, we have been taught in our culture that we are special, each of us unique, and each has an equal chance at the American dream in our democratic capitalistic social system of every man for himself. Of course, this idealism does not work out for everyone, but that does not dampen our independent, egalitarian spirit.

Our meaning and purpose in life depend on this way of thinking. When we became Christians, we did not automatically shed this way of seeing ourselves and how to achieve a sense of purpose and meaning. We think that God has a special part for each one of us in his plan for the world and that we will be successful in our lives when we find out what it is. We have cultural expectations for what that success looks like in life. We feel this "success" is the goal for all of us, and our urgency orientation tells us we need it now. But as soon as we insert our ideas of success into the concept of being in God's will, we are adding something to the Bible that is not there. Finally, in Sunday school, we are told repeatedly that we should expect God to use us in remarkable ways as he did Joseph in Egypt, Daniel in Babylon, or Esther in Persia. Then it falls to us to get from where we are to that extraordinary place in God's will for us. It is little wonder we feel a good deal of stress as we set out on our own to "discover" that situation and arrive at these goals for ourselves. The relief of finding something that might be the strategic key in our search brings as much excitement as not finding it brings despair.

In the last chapter, we dealt with specific terms like love and believe that we, in our Western culture and English language, do not use in their biblical, Middle Eastern sense. Our translation of these words carries Western attitudes and values because that is the cultural system and collection of human and personal experience that gives meaning to those words for us. Other words cause confusion for us as well, and it can be significant for our Christian commitments.

When we consider God's will for our lives, we are again up against misunderstandings of critical terms. Ideas surrounding the words "called" or "calling" or the phrase "God's will for my life" are often popularized in a Western way. The term "called" is used by most to talk about personal direction from God for a person's life, so we must understand it correctly. To take the wrong meaning would keep us at a distance from God's intentions for us. We get much of our thinking from God's direction in the lives of people in the Bible. Abraham's call to leave his country and go where God would lead him,[1] Paul's calling on the Damascus Road and God's direction for his later ministry to the Gentiles,[2] Nehemiah being sent to build the wall around Jerusalem,[3] or Joseph being told to take

1. Gen 12:1.
2. Acts 9.
3. Neh 2:1–9.

Mary as his wife[4] are the kinds of examples that stick out to us in the Bible. Through voices, dreams, burdens, and Angels, God made his will known to them. We think we too should have experiences in our lives that clarify precisely what it is that God wants us to do.

We see these stories in the light of our American optimism, and we interpret them to mean that God's leading and calling for us will result in the same achievements. Our expectation for what God will do in our lives is also colored by the cultural ideals of our pursuit of happiness, desire to be unique, or need to change the world. Our internal locus of control takes over. Our individualism makes us think that we should be in the center of his movement in the world just as these exceptional people in the Bible were. In our informational approach, we want to know exactly what we should do to make that happen. Our culture tells us it is up to us.

We miss as we read these stories that these were, as I said, *exceptional* people. We overlook that God was taking the lead in their cases; they were not searching for God's will. God made it clear to them without their help. We feel that it will require effort from us, a diligent search, and then we expect some special information from God, a sign to confirm his will as he gave to these in the Bible. We miss that the way to serving God in his will was, for many of these, a very traumatic experience. Joseph would not have chosen how God used his brothers to put him in a powerful position in Egypt.[5] Daniel suffered the invasion and destruction of his land. He was taken to Babylon by the warlords of Nebuchadnezzar and his mercenary allies to arrive where God wanted him to serve.[6] Moses did not arrive at his calling to deliver God's people from Egypt without difficulty and was not welcomed in his early attempts to help them. The years of his leadership in the wilderness were not what we in the modern West would call successful.[7]

We also miss in the examples here that these men were chosen by God to be the leaders of critical movements in his plan. They were strategic people in revealing him to the world around them. These particular people had a unique role in God's overall plan. No such revelation came to the vast majority of faithful Jews in the Old Testament or the many honest Christians in the New Testament in their day. We are taking

4. Matt 1:20.

5. Gen 37.

6. 2 Kgs 24:1–4.

7. See the books of Exodus and Numbers.

special cases and making them the norm for the Christian life, making it the rule that everyone must find or receive special guidance or signs for an extraordinary role in his plan. Nothing could be further from the actual situation in that day or ours. Most of the things God is doing in the world are being accomplished by faithful people of whom you will never hear. He often carries out his purposes using people who do not know it.

Many who become convinced of God's will in a matter would explain the outcome of their search as a sense of emotional assurance of God's direction, a feeling of peace, which confirms his will in their lives. Some people find that feeling of confirmation mysteriously and recount how God provided a sign for them to take the right direction or make the right decision, as he did with the fleece of Gideon. Outward success then is often seen as proof that one is in the center of God's will. Many others look on and feel envious, deeply desiring God to speak to them in such a way; that he would clarify exactly what they should do. But in cases where finding God's will is entirely dependent on the unreliable variable of emotions, there remains a great deal of uncertainty. A feeling of peace was not the sign for those biblical examples we introduced at the beginning of this chapter. For most of them, their feelings were quite the opposite.

The achievement values of our self-centered society make discovering one's spiritual gift or one's unique calling a powerful means to advance one's standing in the group. In cultural anthropology, we call it achieved status as opposed to ascribed status. If a person says he has found God's calling to do something, they have achieved a status. People must accept the person's statement; the trump card has been played, God has spoken. But in many cases, what we are seeing is someone's search for social and emotional survival in the Christian life. This is one of the ways achieved status can be seen in the church. We are told of our ascribed status in Christ in the New Testament, but we find it hard to let go of cultural solutions for survival. When we hang on to our culture's individualist conditioning that it is up to us to make something of ourselves, to find our way, we can become desperate in our attempts to arrive at God's specific will for us. It seems to us that we ought to be searching to find that calling. We are problem solvers and achievers at heart, and we value an internal locus of control. When we arrive at something that satisfies these drives, we believe we have found God's will.

Some Christians reach heights of influence and bless the lives of many, helping them understand God's Word and grow in his grace. God's hand on their lives seems obvious. But the calling does not always turn out, to everyone's frustration, confusion, and doubt, to be something blessed of God for the people involved. There seem to be miscalculations. People sometimes feel called by God to a particular post or a lifetime of ministry in a situation but are gone in two years. A promising young couple feels called to be missionaries in a particular country but comes home before their first term is completed. These scenarios cause embarrassment and shame for those involved and create insecurities in onlookers who have wanted to know God's will for their lives. There are plenty of examples throughout history and in the present days of the church that do not seem to substantiate that arriving at God's will in such ways results in his blessing and the spiritual flourishing of the attempted endeavor. And then there is the fear that one has missed God's will in their life because of signs or feelings that never came or feelings that one did not act upon at the time. This is not God's way. What are we missing?

One of the emotional aspects of this search for God's will is the feeling of guilt. Over the years, I have come across many who struggled with the thought that God must want them or wanted them to be missionaries early in their lives. This vocation for God has been put at the top of the list, exalted as the most spiritual and most sacrificial calling one can have. Biographies of great pioneer missionaries and missionaries visiting supporting churches with stories of success and great sacrifice make people feel guilty for not taking up the cross of missionary life. Surely that is what God demands of them as well. Some live with that guilt all their lives. Others give in to it as the only way they can earn God's approval. But guilt and seeking to gain God's approval will not get you through the difficulties of daily ministries in any situation. These are not biblical motives for living in God's will. God has not made it this difficult to know his will for our lives.

J. I. Packer may have said it best when he remarked, "The idea of a life in which the inward voice of the Spirit decides and directs everything sounds most attractive, for it seems to . . . promise close intimacy with God, but in practice, this quest for super-spirituality leads only to frantic bewilderment or lunacy."[8]

Sometimes a devastating emergency is taken as God's sign to us that involvement to help people in such straights is his special calling for our lives. This is accompanied by strong emotional feelings, but a need, even

---

8. Packer, *Knowing God*, 213.

a desperate one, is the opportunity to be who and what God has already called us to be concerning those situations: caring, concerned, praying, and doing the good works that help people and will make our message credible. Situations that demand help will always be with us as Jesus reminds us, "The poor you will always have with you."[9] We may spend our lives helping hurting people. But we do not need to feel a special calling from God for this. Emotions come and go; we must continually emphasize being and then doing as its result. Given our gifts and passions, this might result in going somewhere or staying where we are. The needs for ministry to people are everywhere. They may not seem devastating today in our own surroundings. They may not seem as exotic, nor our involvement as sacrificial or romantic in our own town, but they are there, and they call for our attention.

Feelings must be treated with caution. Just when you need them, they will let you down. They have very little to do with our daily walk with God. That is where truth must have the upper hand. Nowhere are we told we will be called to a specific place in the world to do a particular task. We are not told we are to look for such a calling. We are not told that feelings of peace will be a sign to decide one way or another. We *are* called to live for God and have a part in making disciples wherever we find ourselves. It is in living for him we find our peace.[10] Yes, God chose many in the Bible to do specific things at specific times, which activities set the stage for all the other thousands of unnamed people, who were not called with such specificity for an activity, to live for God in their situation. The call of God to Jeremiah is quite direct and to Nehemiah was less direct,[11] but their callings were the exception in God's approach. Their stories describe God's work in the world and with his people, but they are not prescriptive for our expectation of the same in our lives. These are pivotal people in God's plan at that time and for his purposes. If that kind of call was central to every Christian's life, God would not have left it unsaid in his Word to us.

The call of God on our lives throughout the New Testament is, instead, to a biblical worldview: the true values, beliefs, and understandings that cause us to see the world the way God does and respond in loyalty and obedience. It is simply to be faithful to him and his Word. Our

9. Mark 14:7.
10. Matt 11:29.
11. Jer 1:4–5; Neh 2:1–9.

confidence in him is what brings us peace.[12] Living for him in this way is not a special calling; it is the normal expectation we find in the New Testament. It will not bring us reputation or notoriety. Normal is not valued in our culture. But realizing this place in God's plan and our ascribed worth, identity, and value in our relationship with him frees us to serve him in rewarding ways wherever we go. The faithful life is not without its difficulties. Faithfulness and loyalty have meaning because there are difficulties, temptations, suffering, and cultural alternatives that we do not allow to derail us from trusting him. This is a calling for everyone to a faithful life for God. God's eye is on his people, and he knows every one of us. His providence is shaping our lives. Our testimonies are not usually about spectacular events but about his faithfulness to us and others. It is not that we do not accomplish things in ministry with his help. We recognize it is of him and that he has used a servant saved only by his grace.

This everyday faithfulness is countercultural in our society. Because we find it challenging to leave culture's solutions behind, to give up the idea of achieved value, we find it hard to trust God. And when we do, it turns out differently than our cultural expectations would predict. If God should choose a person today for a unique role in his plan, it would probably not be accompanied by feelings of excitement, they would have no doubts about its origin, and it would come when that person was not searching for it.

Yet, a pressing need remains among us for God's help in particular questions for life. There are so many things one might do, so many careers to evaluate, various people one might choose for a spouse, but how will we know that this or that course of action is precisely what he wants for us? Where is one to look for the answers? Are we missing some secret key? Are we not spiritual enough? It can be a nagging agony today, and tomorrow it starts all over again. Is God hiding his direction from the seeker?

We do not see people in the Bible in such a lather about finding God's will on such questions. We are given what we need to live faithful lives for him, but outside of praying for wisdom, we are given no instructions about finding out exactly what God wants in these common issues. It would be the number-one concern for believers in the letters written to Timothy and Titus as they led and taught the early churches. But God is concerned instead that they are taught to be faithful to the Gospel and

---

12. Ps 71:5–8; Isa 30:15b; 32:17.

continually practice good works. The importance of a life of good works is mentioned five times in the letter to Titus, which takes up no more than a page and a half in the average size Bible. We have noted that some people in the Bible are simply told by God directly what to do in their cases, but the vast majority do not get a voice or a vision. They are the norm, the faithful people who, as Kidner would say, give "dogged attentiveness to familiar truths" without the lights and fanfare.[13] And in the New Testament, those who did get a voice or a vision about something specific were not looking or waiting for it. Paul received a special call, but in the routine decisions of ministry, outside the Macedonian call, how did he know what to do, where to go, who to take with him, what to say in a letter? What are we missing in all this?

There is some mystery in walking in God's will because his providence in our lives is often inscrutable at the time. It calls for trust. But we can also allow too much spiritual mystery to surround the issue of "what to do." Joseph, Daniel, and Paul went through traumatic situations in their lives, but they are never found sweating it out wondering what God wanted them to do. There was a devotion to God that was expressed in humility, prayer, worship, seeking of forgiveness and wisdom, faithfulness to what they *already knew* of God's desires for them, assurance of God's hand on them in his plan, and unshakable confidence in his providence. Notice that Joseph did not choose to go to Egypt, or David to be king, Daniel to be taken into captivity, or Esther to be selected by Xerxes's edict. There are also things in our lives over which we have no control. These things, these conditions and circumstances, are used by God in our lives. We can trust him as those in the Bible trusted him. To ask him for a change in these things is normal and invited. He may intervene, he may remind you that his grace is sufficient,[14] or he may work in your life regarding your prayer in ways you do not expect and therefore do not notice until much later. The ruling attitude in our normal Christian lives must be trust.

Then there were decisions made by people in the Bible with seemingly little if any specific guidance from God: Joseph to be faithful to an Egyptian king, David to expand the kingdom, Daniel to pray in the open when disallowed by the king. In God's providence, each of these events was central to his plan though we do not see the person agonizing

13. Kidner, *Proverbs*, 68.

14. 2 Cor 12:7–10.

over them to make the right choice. Abraham and Moses are exceptional cases among these giants of the faith as they did get detailed guidance from God throughout their lives—Abraham after his calling "out of the blue" and Moses after the burning bush. But who else was getting this specific information from God at the time? These were elected to lead, but those with them, generally unnamed, are following. Abraham and Moses were men like others. Abraham is called when he knew very little of God, and Moses is summoned from his cowardice while hiding in the desert. Abraham learned to trust God's word. Moses' reluctance to follow his specific calling was eventually overcome by his awe of God's power and confidence in his faithfulness. Each was given a particular task that was significant in God's plan for his people. These were the exceptions. The people who stayed faithful to God and his leadership through these men did so without special callings. There was a general calling to be faithful to what God had revealed and trust what he was doing through his chosen leaders.

The cultural pressure in the days of Moses was not an emphasis on self as it is for us; it was the temptation to call on other gods. In both cases, it was and is a lack of trust in God. Trusting God only was the countercultural choice his people had to make then, and it is the choice before us now. Human culture is so easily used by Satan to distract us from the main issues of living for God. We do not have to let culture control our relationship with God, but it is the biggest challenge we face in being faithful.

Seeking signs to confirm God's will in one's life is very much like a kind of "Christian divination."[15] It is performing a ritual that produces a unique signal from him. It involves no relationship of trust. It is seeking God on our terms, not on his. Sometimes people actually define the sign for God. People talk of "laying out a fleece," as Gideon did,[16] as if that passage of his lack of faith was prescriptive for us today for knowing God's will. It leaves out all the teaching we have in God's Word on trust in his providence, obedience to his revealed will, patience, and humility. These are the elements central to knowing God's will.[17] After the choosing of Matthias and the descent of the Holy Spirit,[18] there are no other uses of

15. Waltke, *Finding the Will of God*, 11–12.

16. Judg 6:36–39.

17. See Ps 37; Mic 6:8.

18. Acts 1:15—2:4.

the casting of lots in the New Testament, no other seeking or finding God's will through ritual behavior. The Apostles never used, and no mention is made that others should use anything to seek a sign from the Lord. The emphasis of their teaching is that we become godly people seeking his kingdom. We have all we need to do this.

A heart's desire to please God, honor him, and prefer him to all else shapes us to make life decisions. God looks on the heart while we are concerned about the outward appearance and the confirmation of the right choice. Once again, we see that God's Word is more about shaping the reader into a kind of person rather than providing information and specifics about options. His will is not to be discovered by each person because it is not hidden. He has already given us all we need to become those who honor him with their thoughts and activities. As such, we will find the opportunities before us as ways to honor him, serve him, and express our gratefulness for his grace. There are no shortcuts. We will have to desire his revealed way to have his wisdom in decisions from day to day.

God is more concerned with what you are than what you do anyway. He wants you to know him through all he has given to you in general and special revelation, and then to ask him for, and then trust him for, wisdom. We can then see our world through his eyes when we read the Bible. If our questions are, for example, which college to choose, which person to marry, or what job to take, instead of thinking that only one single option is God's exact will for us, we need to depend on the principles and boundaries he has already given us. Knowing the options, and our own motives, strengths, and weaknesses, we will ask him for wisdom because we want to honor him. Being a godly person is his exact will for you whether you own this or that house, live in this or that location, get this or that degree at school, choose this or that vocation, and, perhaps the most important decision for a person, marry this or that person. Being a godly person is spelled out to us throughout the Scriptures. It is not perfection, but an aspiration to give our whole person to honor him in whatever decisions we make, seeking his wisdom and trusting his Word.

How very un-Western, un-individualistic. This course of life is very different from our cultural concerns for our independence, even as Christians. Part of the offense of the Gospel in the West is its taking of the attention off the individual. Instead of accentuating the self, the Gospel emphasizes God, his power, grace, and providence. This is glorifying God. It will not result in the popularity of the person. Fame and fortune are not its rewards. Most who have been faithful in this regard have gone unnamed in history but were never unknown to God.

Sometimes it looks like God allows things to go wrong in our seeking to honor him. But there are several causes for things going wrong and the suffering that may follow. The reason could be in ourselves. Perhaps we did not have the best motives or desires in a decision. Remember how strong our culture's expectations are and how much we depend on its solutions for survival. In addition, our own heart has its powerful inclination to satisfy the self. If we do not know ourselves and our culture's influence on us, we will likely see God's Word through this lens instead of allowing God to speak for himself. We will lean toward being more legalistic or permissive in the ways we see his boundaries and our freedom in Christ.

There is also the case when we are as faithful as we know how something happens that looks all wrong. But in retrospect, upon reflection, we see it was right in God's plan. It only looked different than we expected. We must not lean on our own understanding but acknowledge his hand in our lives in all our ways. It is a matter of trusting in the Lord.[19]

We must also remember that we live in a broken world since the fall, and we all have our challenges and weaknesses in being godly people. We must be ready to help each other. Lastly, we must always trust God's wisdom and providence. Through suffering, he often shapes us to be godly for him in ways we would never have learned on our own. We become "handmade" by his loving care that provides the occasions to shape and strengthen us. When we give ourselves to him, his intentions will be at work in our lives. It will make us different from other Christians around us, a unique object of his love and care for his purposes. And, of course, in a broken world, we cannot expect to live forever, nor would we want to. Much greater blessings lie ahead.

In summary, His wisdom will help us decide about education, vocation, marriage partner, and how to use our money within the boundaries he has given us. We ask him for wisdom and trust his providence and move ahead with the discernment he provides. The boundaries of God's will in a matter allow more latitude than many realize and more than some of us want. In choosing to serve him in life, the opportunities and our natural talents, personality, training and preparedness, and interests

19. Prov 3:5–6.

and desires form areas within which the specific ministries or vocations we might choose lie.

While we may have a higher regard for a missionary vocation, God's Word leads us away from a dichotomy of higher or lower, secular or sacred domains to a realization that any respectable occupation can be a platform for serving him as salt and light in the world. What we are inclined to, what we have talents or training for, what gives us the best opportunities for incarnating his truth or expressing the Gospel are considerations for this decision, as is his direction that our lives should encourage the making of disciples.

God's Word gives us a description of the kind of people to seek out who will make a marriage honorable to him. Once again, instead of the "there is only one person in the world that God has selected" approach, God gives us boundaries that define the right kind of person to marry. Many individuals are within those boundaries. Choosing a settled Christian growing in grace and away from legalism, syncretism, and mysticism would be of primary importance, but, of course, considerations of personality and habitual behavior should be regarded for compatibility in such a decision as well. Decisions about education, vocation, and purchasing a house, etc., are all made with the wisdom his general boundaries of living for Christ give us.

Instead of our indecision and perceived dilemmas keeping us from knowing God's will, we will weigh the options before us in light of the boundaries and freedom he has already given us. Our natural inclinations will be tempered with a longing to honor him to move ahead with our desires in these areas; the right decisions will become more intuitive. The answers are already there. Our knowledge of God's love and our love for each other are two of the significant boundaries of our freedom.[20] We are not and will not be perfect in carrying out our desire to honor him, but he is looking on the heart, and his grace is as real and abiding as it was the day we chose to follow Christ and receive his forgiveness.

We must have the proper perspective concerning those heroes of the faith we find in the Bible. We often see these spiritual giants as examples of what we should be or do. We live in a culture that highly values achievement, so this comes more naturally to us than to a collective society. We read of the seven thousand unnamed faithful people

---

20. Jesus' words are very clear about the basic rule of love, John 13:34; 14:9–17.

that God revealed to Elijah.[21] God knew every one of them and of their circumstances in life. Being faithful to our God, loyal to his purposes, intent on honoring him, and helping others understand his grace is our goal and task as he has given them to us. If you are what he wants you to be, you will find yourself doing what he wants you to do, with a heart desiring to honor him in everything. Will it be life-changing for a huge group of people? Maybe. Will it be honoring to God if it is faithful, grateful, and humble? Always.

So, does God guide us? Yes, he does. He has given us a great deal in his Word about his plan and program for creation and humankind in terms of decisions made. We might best describe these as his ways. First, there are some things God has already decided about the nature and direction of creation, such as how people become his children, the second coming of Christ, and heaven prepared and promised for his own. There are also the unchangeable results of sin like human death and rejection of Christ, resulting in eternal separation from him. These are absolutes, decrees that no one can undo and will remain despite any cultural change in preferences or worldly pressure to remove them.

There is great value and wisdom in knowing what he has already decreed. From this, we get objective guidance. These are the limits; to ignore them leaves an individual on their own. Setting up your own boundaries where God has already drawn his only results in a very temporary feeling of freedom. Adding to those he has put in place results in a lethal legalism. These can be the tendencies of those who value individualism as we do in the West. Just because you do not like God's boundaries or feel more secure if there are more boundaries, are never reasons to change God's Word and never result in the "ideal" Christianity for which we hoped.

God also guides us by controlling the events of history according to his providence in our lives. Joseph, Ruth, Esther, and Paul are among the many examples in the Bible. He will achieve his purposes for creation, and we can be an intentional part of that plan by allowing him first place in our lives. On the one hand, we can resist being the people he wants us to be; on the other hand, he is at work bringing certain circumstances about in our lives that open the door to just that. The self and culture are pulling in the opposite direction, and we are given the choice every day

---

21. 1 Kgs 19:18.

of our lives to trust his providence or to live by our own ability to achieve what we need.

Then there is his desired will, his intention, purpose, design for us that he has revealed already concerning genuine, honorable, wise, trusting, and common sense behavior for His people. He does not force his desires on us, but neither do we have to discover them. We do have to read his Word and let him speak for himself. But it is already there in front of us. Desire is different than decree. It is what God wants for us, but what we may decide not to follow. It is how we can grieve the Holy Spirit. Jesus lamented the stubbornness of Jerusalem.[22] God does not desire the suffering of his people or any people, but we chose it with the first sin. He does not desire that anyone should perish without salvation,[23] but many choose to do so. He does not want us to lack faith in him, but we often do. God must often encounter disappointed love, but his grace and patience are enduring and his loving-kindness everlasting.

The purpose of prayer is not to pray about his decrees coming to pass, but that what God desires in our lives might come to pass more and more each day. It is not something human logic can comprehend, but he meets our needs and those of others in answers to prayer. He has a plan, and we can enter into it by prayer. His promises of it are many. We may or may not recognize his answers, given our cultural expectations and personal preferences of what that answer should look like. But the answers are always there even if it is the grace to bear what, in his wisdom, he does not change. If we trust his will more than our own, we will be as grateful for this answer as any other.

We gain wisdom from God's revealed decrees and desires, our experience from walking with him, and the counsel of mature Christians. It is a topic worthy of more discussion in the next chapter, but it is an integral part of our topic here of knowing God's will. Wisdom is how we make good decisions that honor God. The church community and advice from mature friends and leaders help confirm God's direction in our lives. But wisdom comes at a price too many are unwilling to pay.

If we are becoming the kind of people he intends, we will find ourselves doing and desiring what he wants us to do and desire. Our desires and preferences, shaped as they were by our worldview regeneration when we acknowledged his grace in the Gospel, are now important to

22. Matt 23:37–39.
23. 2 Pet 3:9.

notice and value. Our natural behavior is becoming more and more in-dicative of our heart's direction and inclination. His desires are becom-ing ours, and we can move ahead with confidence, having asked him for wisdom and to open and close doors to directions we might take. Our desires, interests, and compassions have their place.

Walking in God's will for our lives will not mean we always feel spir-itual. Maintaining that feeling is elusive. This is not the pattern we see in the Bible. We see genuine believers at the height and at depths of feelings of spirituality. "Nobody can always have devout feelings, and even if they could, feelings are not what God principally cares about."[24] Actually, our concerns are to be much more practical. We may need to study a course of action or learn a set of skills; we may need to understand more about that course of life in which we want to serve him. This is the practical side of doing his will, and the humble heart will recognize the need we have to prepare properly. It may or may not be accompanied by the feelings we want, but the intentional desire to serve him, the allegiance to his cause, the commitment and loyalty to his honor must be our motivation. That being said, feelings of humility and gratitude for his grace should never be far away.

As unpalatable as it is in our Western, scientific culture, we can-not exclude God's intervention in our lives in a more particular sense. In unique cases, God has supernaturally guided believers and unbelievers through miraculous means. I am amazed at the many Muslims who have come to Christ through a vision or dream.[25] It is never a new revelation about himself beyond what he has already given, but guidance to it or understanding it to meet a need. God is the one who decides if he needs to provide special information or help. Most of us will never need or ex-perience it and are not instructed to seek it. It is not the norm, but the exception. We need to follow what we already know.[26]

We cannot let talk about "discovering" God's will and calling come between God and us. It is the opposite of his desire for us. Popular Christian talk sometimes prides itself on having the secret keys to know-ing God's will, but there are no secret keys, no magic words. The broad and the narrow path are both plainly exposed. God is not withholding

---

24. Lewis, *Mere Christianity*, 132.

25. See Doyle, *Dreams and Visions*, and Qureshi, *Seeking*, 260–66.

26. See Friesen, *Decision Making*, 233–43.

anything from you that you need to know to follow his will for you. He is not hiding a calling, your spiritual gift, or special power over sin in your life.

Your culture is not friendly to your knowing and doing God's will in your life. Human cultures never are; they have their own solutions for survival. Western people tend to read these ways of survival into the biblical text. Our values on individualism, egalitarianism, internal locus of control, and unlimited good cause us to want to see the biblical text from a particular perspective and to turn its teachings around to meet our personal needs the way we expect them to, the way we want them to for our emotional and social survival, instead of the way they are intended to help us. We must let God speak for himself without allowing our culture to interpret his words.

Non-Western cultures also present challenges to allowing God's will to operate freely in the lives of believers. All Christians have a shared calling that will face different challenges from whatever culture is in control. We are called to be faithful, obedient, loving, self-controlled, and humble as we make disciples among every nation. It is a calling to be godly, missional people. But culture is culture everywhere, and it is powerful. Either you control it, or it controls you.

So, there are no secrets concerning God's will for us, but we tend to let our personal desires, culture, or theological system skew what is in front of us as we read his Word. When we let God speak for himself in the Bible, we get the clear idea that there are priorities in God's will, perhaps better said, prerequisites for later stages. His desire for those who have believed, then, is twofold. He is first concerned about what we are, where our deepest heart's loyalties lie. When we are being what he wants us to be, as imperfect as we are at times, we can do the things he wants us to do, but not before.

When we truly belong to him, his desire is that our lives be fruitful in terms of good works. These prepare the soil of the hearts of those around us, so we can plant the seeds of the Gospel in their hearts and minds. As we read through the New Testament, we see that the priority for doing is, surprisingly, on this stage of good works. Planting the seeds, making disciples of all nations, is clear but less prominent and is predicated on these good works. The order is clearly grace, then godliness, then good works, then Gospel. Ritual behavior has little to do with this. Without natural behavior giving evidence to our faith, we are destroying the very thing that gives it credibility. Beliefs and loyalties are personal, but behavior in the world around us is public. Words are cheap enough; true faith must come out into the light, must be incarnated. There is no secret to it. When we live out these priorities as they are given to us, to the best of our ability, we are, without the slightest ambiguity, in the center of his will for us.

This understanding of God's will in our lives opens the door to freedom that many Christians do not experience. These allow too many distracting worries, false guilt, memories of the past, and legalistic thoughts about God's ways to cloud their enjoyment of freedom in Christ. But freedom from all this can be experienced in its fullness in Christ. The best witness to God's grace is a life lived out in this freedom in the workplace, in the family, in the marriage relationship, and in our service to others.

CHAPTER 17

WISDOM FROM ABOVE
IS WITHIN REACH

KNOWING AND WALKING WITH GOD, trusting his providence, and desiring above all to honor him will result in a pattern of life and reasoning, a sensitivity that is best described as wisdom. Though human wisdom is not perfect, God has given it as his way for us in life. It is discerning the difference between legalism and freedom, mysticism and mystery, and syncretism and relevancy. It goes further to distinguish between natural behavior and ritual behavior, and inclination and duty.

Though it may seem this is cognitive and informational, the characteristics of wisdom are actually quite relational, as we see them in James 3:17. Those who accept its ways are known for being pure, peace-loving, considerate, submissive, merciful, impartial, sincere people noted for good works. Its central theme is realizing a regular stride with God, an intuitive sensitivity to him, and the humility it engenders. Wisdom is actually an engaging of life at a much more meaningful level. A lack of wisdom does not always look like the fool in the book of Proverbs choosing ruin leading to death. It is just as often a going along in one's days missing the deeper things in life, unaware there is anything else, sometimes avoiding the meaningful for the more superficial levels, and perhaps reaping the mediocre and temporary results of popular Christianity. But God, in both the Old and New Testaments, goes to great lengths to show us that everyday life is the context where wisdom is the salt that brings out the flavors of confidence and bearing in the unsettling things of life and expresses itself as the dynamic result of knowing God for who he is and letting him speak for himself.

All our talk about the negative influence of culture on our faith in this book does not negate the fact that we live out our Christian lives, by God's choice, within the framework of that system. There is no expression of anything without a cultural system to give words, forms, and behavior their meaning. God used Middle Eastern culture, and we use Western culture as frames of reference for meaning. Wisdom understands this and, though not controlled by that system, expresses itself, with discernment, within the framework of the common cultural forms available. It must.

The cultural values of any system will fit three categories for the Christian: those that are *negative* and against God's Word, those that are *positive* and good for Christians in each situation to emulate, and those that are *neutral* and do not have an effect on moral or ethical issues but may be very important in the relevancy of the expression of our faith in the situation. An example of negative values in Western culture might be proving our personal worth by our achievements, feelings of self-importance, and a materialist view of the universe. Positive values might be our informal and personable approach to people, our initiative in problem-solving and innovation, or our freedom and determination. Neutral values might be a preference for eating with a fork at a table, enjoying baseball, or feeling a need to mow the grass. Of course, in an informal society, as we have in the West, there are many variations and personal preferences in these matters. It is the substance of wisdom to discern the difference between these categories in any cultural system.

So, we might ask, what is the difference between a person having wisdom and a biblical Christian? Wisdom is the goal of being a biblical Christian. It is an interest, concern, and insight into the things of life that protects the Christian in the difficult environment of this world ruled by Satan's deceptive powers. Having wisdom moves from the starting block of biblical Christian commitments, convictions, and virtues to develop a greater sensitivity about people, intuitive thoughtfulness about life, awareness of surroundings and context, mindfulness of one's emotions, and insightfulness about activities. Wisdom marks a well-founded measure of maturity in a biblical Christian. It is having a fluency for life in a complex world of good and evil.

God's use of Middle Eastern cultural forms might surprise us. Jesus joins a wedding party when he could have revealed his divinity in a less joyful situation. He even made sure that the wedding party was a success for all who attended by providing the best wine when it was about to run out.[1] It was a wedding the couple and their guests would never forget. At the same time, he used the occasion to reveal a central truth of the universe—that he was God. Could he not have done this in a more stoic setting of solemn thought and less human enjoyment? And the creation of wine from water! Was there not a more religious way to reveal himself? Yet this is wisdom, God's wisdom, among us. There is a point to God's use of this occasion. The wise person is not a hermit, but a person engaged in the activities and concerns of life, approaching the everyday things in their lives with interest and insight, enjoying freely what God has given.

Is there any situation that could reveal this more than a wedding? Here two people are joined as the first step into a life together that is intended to be a union of ultimate trust and fulfillment, closer than friendship. Their roles in the relationship would be very different today, but the joy of the occasion was more openly expressed in those times and cultures. Two imperfect people come together and seek to complete each other. Nowhere is a relationship more intimate and complete in the emotional, mental, and physical aspects of two human beings. God's design is at work here. Delight is expected in every realm of the event and ongoing lives, and wisdom only heightens its meaning and enjoyment. Jesus is there, adding to the joy of the event.

Marriage will be an analogy of Christ and the church going forward as it was of God and Israel in the Old Testament. Two joined together to become one.[2] It was the perfect event for his revealing and illustrating what to do with that information about himself: becoming one with God in Christ. He is to be the groom and his followers the bride. Wisdom is in the bride never taking her eyes off her husband.

So, he is at a wedding, and at a midnight meeting with a troubled Pharisee, at an encounter at the Sychar well with an untouchable woman, then we see him at the pool of Bethesda with an invalid.[3] Later he is at the healing of the man born blind and attends the funeral wake of Lazarus.[4] He is involved in the celebration of life, concerned in moments of deep confusion and denial, present in the experience of suffering, and

---

1. John 2:1–10.

2. John 15:4–5; 17:20–23; Rom 8:1; 2 Cor 5:17, 11:2; Rev 19:7.

3. John 3, 4, 5.

4. John 9, 11.

understanding in times of sorrow and loss. His life was filled with these encounters; he had a fluency in the affairs of life. In these moments, he incarnates the wisdom of God in the daily lives of ordinary people.

We could go into any area of everyday life because that is where wisdom applies itself: in friendship, vocation, neighborliness, the business deal, marriage, the family, anywhere and everywhere. As the proverbs tell us, wisdom is calling us to follow its path.[5] The meaning of the word has become hazy and even irrelevant for Western Christians today. We have moved away from it and devalued its use. We live in a culture of pragmatism, independence, accumulation of information, personal achievement, and self-centered gratification. There is little attachment to character and a scarcity of honor in the owning of worthy values. Life for Western people is more about doing than being. Wisdom does not seem to fit anywhere. But this comes from our inaccurate thinking about it, absorption with logic, internal locus of control, and our independence. We just can't make sense of the idea that the greatest freedom comes from letting the self go. Some of the hardest words for the Western person are the many places Jesus talks about the theme of this death, but the seed must die if we are to harvest the wisdom God intends.

Today the church puts little emphasis on the wisdom literature of the Bible. Though reading any part of the Bible is a cross-cultural experience, wisdom literature is most foreign in our modern situation. We know nothing of established tradition and have little respect for age. Our Western longing is for innovation and our value on youth. We cannot expect to walk into the world of the ancient sages with any familiar feelings. It seems dry and irrelevant. Wisdom is not part of our Western world.

It is an emphasis noticeably absent in the teaching of our young. An awareness of wisdom's value and its corresponding humility in our relationship to God and to others, as well as the events of life, is unknown to them. Students in our Christian schools are packing away a great deal of information about God and his Word, but there is a danger in this without an emphasis on wisdom. There is a strong inclination in the West to accumulate information without seeing its significance for life. Our individualism tells them they must make something of themselves. Our value on objectivity pushes them to a logical arrangement of that information into systems. Finally, our feelings of competence at accomplishing this process result in knowledgeable students who lack the essentials

---

5. Prov 8:1–11.

of wisdom. The use of the information then adds to the establishment of identity and feelings of worth. Rather than humility, the result can be pride that we are the ones who know the answers. We may feel that all is done now, and we can move ahead with a profession of delivering this information to others without considering its implications for day-to-day life. This has the likely outcome of only popular Christianity.

The Proverbs tell us over and over that to refuse wisdom is to court death.[6] It means that primarily in terms of separation from the blessings and benefits of a full and healthy life—the fulfillment we seek in life, the guided pursuit of contented wellbeing. And those proverbs make it very clear that this wisdom is the choice of a particular path concerning God and that its fruits are hard-won by the determined effort of the seeker.[7] It may be that, in the West, the idea of grace makes us feel that all is done for us and there is nothing left for us to do. We may think we can let go, and God will bring about all the results he desires. But that grace through Jesus Christ opens a door whereby, in our newfound forgiveness, we are given the chance, with his help, to intentionally become all he has purposed for us. Rich and poor alike, learned and unschooled, man or woman, regardless of ethnic group, we all will choose to move ahead in this wisdom of godliness or to be waylaid on our journey by our persistent culture and lose forward motion against the barrier of the self and its demands on us. We might opt for information only or for a position of status in our faith, but we will have forfeited the way of awe and intimacy with God that leads to true understanding—that fear of the Lord and knowledge of God that is the beginning of wisdom.

The way of wisdom is held out in Proverbs as a choice that is often discarded. The book is written to the godly and the ungodly in Old Testament societies. There is no middle ground of someone being a Christian and yet not having entered the house of wisdom as we have today. Given the context, people are either pursuing an understanding of life with God at the center, or they are taking the path of the fool, whether senseless, stubborn, proud, or lazy.[8] It is a choice between honor and shame, true riches or human folly, life or death. It can still be so for the ungodly of our day, but God's grace is not the end of the journey for Christians. It opens the door to a life of wisdom. We choose to enter and pursue wisdom, or

---

6. Prov 8:34–36; 14:12.

7. Prov 4:5–8; 1:7; 9:10 with Matt 6:33; 13:44–45.

8. See Waltke, *Book of Proverbs*, 109–116. See also Kidner, *Proverbs*, 39–43.

we bask in grace and information about God and let the world go by. Popular Christians remain in the way of self and culture.

The Western reader of today may see very little value in the wisdom found in the book of Proverbs. It seems foreign and removed from real life in our day. We find its Middle Eastern flavor tasteless, perhaps even disagreeable. But if we allow ourselves to be satisfied with a superficial Christian life, we miss the point of Proverbs. It is to live deeply with integrity, faithfulness, humility, and insight. In the New Testament, Paul struggled with the people at Corinth to bring them to this level of the wisdom of godliness.[9] The struggle is plain among the seven churches of Asia Minor of whom God gives his assessment.[10] Godly wisdom must be part of our lives and ministries. Harsh as it sounds, Proverbs only gives very unattractive alternatives to the person who chooses against wisdom.

The blessings of wisdom are found through persistent discipline, leading to understanding and insight for discretion in skillful living. Wisdom grows, and no one in their humanness reaches its end. As Ezekiel was told by God to eat the scroll[11] and Jesus told his hearers that they must eat his body and drink his blood,[12] we must ingest the truth from God's Word; it must become part of who we are. As it becomes part of our natural behavior, it influences our experience and relationships in everything we do. It has become wisdom, giving us discernment and insight concerning God's ways with people, events, and circumstances in life.

An important aspect of wisdom is that knowledge is never an end in itself. The ultimate goal of learning is not simply to gain information but to see its meaning in our lives. We must understand when and how that information should be used and what function it should have. So, knowledge becomes understanding. Our status in the social circles of our day has no bearing on this. A godly person in Proverbs may have the wisdom of Solomon or a tenacious peasant shrewdness. These will look very different, but the commonality is that they find their source in God and reflect his character.[13] It is not about an informed mind by itself, but about an attitude, a perspective that comes from the fear of the Lord and trusting God's providence that puts accumulated information to its best

9. 2 Cor 13:5.

10. Rev 2–3.

11. Ezek 3:1–3.

12. John 6:48; Matt 26:26–29.

13. Jas 3:13–18.

use. A definition of wisdom might be: a state of being, beginning with humility and the fear of God, followed by disciplined and patient learning, that results in right and skillful living, with the embedded qualities of discernment and integrity, resulting in gratefulness before God. In his commentary on the Book of Proverbs, Derek Kidner says it well, "Knowledge, then, in its full sense, is a relationship, dependent on revelation and inseparable from character."[14] Bruce Waltke sees wisdom from the Book of Proverbs as "the model of curriculum for humanity to learn to live under God and before humankind."[15] Curtis and Brugaletta add balance, priorities, diligence, and resolve from the book of Proverbs to the practical side of the way of wisdom.[16]

In summary, wisdom is not doing something or knowing something but is first a matter of being something. Reading God's Word is to shape us into the image of Christ, we who were first created in the image of God. Wisdom is costly in the book of Proverbs, but we are counseled to find it whatever the price: "Wisdom is supreme, therefore get wisdom. Though it cost all you have, get understanding."[17] "Wisdom is more precious than rubies, and nothing you desire can compare with her."[18] This is the root of the tree, the mainspring of the watch. Wisdom speaks for herself: "I love those who love me, and those who seek me find me. With me are riches and honor, enduring wealth and prosperity. My fruit is better than fine gold; what I yield surpasses choice silver."[19]

There is a process in gaining this kind of understanding and prudence. It takes persistent effort with the goal in mind: "If you call out for insight, cry aloud for understanding, look for her as for silver, search for it as for hidden treasure, then . . . you will understand the fear of Yahweh . . . which is the beginning of wisdom."[20] This process is gradual over time, and access to it is granted by the desire for it from a God-centered perspective, the discipline to pursue it, the fear of the Lord, and his help along the way. The pursuit must be genuine and begins with asking for

---

14. Kidner, *The Proverbs*, 59.

15. Waltke, *Proverbs*, xxi.

16. Curtis and Brugaletta, *Discovering*, 65–103.

17. Prov 4:7.

18. Prov 8:11.

19. Prov 8:17–19.

20. Prov 2:1–6; 9:10; Job 28:28.

it.[21] The ways and means of God in granting that request will undoubtedly be different than we might expect or desire. If you ask for wisdom, you'll need to fasten your seatbelt. The creature must remember his creator and entrust life and all his pursuits to him.

As I have said, the idea of biblical wisdom does not resonate well, if at all, with Western culture. But wisdom is an approach of caution with the intent to honor and trust God that can withstand any weapon culture levels at it. Walking in wisdom does not, however, mean there will be no difficulties in life. It may bring some loneliness in our day and culture, and you may feel out of stride with those around you. But wisdom gives us a way to approach these difficulties. We will face them with an entirely different perspective—with confidence in God's grace and providence and with a sense, deeper than the need, of contented wellbeing despite our circumstances.

I thought wisdom was knowing a great deal about life and our part in it in my early years. But wisdom is as much about accepting what we don't know and being content that God does and has a plan for all things in the world. That drama is bigger than us, but we today have a valuable part in it for which we must trust him. This was the outcome for Job as well as for the author of Psalm 73. Wisdom is desiring that plan to be carried out more than anything we prefer—a desire for his will to be done among us as it is done in heaven, of which we know very little.

So, wisdom is a complete trust in God's purposes and providence such that concerns about self and cultural expectations dissolve, and one is released to enjoy the freedom and confidence we have in Christ. It is a fruit of our salvation while we remain on earth. It is the incarnation of the truth we have learned in his Word. We will not be perfect at living in the new worldview, but we will look different to others—like we are second-generation immigrants, relevant in this culture, but with roots in another.

The character qualities of a person who lives by wisdom from above in James 3:13–18 are striking and noticeable. The central virtue of this "good life" is humility. Wisdom is not possible without it. It is the same with all the biblical expectations for us as followers of Christ. Years ago, I came across a description by C. S. Lewis of those who have come to Christ. It describes people with a wisdom about life that comes from their unqualified trust in God. It is not the only description and is a generalization, aspects of which are seen here and there among people who have

---

21. Jas 1:2–8.

come to see the world differently than the rest of us—people of wisdom. I have come to appreciate these words more over the years. People of this kind of wisdom will seem

> stronger, quieter, happier, more radiant. They begin where most of us leave off. They will not be very like the idea of "religious" people [you have seen]. They do not draw attention to themselves. You tend to think you are being kind to them when they are really being kind to you. They love you more than other people do, but they need you less. They will usually seem to have a lot of time; you will wonder where it comes from.[22]

The desire that leads to the steady growth of wisdom comes from the person's heart, but the elements needed are in God's Word and a trusting relationship with him. Psalm 1 compares a person of this wisdom to a tree well-rooted by a stream of water, the nutrition and moisture deep in the soil (of God's Word) causing it to bear fruit at the right time and with healthy foliage. Whatever this person does prospers in God's plan. And as the Proverbs tell us, it begins with the fear of God[23] and is followed by a decision to intentionally pursue that wisdom.[24] To move into a life of wisdom, we will have to be willing to let God be God. We cannot let the expectations of our culture, even our Christian culture, our theological system, or our personal desires for what we want God to be or do keep us from the desire for *his* plan in the world and attentiveness to our part in it. He is in control of his plan, though he has not revealed all the details to us. He will carry that plan out in ways we do not expect since our cultural and human expectations are just that, cultural and human. He is far above all that. He has a part for us in this plan if we will acknowledge him in all we do.

Though rooted in the fear of the Lord, Wisdom reveals itself mainly outside the church, in the everyday activities of life. So, as I have said elsewhere, it has to do with natural behavior, not ritual behavior. It shows itself during the week when we are at work, at the market, in a business deal, with our neighbors, in our family, with a group of colleagues. The streets of the town are the stage on which wisdom is played out in the book of Proverbs. It is there that concern for God's honor in contrast to self-interest and cultural expectations must become characteristic and

22. Lewis, *Mere Christianity*, 223.

23. Prov 9:10; 15:33.

24. Prov 2:1–6; 3:13; 8:10–11, 17, 34.

loyalty to him unmistakable. Humility, patience, contentment, and understanding are demonstrated in the mundane affairs of life and cause people to show honesty, kindness, justice, longsuffering, consideration, and decisions with moral direction when wisdom from God is demonstrated. There is plenty to do for God, but this is becoming something—being something that precedes doing something.

Becoming this sort of person in the ups and downs of life is not something we do entirely on our own, but it never happens by itself either. As we have said, it begins with the fear of God, and then we must desire it, make the sacrificial decision for it, search for it in God's Word as for treasure worth more than silver or gold,[25] and above all, trust God for it. He gives it to all those loyal to him[26] and willing to step out beyond self and their culture with diligence to honor him and "pay dogged attention" to the old truths while avoiding legalism.

Many things are set in motion through the lack of wisdom, which, even when we finally accept God's way, cannot be undone. If our culture and self have had the upper hand in our lives in this way, and they have, then we can only begin where we are and trust God's providence to use us as we are from that day forward. He can and will. Only a few have had parents who started them down this path as the book of Proverbs would beg us to do, so most of us must begin where we are when we once allow God to be God. But he is not unaware of our situation. He knows our intentions and has been watching and waiting for us to turn our heads in his direction. That is the beginning of wisdom.

A practice of godly, Middle Eastern people who had wisdom in their lives had to do with another concept that is not common to us in our culture, meditation. Non-Western cultures have a tendency to value reflection while Western cultures veer away from its value and replace being with doing—with achievement through an inner locus of control. Our value on time makes it nearly impossible to be still and know that he is God and that we are his people.[27] To actually take time to think deeply about one thing that God has given us and nothing else seems a waste of time. To do nothing, even for a few moments, has been drilled into us by our culture to be wasteful, unproductive, wrong. We can feel guilty. We are so distracted by concerns for our own happiness and fulfilling the

---

25. Prov 3:13–15; 8:10–11, 17–21.

26. Jas 1:5.

27. Ps 100:3.

demands of our culture and the expectations of those around us to get it that we ignore the training of our minds to think on things above,[28] the things that actually provide for that happiness. Once again, culture and self separate us from God. The superficial satisfaction of popular Christianity without serious thought about God and his intentions is all this approach can be expected to yield.

Of course, meditation is used in some cultures and religions to cultivate or eliminate the self without a thought of God. There are those nagging images in our minds of stoic Zen Buddhists in a lotus position for hours in silence and Hindu Brahmins, mind in a trance, body in a twisted *raja* yoga position. We hear talk of chakras, magic sounds, renouncing all of life, incense, and entering non-existence or ultimate reality.

These kinds of meditation expressly reject the creator God of the universe revealed in Scripture. Meditation for the Christian has nothing to do with these forms of it so foreign to the Bible. It has value instead based on its focus on God. It is not a trance, but wide-awake thought on his person and works, his revelation of himself, his teaching, and the examples of godly people we have in the Bible. For the most part, it is time spent simply focused on the truths we have, mental and physical distractions removed, selfish and cultural influences put aside. It is a time of looking inward to our weaknesses and needs so God can forgive and work in our lives to accomplish his plan. It is looking beyond information to its meaning and allowing its full implication to impact our lives. It is centering ourselves once again on his will and seeking his help to see it done. In this way, we are letting him speak for himself.

Meditation on one thing means not being distracted in our minds by other things. It is the practice of letting go of all the distractions in our minds to concentrate on the things God is telling us about himself or ourselves. It is a learned and intentional behavior, and it takes time like anything else. It is refreshing to think about God's creation of everything, his grace and forgiveness of our sin through Christ's death, his providence in our lives, his trustworthiness in everything, or his love in contrast to our selfishness. We come away with a new perspective on the things about which we were anxious and stressed, or impatient, frustrated, and angry. As we do this more and more, it will become habitual for our mind to go back to these thoughts when stress begins to dominate, anxiety threatens our peace, impatience makes us irritable, or frustration makes us angry.

28. Col 3:2–3.

Meditation brings health and stability of mind and creates a harmony between God's desires and ours. It closes the gap between God and us, letting him be God and not our worries and concerns for ourselves. We are learning to "Seek first his kingdom, and his righteousness, [so that] all these things will be given to you [us] as well."[29] It is a hard fact of life that the results of our efforts are not often immediate. But the discipline and practice of today become the welcome results and often the habits of tomorrow. Training ourselves in godliness is the only thing that will move us from the superficial Christianity of our day to a walk with God rooted in his being rather than in our engineering. And this is not a blessing for us alone, but for those around us and those closest to us. Being less distracted by our concerns for self, we are now freer to take a genuine interest in their wellbeing.

In the New Testament, we are given many instructions for our spiritual welfare that cannot be achieved without some form of careful consideration, serious and thoughtful attention, or in a word, meditation.[30] When we are told to let the peace of Christ rule our hearts and his word dwell in us richly, the idea is that the resulting peace and comfort should overwhelm our thoughts to guide our actions.[31] Setting our minds on things above, casting our cares and anxieties on him, and being transformed by renewing our minds will not happen without training our minds and hearts in the right directions.[32]

The Bible tells us in the Old Testament to meditate often on the law of the Lord. It often refers to this as writing his law on our hearts—his will indelibly on our innermost being—so that we never forget it even in the toughest moments. Remembering, acknowledging, being loyal to his ways are the outcomes of meditation motivated by desire and not simply ritual. Memorization and repetition can be ritual behavior and may or may not engage the heart. We must think about what we know.

Meditation is important to life. But note, it is not just thinking about the words and agreeing with God's love and wisdom and leadership in our lives that they describe; it is the life direction, the activities they call us to, the behavior expected by those words. Knowing calls us to being, which results in doing, and in this case, that is wisdom. If meditating on

---

29. Matt 6:33.

30. Josh 1:8; Pss 1:2; 48:9; 77:12; 119; 143:5; 145:5; Col 3:2–3, 15–16; Rom12:2.

31. Col 3:15–17.

32. See Col 3:1–4; Phil 4:5–6; Matt 6:25–34; Rom 12:1–2.

words does not lead to inner transformation or motivate honest, godly behavior, they remain words no matter how good they are. It is not magic. We must meditate with the intention to follow through with deeds. These are the good works that are an obligatory result of faith. There is no promise of blessing without them. There is no way to clothe ourselves with "compassion, kindness, humility, gentleness, and patience" except to clothe ourselves, and therefore our lifestyle, with "compassion, kindness, humility, gentleness, and patience . . . and love."[33]

Let us be careful not to confuse busyness with godliness, doing or knowing with being, sound with the need for silence, entertainment with meditation, and cultural absolutes with biblical absolutes. Often it is an effort to be relevant. But we must not hold on to the values of our human culture when they hold us back, not even in an effort to be relevant. People beginning to seek God are not looking for superficial conformity to the behavior of others; they want the real thing, the answers. We cannot expect to win favor easily with those around us in a culture headed the other way that controls their decisions—a culture putting self-survival at the center. Effective witness must show the world that the solution to wellbeing lies in the opposite direction. Being what we have called relevant is not working. Our confidence and strength are not in ourselves or the world around us but in the quietness of knowing and trusting God.[34] Wisdom moves us above and beyond the ordinary to see it all through a different lens. One that filters out the superficial and allows the significant to come into focus.

33. Col 3:12–14.
34. Isa 30:15; 32:17.

CHAPTER 18

GOODNESS, PROVIDENCE, AND SUFFERING

MANY RELIGIONS BEGIN WITH THE problems of mankind and seek a solution to being right with the forces of the cosmos, ancestral or nature spirits, or a god or gods that control their circumstances. Over the centuries, they have a sought ways to overcome the suffering and meaninglessness of the human situation. There is some truth and insight in nearly all of them, but there is no saving truth in any of them. The truth we find in them generally has to do with the nature of humankind. All people are up against common human problems and questions for survival on physical and emotional levels. If we temporarily set aside what they did not have right, the common themes in the religions reveal humankind's suffering and hopeless situation and the great need for supernatural help for people in our condition.

Gautama the Buddha, for example, was an atheist; his religious teaching was self-centered, but he had one thing generally right: attachment to things for self leads to grasping; it is fueled by desire, and it ends in anxiety, stress, emotional pain, and feelings of loss. So, unless a person makes the right choices and has a mind clear of the clutter of attachment to things and concerns for the self, life *is* suffering. The Buddha's answer to this suffering was, however, entirely human. It emphasizes detachment from the world for a peaceful spirit.[1] It distracts people from their misery

---

1. See Corduan, *Neighboring Faiths*, 314–21.

and despair temporarily, then leads to eternal separation from God. It falls terribly short of the actual resolution that God provides in Christ, and it does nothing to help others who suffer. Each person is on their own in their search for deliverance. This can seem natural for the self-made individualist.

In another effort to deal with suffering, Confucian wisdom teaches that people should not express any extreme. There is always a *middle way*, a moderation of any action, of any emotion, that creates harmony and balance in life and relationships. It is called the Doctrine of the Mean.[2] It is an unnatural view to Western people and is absent from their individualist cultures. Asians live by it in a human effort to maintain moral balance in their lives and the virtue of harmony with their collective communities. It is about the cultivation of the self.

There is some truth here once again. Many extremes in human experience bring suffering. Biblical wisdom understands that attachment to the wrong things, or to good things in the wrong way, or without self-control or moderation,[3] brings suffering for the person and the group. God gives us the essential element of practicing moderation out of love for those around us, which honors him. It does away with vulgarity on the one hand and legalism on the other[4] and puts interaction with honest and *agape*-based intentions on a particularistic level.[5] We have a reason to be measured in our self-expression and a greater encouragement to do so than community recognition and harmony. Confucianism leaves this on the human level of works. For Christians, it displays our trust in his providence instead of our works. We can wait on the Lord instead of asserting ourselves in our situation.

There are honest religions and dishonest religions in this search for relief from pain and the human condition. Honest religions are searching for an understanding of life and the solution to the suffering of humankind. They begin with good motives but do not come to the truth as they rely only on man's ways and wisdom. Other religions are dishonest from the start and more like cults. They are the making of clever and controlling, self-consumed leaders seeking their own promotion and power. From the outset, often beginning with a delusion, the cult's purpose

2. Confucius, *The Doctrine*, 95–115. See also, Confucius and Legge, *The Analects*.

3. See Phil 4:5 for the biblical perspective. The *KJV* uses "moderation" in this verse. The *ESV* uses "reasonableness." The *NIV* uses "gentleness."

4. See Eccl 7:15–18.

5. See 1 Cor 6:12, 10:23.

becomes the control of the followers to the glorification of its founder. This is used by Satan to deceive and distract people from the true nature of reality, trapping members with fear and social pressure. There is no truth or light in a man's search for power and controlling others to get it, and no solution to human pain or answers for survival.

Religious systems exclude God as he reveals himself in the Bible but include human wisdom and human truths by which people are easily deceived.[6] Desperation makes them easy to believe when alternatives have been discredited. But this human wisdom only goes so far, which is why there are so many human religious systems, each trying to convince people of their answer, and none of them having a real solution. They often become institutionalized, politicized, materialistic, or simply systems of legalism. They lose their core values regarding human suffering, leaving members searching for emotional support in their misery.

Christianity is not, as we have said, a religion. Instead, it gives us the true nature of reality, and at its core is a relationship with God. Unfortunately, it can be made into a religion: a human system, professionalized, even politicized, or an empty, ritual-filled, or legalistic lifestyle, but that is never the intent of God in our lives. Made into a human religion, institutionalized Christianity can no longer answer the question about human pain. It keeps thoughtful people at a distance from the truth. It becomes just one choice among many for the answer to suffering and, on its popular or folk level, it is not a very convincing one. Many people are caught in this deception and miss the realities of knowing God. They are no better off than those trapped in any other human religion. For them, suffering continues to be God's fault, unfair, and undeserved. Though there are many differences between Christianity and the religions, the significant difference is God's grace. Satan has not been allowed to clone this central theme of God's attitude and actions toward humankind. Grace cannot be institutionalized, and it is our hope in the human situation where suffering abounds.

In our lives, God's Word would produce a lasting and enduring answer amid our circumstances if we would but learn to trust his grace and providence and walk in the wisdom he offers. Too often, we let our culture and our preoccupation with self-survival keep this wisdom at a distance. We read the verses, and when we close the Book, we go back to controlling our lives and circumstances. When we see a Christian from

6. 2 Cor 4:4; Eph 4:18.

another culture return to his animistic practice in a syncretistic effort to make sure everything turns out okay, we don't understand it. We don't realize it can be in our habits and patterns of survival as well to go back to old solutions. Religion in any form does not undo suffering in more than a superficial, temporary way.

Culture does not leave us alone in any area of life, and the question of suffering is no different. In the West, we feel that happiness and prosperity are a right, that any downturn of events is wrong and should be removed from our lives. At the same time, we know that life can be full of suffering. When things are going our way, we don't give it much thought, but then we have stress or pain and think it is unfair. Many think that if there is a God, it is his fault. It is true even for some Christians, and it makes the gap between God and Christianity greater.

To choose God is, by definition and logic, not to choose self or culture as the frame of reference for life. God has a purpose for our lives and knows how he is going to achieve it. He works in the most unexpected ways since our expectations come from our cultural values and personal preferences. He is outside these limitations and his ways beyond their dictates. When we allow him into our lives, we must let go of our own control and walk by faith in his goodness, power, grace, and providence.

The Bible tells us of the temporary nature of the physical world and its pain and the permanence of the spiritual universe without grief or anguish. Though created perfect, in that creation, God gave humankind free will so that love and trust in relationships would be possible. The result was that the original design was spoiled by the human choice not to trust him. The human heart, given the freedom to choose and distrusting anyone who might withhold something from it, wanted to know both good and evil, and now we do. We live in a broken world. Satan is still at work deceiving us and creating doubt about God's Word, using suffering as one of his many tools to blind the minds of people to its only answer.

But God chose not to end his relationship with his creation, and he continues seeking the trust of his creatures. Though we brought a great deal of suffering on ourselves in Eden, our present world is now the context within which to live our lives in a relationship of love, submission, and trust with our Creator. We can still see his hand in creation. We can experience and are humbled by his continual grace to us in it. We are to use it in ways that honor him but not set our hearts on it because it is not the permanent state of things in the true nature of reality. Here we embark on our journey and travel our chosen road, but it is not our destination. It is where we learn to live in a relationship with God. Here we can choose loyalty to God and trust in his power, providence, and grace amid the suffering sin has brought us and the idols surrounding us. We know it is neither an illusion nor the permanent state of affairs, but it is that place where we must choose to give our allegiance to self or to God.

Humankind makes the decision to choose God or reject him. If he is evaded, people are left with the pursuit of happiness in their culture on their own, trying to find ways around suffering. Some seek relief in the excesses of religious asceticism or worldly hedonism. God's way is very different. We are to become preoccupied with God and his plan, but our humanity is not forgotten. Not all desire leads to suffering. God created all things good[7] and for our enjoyment when bounded with gratefulness and love for others.[8] They may be twisted and abused in the world and misunderstood by Christians in their legalism, mysticism, or syncretism, but they are very real.

We have freedom in Christ from these abuses and misuses of what God has created for us. His created joys bring the needed rest and relief along the way, often speak of his power and grandeur, and reveal the deep-seated beauties of his design and love. They add to our contentment even in suffering. These are only encouragements along the way, however, not the destination. So, we are free, and our desires have a place. Passion for honoring God allows us to order them with wisdom, and knowing God's desires paves the way to true fulfillment of our own. He gives us boundaries within which to enjoy all he has given us. We must be careful not to call bad what God called good at the creation of the universe. Paul would say we are free to enjoy all things with gratefulness, but some are not always beneficial or constructive. We can drink deeply but not self-ishly from the fountains of blessing God has given us.

We may cause our own suffering, it may come from natural causes, or it may be triggered in our lives by others. For many of us, our disordered, self-centered values and desires, fueled by our individualist cultural system, cause us a great deal of suffering as we embrace idolatrous attachments.[9] John called it loving the world, and James says it is spiritual

---

7. Gen 1:31.

8. 1 Tim 6:17–19.

9. Older authors were good at revealing our attachment to self and the suffering it engenders. Particularly George MacDonald and G.K. Chesterton. Modern authors also warn us about idolatrous attachments such as Keller, *Counterfeit Gods*, and Newkirk, *No Gods But God*.

adultery and makes us enemies of God.[10] These false attachments damage our souls. They are uncritical addictions to self-love—self-preoccupation and the control of our situation—that filter God out of the picture and lead to more attachment to things around us and our efforts to attain them. This gap between God and us grows, as does the distance between other people and us. The warning of 1 John 2:15–17 reminds us of the temporary fix these attachments bring, for all things connected to them pass away. Love gone wrong is blinding, numbing the mind to the realities of the human condition.

This attachment to self must be confronted first of all, for from it comes all manner of suffering. To attribute this pain to those around us is to evade our responsibility for our own hearts. Desiring or requiring for self what it is not meant to have or expecting everyone around us to behave in ways that only add to our own happiness causes us and those around us misery. In return, their careless and unkind treatment triggers more negative responses. But, it is in our control to allow this to bring on stress and resentment or not. An inordinate concern for our wellbeing, even when we are right, can lead to suffering. Our faith must be framed by humility, our freedom ruled by love.

Whether it comes from dangerous loves, ill-health, the loss of one we loved, the selfishness of one we thought a trusted friend, the unfaithfulness of a spouse, the waywardness of a child, our response must be humility and faith, not resentment. God's purposes and providence in our suffering may only be known to him, but we can trust him. His grace *is* known to us and does not diminish in suffering. What we cannot do is trust ourselves or our feelings. We must not doubt his goodness as Adam and Eve did. Only an undiluted relationship of steady trust and unbending loyalty with God can meet our needs as we join his plan in this world and walk with him into the next one.

We must respect the priority of spiritual values lived out in a human context that is both physical and spiritual. The physical is God's gift and must not be ignored. Nor can we ignore the physical needs of others or the responsibilities our roles give us in relationships. God purposes that we live out our faith in him and our commitment to one another in the physical world with its pleasures and pains. It is a choice to live for him regardless of circumstances. He knows the pain we experience in our lives. It is our primary opportunity to trust him. If he says, "my grace is

10. 1 John 2:15–17; Jas 4:4.

sufficient for you, for my power is made perfect in weakness,"[11] we must trust him and not doubt his word as Adam and Eve did. This world is temporary; the realities of the spiritual universe are lasting; trusting God is everything.

So, instead of resigning to a life of hardship, suffering, and sacrifice in legalism and a bitter spirit or demanding material, emotional, and physical blessings, we must let God be God. We are to accept whatever life brings that we cannot change as his providence for us, embracing both the good and bad in life as ways of knowing and serving God. We must accept that our judgment of these things is limited. Jesus speaks of both hardship and blessing ahead of us. To seek only one and be embittered by the other is not in the Book. Job's words to his wife ring in my ears, "Shall we accept good from God and not trouble?"[12] God allows suffering sometimes to strengthen our faith, sometimes to glorify himself as with the blind man in John 9, and sometimes to show us that his grace is sufficient, that his power is made perfect in weakness, as in the life of Paul. Having the correct perspectives on these things is a large part of wisdom. Proper concerns for our own health and safety and that of others are appropriate and evidence of a godly perspective, but bitterness, worry, and dread are signs of not recognizing God's providence and care in our lives.

This, too, is suffering. We are drifting away from the big picture, from trust in God's goodness and in his plan and purpose. We are insisting on our own way and forgetting that his way is different. This puts us at a distance from God's purposes, and that distance increases our suffering. Physical and emotional pain is real in this life but no more real than the life without them that he has prepared for us—the true and eternal life that follows this temporary one. Culture's solutions leave God's intentions and purposes out of the equation, as in Maslow's hierarchy of human needs.[13]

Christians do not get a pass. Suffering can come between God and us if we let it. The peace and security we find in trusting God and his providence in our lives will always be punctuated with grief and pain in this fallen world. Suffering and death are part of human experience, not because God wanted it that way, but as the result of mankind's choice.

11. 2 Cor 12:7b–10.

12. Job 2:9–10.

13. See Figure 14.1.

He could have created a world with suffering if he had wanted that, but suffering is not God's desire for us. We have caused it—chosen it against his will. The wish to be in charge of our own happiness and survival and the feeling that it is better than God can supply, the desire to be like God and in control, has brought about all the evils in the world that cause our suffering. Though God is blamed for it all when we say, if he is love and is good, he would not allow it, we bear the entire responsibility for it ourselves and would choose it again if God stepped in and stopped all the present suffering.

So, humankind committed the crime, but we sue God for the damages. God did not walk away, however. This present suffering shapes the context within which he continues to offer himself and his way, forgiveness, and a way back to himself. So gracious is our creator God after we reject him. C.S. Lewis called it his insufferable kindness when he said, "He has paid us the intolerable compliment of loving us, in the deepest, most tragic, most inexorable sense."[14] His arms are still open to us, waiting if we will but look in his direction. It is within and sometimes because of suffering we will know his undeserved kindness and see he is right. There is no happiness outside his love and care, his forgiving grace, and there is no suffering that can snuff it out.

Suffering can become an avenue back to him if we allow it to be so. But pride and selfish ambition will not easily permit it. Our culture puts us in charge, and its habits are difficult to break. All the safeguards we have put in place to secure our survival and personal happiness will not survive in suffering. God will see to that. He leaves us with no options but nonsense or to see it as his hand in our lives. If we come to the end of ourselves, we can come to the beginning of him. If we welcome him, it humbles the self. We become weak with gratitude when we catch a glimpse of our terrible arrogance and selfish ambition and his unbelievable grace still held out to us. We can actually come to thank him for the suffering allowed in our lives that we might know him better and serve his purposes.

So, the question is, given our propensity to serve the self, is it even a good idea that God should stop all suffering even though he can? Is our God not a God of providence? We caused the suffering, but he can use it, as he can use anything for our good. Many in the world are still trying to defend their choice and, in desperation, expend every effort to make

---

14. Lewis, *Problem of Pain*, 29.

the world and life seem something other than what God says they are. But we know the true nature of reality and can have contentment in the broken world man has scarred with his willfulness because we have him. He brings joy even in desolate places.

Our competitive individualism must die; our trust in him take over. We cannot let down our guard. Pride is everywhere and may be the individualist's worst enemy. Make no mistake; it is as common in the church as it is in the world. As long as we think in our individualism that we can do it, make something of ourselves, and survive on our own, we will never allow him to "spoil" it all for us. To be proud is the opposite of knowing God. Our pride may seem restrained to us, but we must not trust ourselves in this matter even at the best of times. We are all capable of it. It is always hiding in the wings, ready to come on stage. God is more concerned about a faithful heart than he is about our "spiritual" achievements on stage. Beware of pride that takes over God's rightful place in our lives and loyalties—his prerogative to be God. It will indeed result in pain and misery.

In the face of suffering, we often hear people say that God will do what is best for us, that he is at work in our lives to glorify himself. There is truth in this: God can and does show his grace and faithfulness at these times. His providential intervention in our lives and in the world does reveal his glory. And few things contrast our weakness with his strength more than his hand in our lives when we are suffering, whether to bless or use us to bless others despite our weakness. But the truth ends when we try to make suffering into something God wants for us. He is pleased when we express our faith and patience when waiting on him in our pain. We can grow in our trust in him when there is no outward blessing in it for us. But God would rather we did not suffer and has prepared for us its removal in the coming days.

Though God does not want suffering, he does want us to know the loyalty, the faith, that can only be expressed if there is mystery, uncertainty, lack of comfort. Without the need for help, without things we don't understand, there can be no faith, no trust. When we can walk by sight, when there is enough light, we feel we do not need to depend on God. I am reminded of Isaiah 50:10–11, "Let him who walks in the dark, who has no light, trust in the name of the Lord and rely on his God. But now, all you who light fires and provide yourselves with flaming torches, go, walk in the light of your fires...[but] you will lie down in torment." Just as there cannot be love or obedience where there is no freedom of choice, there is no faith where there is no uncertainty. We are told to walk by faith rather than by sight.[15]

There is risk to the self in trusting God when seen from our limited vantage point. We have spent a good portion of our lives coddling the self and making every preparation for its survival and pleasure. Much effort has and is put into avoiding uncertainty and reducing risk, minimizing our liabilities. Naturally, we have an aversion to the risk involved in setting aside our trust in all our strategies for a promise, even though it assures us of more and better than we can ever attain for ourselves on our own. Knowing there is no way back and no off-ramp makes us uneasy. Yet, God allows one opportunity after another in our lives for us to trust him. Suffering is another chance to do so, perhaps the most poignant but the most effective in our lives. It does not mean we do not do all we can to deal with the difficulty, but it does mean that ultimately, we know, we really know, and are content, that the situation is in God's hands. And even if it does not work out as we want or expect, we will be content with the outcome because of this faith. Daniel's three friends are an example of it as an intentional and ultimate choice of confidence in his providence.[16]

But, once again, it was not God's will that Adam and Eve experience suffering. It was his will that they live in a perfect place in perfect peace and happiness. He had prepared that for them. But it was also his will that they choose to trust him entirely, so he gave them the ability to choose, describing the results of not trusting him as death. The consequences could not have been more explicit. But the temptation of having the power and control that belongs to God alone was too much even for those who knew no other sin, those who walked with him in the garden. We must never think that we are equal to the inducement Satan puts before us. We will have to trust God's grace and power in the best of times as well as in the worst of times.

God's redemptive purpose is to bring all things back to that perfection he created. He promises us perfection in his presence; all suffering will be done away, perfect happiness restored. It grieved God to see Adam and Eve lose it. Since they did not trust him and the goodness he had provided, he allowed them the *fulfillment of their choice* to know evil. His gift of free will would not have been valid any other way. We are not told of God's sorrow at this event. Perhaps we cannot understand divine grief,

---

15. 2 Cor 5:7.

16. Dan 3:16–18.

but trust cannot exist unless there is a possibility not to trust. His grace and intent of redemption were made clear at the same time as suffering came into the world.[17]

God has made the end of our travels like the beginning, a perfect place.[18] That means primarily a place without the effects of the fall, but also a great deal more that we cannot imagine. Along the way, we suffer amid various blessings of his hand in our lives, but he does not bring the results of Adam's choice into our lives; they are already there. His plan is for their removal, total redemption, perfection, heaven. We are not given much information about this destination, and what we have uses a good deal of allegory. He gives us just enough to require our trust in his promise. God's one desire for us in this life is that we trust him and let him be God in all things. This is the one thing that our logical, scientific, information-driven culture rejects at its mention. The choice is ours as it has always been since the garden of Eden.

Let me remind us one more time that we have an enemy who has always wanted nothing more than for us to doubt God. The sufferings he has managed in the world give him plenty of ammunition. But, in all his strategies and power, Satan cannot stop God or the trusting Christian in this life though there is suffering along the way. We make that choice.

We do not anticipate that God can bless us in and through our suffering or that he can use our suffering for a cause we do not expect, but he can and does. And always with the promise of removing it all in his time. But he also alleviates suffering to reveal his love and care, his power and providence to us and those around us to enable his plan for our lives or ministries to others. In his providence, our life story may have more or less suffering than another person's, but his purposes for us each are different. But everyone lives in a world of suffering. We have unending opportunities to love our neighbors by helping them in their pain. This imperfect world is that place of ministry to one another that reflects Christ's love. How else would it be possible?

God often intervenes in our lives, but he never removes us from the context of the general conditions of humankind, from the fallen world. He does not intend to do that until the end of the road. He has his purposes. Jesus prayed that he would not take us out of the world until those

17. Gen 3:14–15.
18. Rev 21:1–14.

purposes were fulfilled.[19] These are the only conditions under which we can choose to trust and love him—show our allegiance and loyalty in their true perspective—and love and serve our neighbor.

Now that we have decided to know good and evil, we have the opportunity to trust him for one in the face of the other. Once doubt was introduced in the garden, we have ever since been on a journey of choice, knowing the alternatives but having his word. We trust his wise and loving providence, or we do not.

19. John 17:15.

CHAPTER 19

CLOSING THE GAP, LETTING GOD BE GOD

CULTURE HAS POWERFUL, CONTROLLING, AND subtle effects on people. The results of ignoring its impact on our lives and ministries are too severe to go on as if there was no connection. Syncretism is lethal for Christianity. We must counter its effects on the church and its mission, on our lives, and on our message.

The self in our individualist culture has been elevated to the role of savior—its assertion is our only way of personal, emotional, mental, and even physical survival. Some of my readers may feel frustrated, even exasperated at the very mention of the intrusion of culture and this culture-shaped self in our Christian lives. But that risk is worth it. We must change, put culture in its place, let God be God, and return to a missional lifestyle. Please take a closer look. We have been suffering from this deception of cultural absolutes and self-survival for too long.

Some readers would have preferred that I be more black and white about our relationship with God, more objective about its requirements for each of us. Though our forgiveness through trust in the sacrifice of his son is an absolute promise, our ongoing relationship with him is beyond the black and white language or list of propositions we might prefer. It is not a tit-for-tat agreement, a contract with terms signed, sealed, and delivered. Information is essential, but by itself does not result in a relationship. That will take genuine trust. Relationships have some objective elements but are more qualitative than quantitative. The primary factor required is this trust, especially when there is so much we do not know.

Actually, our discussion in this book is not about anything new. Many have gone before us on this path to understand God's will and ways and mind and became missional people in this world for him, in his way. They let God be God. Yet, they are few compared to those who have not realized the effects of culture on their faith. These live Christian lives partially syncretized with their culture. They want to be biblical but are out of step with God's Word, not seeing the contradictions of their culture in their lives and church. Others have had only a casual interest in God while in love with Christianity. They are popular Christians, unaware that God is active in the world and waiting on their hearts to turn toward him. They readily welcome the latest influence of culture and adapt to it as needed. The world around them is their second love.

These may not be seen readily by others in this life, but God looks on the heart. Honesty is the only way to come to terms with the self and the only way to pass inspection. But every care must be taken. The heart is cunningly deceptive[1] and can put up an enormous defense of its habits. But it would be better to move ahead without our right eye or hand than to ignore its influence.

Others have misused or exploited Christianity. Some have disfigured God's intentions for us by their emphasis on ritual behavior or drummed-up emotions to "feel closer to God." These ways are easily detected and appear as cold legalism and superficial mysticism to the outsider. The image they have created has made Christianity distasteful to the watching world—something to be avoided at all costs. No religious slogans, pictures, or vocabulary will impress the world with an understanding of God as he really is. These sometimes contain a good thought or idea about God, but they do not penetrate the worldview of our day. They are not relevant to the deep, felt needs of the lost and work against our missional purpose in the world.

Are we putting the gold ring of true faith in the pig's snout of a church syncretized with the world and personal values?[2] Jesus' words are not kind toward these attitudes. They deny him in every way.

1. Jer 17:9.

2. The reference is to Prov 11:22. The church should be a beautiful woman as the bride of Christ, but if she lacks the deep grace and relevant truth that came through Jesus Christ, she will be detestable in the eyes of the world as she should be in ours.

If we are going to close the gap between God and Christianity, we must change our approach to the Christian life, church, and doing mission. We would better be involved in ways that touch the real felt needs of the world around us. Instead of larger buildings for our own needs, what might we do in our communities to show God cares and provide sustainable help to those in need? We need more missional people in the marketplace and among professionals being and doing the right things and caring for their patients, clients, students, and customers in ways that leave an impression of God's care. Home repair and service people are called into the homes of many in the community every day and can leave a taste of new wine—an impression of God—in their wake and put the truth within reach of our neighbors in a relevant way. These are our missionaries in the Jerusalem and Judea of our world[3] like the itinerant Christian messengers of 3 John 5–8. How is our church helping to prepare them, send them out, and help them on their way? We must infect the world with lives lived for God in relevant ways. This is the salt and light of mission. Without the credibility that good lives and good works provide, the times we are given to speak meaningfully of God to our neighbors will not impress the truth on their hearts. We must get beyond superficiality to substance evidenced by genuine care and *agape* love for our neighbor. This is the essence of being missional.

Knowing and walking in God's will is a way of life. We must approach the world and go through life's everyday events with God's priorities in mind. It means denying the selfish ends culture puts before us as individualists for his greater purposes in those events and relationships but *never* means legalism. It is a way of seeing and going about life, not a list of things to do or not to do. It is about becoming the kind of person that does or does not do certain things because of a relationship with God that puts self second. It will take faith of a higher order than we find among popular Christians to trust him for his way unconditionally. But only this will close the gap between God and Christianity.

We do not know his plans for the future or how they will affect us today. We do know that without faith, it is impossible to please him— faith in who he is and in his providence for us. "When Paul prayed that the Colossians 'might be filled with the knowledge of His will,' he was not praying that they would receive revelations or 'calls' regarding vocations or locations. He desired that they be filled with the knowledge of

---

3. Acts 1:8.

God's will 'in all wisdom and spiritual understanding.'"[4] This was for a life honoring to him anywhere and everywhere, in any and all circumstances, with any and every person in our lives. We are the ones who have put the "call" to be a missionary above that of being a Christian student, secretary, or piano tuner. And we have turned passages like this one into a call to discover God's secret will for our lives. We Western Christians have been more concerned about feeling good about ourselves and impressing others than honoring God in the way we have discussed in this book.

J. I. Packer says, "Wisdom is the power to see, and the inclination to choose the best and highest goal, together with the surest means of attaining it."[5] It seems there are two main components, a trusting relationship with God that allows him to speak for himself and living our lives as part of his plan instead of making him part of ours. I refer to both as aspects as being missional.

Being missional has to do with living our lives as part of God's mission in the world. Pastors, missionaries, teachers, plumbers, police, bankers, or soldiers, as Christians, all of them are to be part of God's missional plan for the world. They are all to be a *full-time* part of that plan. Being a Christian is not a vocational choice; it is about being missional in any choice of vocation. Missionaries, pastors, and teachers train others to be missional in their vocations, communities, and families. These take the message to the world in an incarnational way. No one role is more vital than another. All are necessary for the making of disciples; all are full-time.

The message we bring to the world is of the utmost importance. Teachers training others to be missional, and the missional people in their vocations are called to responsibility for the kingdom. Teachers must be accurate in their training and careful in their examples.[6] Missional people in the world must be careful to protect the integrity of the message and incarnate it faithfully.[7]

But all missional people are not alike. They each have choices they make regarding how they incarnate the message of God. God's providential particularity with each person is central to our wellbeing in Christ. Many are kept at a distance from God's will for them by comparing

4. Smith, *Can You know God's Will*, 16. See Col 1:9.

5. Packer, *Knowing God*, 80.

6. Jas 3:1–2.

7. Rev 22:18 can be seen as speaking of the whole message of the Gospel and our examples of it in life as missional people.

themselves to others, not realizing God's providence in their lives will be different from any other person in the world. The conversion and subsequent lifestyle will not entirely conform to the lifestyle of other Christians. Though there are essential truths, there is no absolute pattern of how a person comes to Christ, how they will express that faith, or the turns in God's plan for their life as a Christian. The woman at the well, Nicodemus, the disciples, Zacchaeus, and the Apostle Paul each came to Christ differently. They had different challenges to deal with in allowing God into their lives. They had different personalities, abilities, and life experiences that influenced how they would live out their lives for God. They had diverse social conditions within which to express their loyalty to God. They each had distinctive ministries that God in his wisdom had laid on their hearts that used their backgrounds, the various influences that shaped them, to fulfill his particular desire for them in his plan and purpose. There was great diversity among them, even though the individuals shared a similar cultural frame of reference. This is the providence of God at work before, during, and after conversion. They all chose God for their lives, but their choices to honor and serve him after that were all quite different.

So, there are central truths about God's intentions for the creation and his work through Christ on our behalf, but there are also general blessings for believers that all enjoy in their own way. All experience the same boundless grace of God enrobed in unconditional love, but each relationship with God is individual, particular to that person. It is their story. Each person has spiritual needs that differ from the next Christian—different struggles in their lives. What each person will need to keep them growing in Christ will be different. Each must make choices different from another. We must respect this in each Christian we meet. Though the characteristics of love, humility, and trust of God are common among us, the demand for conformity in living out our faith is a legalistic limitation on God. To expect others to do exactly what we do in our walk with God or in our service to the body of Christ or the world around us is not a biblical example. Each makes the decision to follow Christ. After that, each must make choices as to how they will live by grace.

In God's Word, we have the non-negotiable essentials that all Christians share and around which they can have fellowship. Though our theologies can delineate them in endless complexity and abstract vocabulary, they are fewer than we think. There are, of course, those who misunderstand or misrepresent an essential truth of God's Word. These lines of thinking must be corrected with diligence and exactitude. The essentials of God's grace and the value of the death and resurrection of Christ cannot be misrepresented in any way. The inspiration of Scripture and the need for personal faith cannot be watered down. God's creation of man and woman as distinct genders and his intention for marriage between them cannot be missed. An individualist, informal culture's craving to put humankind in the center and make their own rules about the order of the universe and society in it is a human distortion of God's intentions. These are not free choices. Ordained by God, they and other like doctrines stand at the center of a relationship with him. The Gospel is his message of love for all, however, and one we must take that message with love to the dysfunctional society in which we live, to the world that is looking the other way.

Obedience to his will for us is not optional for the believer, but its expression must be personal. So, in terms of behavior, the expression of loyalty to God is one of the non-negotiables. But the application of that loyalty to God in life will take on different behaviors for each person. John 22:17–22 is a passage not always seen in its real significance. God's requirements on Peter would not be the same as those on John. Their lives would be divergent after all this. Each will make choices in their obedience.

For a few, it will be a public ministry, but for all it be will be living out a life of personal loyalty to God in our different venues in a way that honors him and that will attract others to Christ. Conversion is a process rather than an event. Set requirements, patterns, and formulas of how people must come to Christ are not helpful. If they result in people actually coming to Christ, it is almost by accident. More often, the result is a syncretistic Christian than a biblical Christian. The same is true of our subsequent walk with God: lists of behavioral requirements take God out of the picture and put personal achievement in the center. These choices come from syncretism with our Western cultural universalism, not the Bible.

Not only should we not require other Christians in our culture to be like us, but we must give even more room to Christians in other cultures. When the cultural frame of reference for the meaning of behavior and communication for Christians changes, the differences for living a life loyal to God between that frame of reference and our own can be enormous. People of different cultures will display different particularities.

There is no room for legalism, superficiality, mysticism, or syncretism. Loyalty, love, and trust will cause people to begin living in harmony with who God is and in the perspective of the life to come while still in this one, no matter their cultural frame of reference. The choice of behaviors must be theirs. Inestimable harm has been done by explaining God and his will for us in another culture using our own cultural frame of reference. But we must each live for him in our own cultural context. It is the only way people can be authentic and relevant in their incarnation of the truth to others in their own cultures.

Institutions choose their approach as well. Some churches have become part of the problem instead of the solution by substituting information about God, lists of beliefs, popular values, and ritual behavior for knowing God in a personal relationship and living in his will. People get locked into these definitions of what a Christian is and does. For these, ritual behavior is all-important, and natural behavior expressing their faith in everyday life is missing. These have chosen to syncretize cultural values on objectivity and uncertainty avoidance with biblical values to make Christianity what they would like it to be, or for less honest leaders, what they need it to be for their success or the survival of the institution. Sometimes this choice is made out of fear that if the church genuinely becomes God-centric, they will lose many in attendance. It reminds one of Jesus when he called for deep buy-in, and many of his disciples turned back from following him.[8]

If the church has been irrelevant, syncretistic, legalistic, or mystical as we have defined these terms, it has encouraged the post-Christian movement as society turns its back on it. What choices have we made? What decisions have we been pressured to make by cultural demands and expectations of popular Christians in the church? What changes have been necessary for the institution's survival that were not quite what biblical Christianity calls for?

In our Western Christianity, we have seemed to miss that living in God's will—being a godly person—is not necessarily religious in terms of ritual behavior. In fact, ritual behavior, and even what we often call spiritual disciplines, can actually insulate us from a meaningful relationship with God when they are an end in themselves. When we turn to these things out of our need for affirmation and reputation, our need to be in control, or for feelings of achievement, we syncretize our lives

---

8. John 6:66.

with cultural values. We are missing the whole point and turning spiritual disciplines into ritual behavior or for self-centered advantages. We do have a choice. Instead of letting our social insecurities or drive for personal achievement have the upper hand, we can choose to trust God for our wellbeing and that of the church or other ministry he has given us. Thinking people can see through our ritual behavior, and they are less interested in Christianity when they do.

God's will in our lives is most evident in people when they are not doing religious things. It is more about being something than doing something or going somewhere. When we are becoming what God wants us to be, we will be doing the things that give evidence to our growth in Christ wherever we go. Our natural behavior in the ups and downs of life, our everyday experience, is the evidence of taking this path in our lives. Religious behavior, what I call ritual behavior, cannot be trusted to reveal the heart's true intentions. In fact, it may disguise them.

We might run a checkup on our institutional values, our syncretism with cultural absolutes, and our legalism with denominational preferences. We're in pretty deep, so there are risks involved. It may be that an intervention is necessary. Not everyone will enjoy the process. But if we have not noticed the numbers leaving our churches across the nation in the past few years,[9] we will not be able to ignore the growing exodus in the next ten years. We will have missed the crucial moment, the opportunity to reshape the church for this century and reach deep into the personal needs created by a society changing values on what is authentic and becoming more dysfunctional by the day.

In this closing chapter about the gap between God and Christianity, there are seven important things to review about being missional once God is the center of one's life: 1. The biblical priority is on what we are rather than on what we do. 2. Being missional does not depend on feeling spiritual. 3. Being missional depends entirely on our motives and goals, the intentions of our hearts. 4. Being missional means becoming part of God's plan rather than letting him be part of our plan for life or ministry. 5. Becoming a missional person started long before we chose to be so. In God's providence, all that has gone before, our strengths and even our weaknesses, in one way and another, become part of our preparation that

9. Sixty-five percent of polled American adults identifying themselves as Christian in 2019, was down twelve percentage points from a decade earlier. "Decline of Christianity," Pew Research Center, accessed October 2, 2020, https://www.pewforum.org/2019/10/17/in-u-s-decline-of-christianity-continues-at-rapid-pace.

makes us the sort of missional people we become. 6. Missional people are not all alike. Aside from the essentials of the faith, each is very different in how they fit into God's plan and express his will in their lives. 7. Missional people are in every walk of life. No particular vocation, personality, or physical makeup is more likely than another, no one person more advantaged than another, no one especially privileged to become missional. In fact, it is usually the more unlikely people that will allow God's hand on their lives in this way. It is more often the weak, those foolish in the eyes of their culture, who respond to God's call.[10] These God will use to glorify himself, though they may not know how or when, or whom God will affect through them. Most of their names will never be well known except to God.

To summarize, the great commission is not about going somewhere. It is not primarily about evangelism. It is about making disciples and teaching them to obey all that Jesus has taught us as we go along in life.[11] This means, among other things, teaching others how to be missional, to see themselves as part of God's plan instead of God as part of their own plans, to see his providence in their lives as his shaping of them for mission and using them in his plan, to see their talents as his provisions for them to be on mission. Living this out is more than doing something; it is being something. Instead of going to strange lands as missionaries being special, every Christian needs to be a missional person. Timothy Tennent reminds us that mission is not about what we do but about who God is.[12] Everything depends on that one question. To have it wrong is to misunderstand his mission, our part in it, and the only pure motive for its achievement.

None of this is possible unless we let God be God. As we have said, we have our cultural expectations. Our culture programs us with values and preferences that do not always align with his ways of caring for us and meeting our deepest needs. It trains us to employ logic and self-assertion when solving problems and making decisions. Though it is helpful in our Western day-to-day activities, God's ways are far beyond our small minds and logical preferences. This cultural conditioning becomes habitual behavior and that, in turn, becomes an addiction. It will be harder to leave it behind than we think.

10. 1 Cor 1:26–31.

11. Matt 28:18–20.

12. Tennent, *Invitation*, 105.

Western people can become addicted to self-assertion, pride, independence, and control. These may have rewarded us with some semblance of self-worth, and we turn to them without thought to get the next fix. There are other addictions to Western values that do not seem so base. Think of our values concerning time as an all-important element in task efficiency and measuring progress. Yet, it is behind our addiction to personal achievement and self-approval. It is hard to think of God as unlimited by the boundaries of time and space so important and necessary to us. Our cultural preferences are so important that we cannot think without logic, time, and space to organize our world. In fact, we feel insecure when things in our lives are not logical. We have difficulties with ambiguity, not knowing the time or place of our lives' events, and not knowing their outcomes in advance. But letting God be God removes the "what ifs" from our lives and replaces them with trust in a God who cares and has a purpose, an unalterable plan for the consummation of all things. He will carry out his plan regardless of what things may seem to us, in his own time, our personal achievements aside.

At the same time, God is very personal. He acts in our lives in response to our prayer, and his providence is at work when we least realize it. His answers to our prayers are different than we thought they would be, and we often are not aware that he answered at all until we look back on it one day. But we must have full confidence in his providence and love, have eyes of faith and move ahead knowing he hears us and acts on our behalf that his will might be accomplished.

Yes, the future *is* unknown to us. We, in our culture-bound humanness, are concerned it may not work out as we planned. God is at work, however. He awaits our participation in his plan and purposes, and he welcomes our prayers to that end. God does this as an act of his sovereignty. He has chosen to answer the prayers of those who know him, giving them a part in the changing events and circumstances within his desired moral will. Human logic fails at this point, but God is not bound by our limited understanding. We are in his hands, and they are hands we can trust.

In this book, we have been talking about the dangers of culture's intrusion into our Christian faith and practice. But we must not underestimate the importance of cultural relevance in all of this. Our model for this is Jesus himself. He was God's contextualization of himself for humankind. He revealed God and God's desires for us in a way humans could understand, using their socio-cultural forms and concepts, their language and cognitive domains, those things and experiences familiar to them. So, as God sent Jesus into the world, he is sending us. We must contextualize God within that cultural system where we find ourselves. We must use its forms skillfully while avoiding its control in ways that hurt the message.

To be relevant in closing the gap between God and humankind at the deeper level of their worldview, we will have to use the cultural forms common to us all. Charles Kraft would tell us that any culture is adequate as a vehicle for the Gospel, and its forms must be considered for their potential to express his truth.[13] Critical contextualization can help evaluate these expressions.[14]

At the very bottom of it all, knowing and trusting God as God is a foundation that must be built upon, or all our efforts at closing the gap between God and Christianity in its popular form will ultimately fail. Throughout this book, I have mentioned that being is more important than doing in the equation of God's will for our lives. Let me give a summarizing analogy. A few today still wear a mechanical watch. Those of my generation remember when there was nothing other than such a device for keeping time. Some of my younger readers may want to consult Wikipedia to get the full thrust of my analogy, but I think it still serves its purpose to give us a framework for understanding.

A mechanical, analog watch is different from a digital watch or cell phone for keeping time. It has moving parts made of metal alloys. In a good mechanical watch, there are jewels that make durable pivot points for the moving parts and provide for smaller tolerances, not only creating more accuracy but because they are harder than metal, giving longer life to the timepiece. Mechanical accuracy and longevity for a watch show us something about accuracy and longevity in the Christian life.

To keep with our analogy, how do I maintain biblical precision in my life? How do I maintain accuracy in reflecting God's desires for the various areas of my walk with him? How do I maintain the endurance of godliness in my life and ministry? The Bible offers us certain jewels necessary in the Christian life that can keep us more accurately reflecting God's desires in our lives. These gems are rare, but more so in a Western society of self-achievement where they are counter-cultural to the success of the individual's efforts. They are not commonly found even

13. Kraft, *Appropriate Christianity*, 3–14; 67–79; 169–82.

14. Hiebert, *Anthropological Reflections*, 75–92.

among many evangelical Christians. They are rare because, though they are accessible to anyone who searches for them, they are costly in the disciplined effort required to make them the pivot points on which the aspects of our lives turn. They are part of the being that comes before doing at the center of his will for us.

Other Jewels could be mentioned, but four jewels become pivot points on which others turn. Assuming a genuine faith in who God is, those jewels are humility, patience, contentment, and submission, and the parts of our lives pivot and turn on them, set in motion by the main-spring of wisdom in an unmarred case of trust.

Humility is a rare jewel in our day, in our culture. It is hard to find in a society that worships the individual and achievement. Yet, it is the most essential aspect of a life of contentment, patience, submission, and wisdom. People who have it do not feel humble. They humble them-selves[15] and feel humbled by God's grace in their lives. For God saves the humble.[16] They may be lowly in this world, simple in their approach to God, but he lifts them up.[17] Only the humble know him, for there is no promise of salvation for the proud.[18] The humble know they have no right to anything, only privileges. Knowing they are deserving of noth-ing makes them content with what God allows to come their way for his purposes.[19] Not that they do not move ahead with life like others, resolv-ing problems and changing the circumstances that can be changed, but they do it with an entirely different attitude. Humility makes them more intentional in their waiting on God and more aware of and submissive to his providence in their lives. This is a facet of wisdom often neglected.

The jewel of patience on its own is equally rare. Our culture tells us that we need immediate gratification of our needs and markets many ways to achieve that. The habit of expecting that immediate servicing of our day-to-day needs causes us to expect speedy results from God in our lives. But many things, many worthwhile desires, take time to become a reality if we want substantial results in our lives. Christians should have a long-term orientation for their desires that allows the time needed to see the bigger picture of God's plan. This will lead to satisfying our needs

---

15. 2 Chr 7:14; Matt 23:12.

16. Ps 18:27.

17. Jas 4:7–10.

18. Jas 4:6.

19. Ps 16:5–7.

at the most appropriate times for the best results in our lives, results that honor him.

The jewel of patience is pivotal in the watch works of the life driven by wisdom's mainspring. As Proverbs 19:11 says, "A man's wisdom gives him patience. It is to his glory [or adds weight to his significance] to overlook an insult." This patience comes with a knowledge of God's will as we have it in His Word.[20] It is one of the jewels of the person who is indeed "clothed with Christ."[21] It is a prominent part of the fruit of the Spirit and a central characteristic of love.[22] Can impatience ever bear the fruit of honoring God? And yet, it runs many Christians' lives.[23]

Contentment is as rare a jewel as the others. Our culture tells us we need more and we need better, that what we have is inadequate and does not reflect the current values and trends. Our culture tells us we are not changing with the times, that we are not achieving. We fear the criticism and being left behind as the rest of the world moves on. The discontentment fires our desire to be accepted until we are unhappy with what we have and seek ways to get better things and more of them. Democratic capitalism counts on this attitude of materialism to function. Even the government wants us to spend more and buy what satisfies our urges.

Many Christians in Western culture are missing the rare jewel of contentment that comes from a biblical worldview. Paul reveals his contentment with his circumstances and that it was something he had learned. It didn't just happen. He grew into it.[24] Learning this peace with our circumstances needs to be on our list of spiritual qualities to cultivate.

In the New Testament, we see that contentment is connected to godliness and that even Christians may fall into that trap of desire that results in grief and tears.[25] We can be discontent with the lack of recognition, unhappy with how much money we have, dissatisfied with our social situation when God ought to be our contentment in everything. The Proverbs tell us that contentment is evidence of wisdom. We are better off with less while knowing the peace of God in our lives than to have much

---

20. See also Col 1:9–11.

21. Col 3:12.

22. Gal 5:22–23; 1 Cor 13:4.

23. See Rom 12:12; Eph 4:2; 1 Thess 5:14.

24. Phil 4:10–13.

25. 1 Tim 6:6–10.

and suffer the pain and corrosion that can result from discontentment.[26] Yet we find ourselves working harder and faster and failing to remember that busyness is not the same as godliness, and pursuit of the world is a "chasing after the wind."[27]

Perhaps the hardest jewel to put in place is submission. We are proud as self-made, achieving, "independent individualists," and our culture labels submission a weakness. When I surveyed Christian college students about their values, submission was ranked very low for its importance in life. The self-assertion needed for survival in our individualistic society leads to feelings of fairness regarding our personal rights or our personal pursuit of happiness. When we talked about a real-life injustice and connected it with Paul's statement concerning Christians using litigation against other Christians, "why not rather be wronged . . . ," [28] the students were stunned speechless. Submission to God's providence was not on their cultural list of options.

These jewels are the pathways to wisdom as well as its demonstration. Wisdom, in turn, reinforces and encourages them. They are clearly spelled out in God's Word, but our cultural bent steers us away from them. As we said in chapter 17, we simply do not belong to a culture that values wisdom, so we do not comprehend the Scriptures talking about it to any significant degree. We attempted a definition there. Here let's put together a description. We might say this wisdom is a state of being, beginning with humility and the fear of God followed by discipline and patient learning, resulting in right and skillful living, with the embedded qualities of discernment and integrity, leading to a life that honors God. It is a little long, but it covers all the bases.

Psalms and Proverbs, historical accounts of godly people, and most of the New Testament keep wisdom before us. But it is far off in our Western worldview of materialism, search for identity, immediate gratification of needs, internal locus of control, rational logic, and achieved status. Our Western culture simply puts wisdom and the jewels that both engender and reveal it outside our range of perception. We must come to terms with our culture and its influence on us, penetrate the façade it puts over life and see it as it really is, as God sees it. Only then can we pursue

26. Prov 15:16–17; 16:8; 17:1.

27. Eccl 4:6.

28. 1 Cor 6:7.

wisdom from God as the Ancient Hebrews, under his hand, laid it before us. It is costly,[29] but it is the root of the tree, the mainspring of the watch.

We must close the gap between God and us. We need to see culture and self from the biblical perspective. We need an unmitigated trust in God's providence and undying allegiance to his person and purposes in the world. His majesty must be our awe, his mystery, our wonder, his grace, our gratefulness, and his ways our delight, no matter how these may be seen by our culture or popular Christianity. It is up to us to choose to let God be God in our lives and ministries. He does not force his way on us. It is one of the choices he gives us.

29. Prov 4:7; 8:11, 17–19.

Glossary

The following descriptions of cultural characteristics and values are brief accounts of various cultural values and understandings highlighting the differences between people of various cultures, including the Mediterranean cultures in biblical times. References here will help the reader understand the terminology in the book and interpret the cultural profiles of Appendix 1. Most cultural values fit on a continuum somewhere between the polarized extremes. Values show up as clusters in cultures, such that some values in the following list are nearly always found in individualist cultures and others nearly always in collective cultures. Certainly, we can see the Western/non-Western characteristics of the extremes. All descriptions of these cultural values, assumptions, and expectations must necessarily be generalizations. Individuals in any culture may deviate from the central value tendencies of that culture, even be characterized by the opposite tendency. But this does not change the generalization. Most values here are followed by a note to compare them with their opposite extremes on each continuum. Descriptions may include other values in the glossary. These are italicized for the reader's convenience. The terminology used in this paper and recurring in this list is particular in its usage in the field of cultural anthropology. The terms may have other definitions and descriptions in other fields of study. The list here is intended to give the reader enough background to understand comments in the book, but further reading would be necessary to understand them in their full significance.

Achieved Status: This value describes people for whom status, rank, and respect must be earned. Western cultures accommodate this need, emphasizing people being respected and promoted based on their performance or achievement. Production in the workplace and achievement in school are rewarded. Those who win competitions are presented with awards and trophies. Non-Western cultures, having *ascribed status,* value harmony in relationships more than personal achievement. As a western value, the process of achieving status operates on *individualism, self-assertion, internal locus of control,* and *unlimited good.* The value of achieved status has positive outcomes emphasizing hard work, commitment, and self-discipline that result in the success of the society. But it can get out of balance and take over the lives of individualists. Getting results can become more important than how a person gets them. Relationships may be opportunistic or competitive. Even friends and family may be overlooked so as not to interfere with attaining a coveted personal identity and winning the approval of others. However, people of important positions do not generally act superior to those of low status because the value is combined with *egalitarianism* in *Western cultures.* Achieved status is relative and insecure, while ascribed status is traditional and stable. (Compare with Ascribed Status, Harmony.)

Ascribed Status: This describes people for whom social class, family name, age, kinship group, or seniority grant status. People of high status are respected. It is not based on one's efforts but is ascribed by the community because of factors that have come to exist on their own and are often connected to one's personal honor. Ascribed status is traditional, stable, and hard to change, while *achieved status* is relative, insecure, and modified frequently. Ascribed status can occasionally be lost but not usually augmented. One should not behave above or below his ascribed status. It is often found in *non-Western, collective,* and *traditional cultures* and *cultures* where wisdom is valued. Central African, Ancient Middle Eastern, and Japanese cultures are examples of those that value ascribed status. (Compare with Achieved Status.)

Assertive Orientation: This value has to do with a *culture* that values self-assertion for personal achievement, quantitative production, competition, and progress. Successful self-assertion in this system affords feelings of self-worth and accumulates status. Valuing self-assertion is an *individualist* form, but it is not necessarily absent in *collective* societies in some form if it results in saving face. Assertive *cultures* are typically Western and more competitive for personal resources and gain, while non-Western cultures are more cooperative, seeking harmony in the group. (Compare with Non-Assertive Orientation.)

Being Orientation: Many in *non-Western cultures* value controlling and disciplining human nature over being busy. It is what we call a "being" orientation instead of a *"doing"* orientation. This self-control has to do with status, rank, and role meeting certain social expectations of the group. There is also an emphasis on wisdom and meditation, attaining internally instead of externally, and achieving a state of mind and conscience independent of circumstances. It is not about what you do, but what you are and what guidance you afford to others on their way. Self-awareness, caution, and self-development are central to these people. They have the present in mind. (Compare with Doing Orientation, Unrestrained Orientation.)

Cautious in Relations: There has been much information published on warm *cultures* versus cold *cultures* regarding relations between people, but the problem is that it does not usually account for a value outside these of caution in relations. While Caribbean, Mexican, and Asian Indian *cultures* are warm in relations, and Northern US and German *cultures* are considered cold, traditional cultures such as Confucian background Asian and Native American cultures are cautious. People in cautious *cultures* feel they need to know more about a person they meet before responding to them in a welcoming, personal way or a formal, distant way. Once they come to their conclusion, their decision may be final and enduring. These people do not confront others. They conceal their feelings and prefer compromise over winning in order to honor tradition and maintain harmony. (Compare with Warm in Relations, Cold in Relations.)

Cold in Relations: Some *cultures,* such as the northern US, German, and English cultures, are considered cold in relations. The people have a general tendency toward objectivity, factuality, planning, and scheduling. Decisions are based on rational analysis and logic and often depend on benefits for self. Social relations are affected by competition and a value on achievement. The people in these *cultures* are mostly time and *task-oriented*. A fundamental description would be that they are more *monochronic* and have a need to control their surroundings. (See *Internal Locus of Control*.) When these people confront others, they use propositional logic to win the argument. (Compare with Warm in Relations, Cautious in Relations.)

Collectivism: The idea that people should prioritize the good of society or social group over the welfare of the individual is called collectivism. It depends on the belief that the individual's identity and feelings of worth come from their group. Collective people are interdependent with the group. Actions must be such that they promote harmony within the group where norms and duty are guides. Relationships and loyalty are also of high value in the tribe. This emphasizes fluency in social obligations that is connected to one's honor or face. Emotional, mental, social, and physical wellbeing and survival depend on the group's acceptance of the individual. They are sometimes referred to as interdependent as opposed to independent. (Compare with Individualism.)

Compartmental: Compartmental *cultures* refer to those whose members see life in its pieces rather than its whole. People in these *cultures* value being compartmental (dichotomistic) in their thinking; they analyze and break down the whole into parts and then organize them into categories often referred to as cognitive domains. The members of this *culture*, generally *Western*, tend to be more objective and have difficulty managing ambiguity. (See *Objective Culture*.) Their thinking is more polarized between extremes than holding to values in the middle of a continuum. They understand life as divided into domains such as secular and sacred, public and private, achievement and failure, and those divided into yet smaller parts. (Compare with Holistic.)

Contextualization: *Cultural* forms and the words of a language are at home in their own situation. The people of each *cultural* context give them meaning and use them in their experience and communication. When we try to use ours in another *cultural* setting, another context, they have to be adjusted, calibrated in the new frame of reference to retain their original meaning as accurately as possible. This process is called contextualization. This is especially important when taking biblical truth from the biblical context to understand and apply it in our *culture* today. It is just as crucial to the process of taking that same message to another human *culture* for understanding and application without contamination of the messenger's culture. Care must always be taken to avoid *syncretism* in either case. God did this when he sent Jesus as his incarnation in the Ancient Middle Eastern *cultural* context. We, in turn, are to incarnate his message in our own and sometimes in another *culture* in ways that are authentic to the original message and relevant to the people in the host context. (Compare with Syncretism.)

Cultural Legalism: Cultural legalism is the requirement of the application of God's Word in one culture of believers in a different culture. While God's Word is inspired the same for all people, its applications are specific to each context. This is because the meaning for behavior is particular to each context, and God's Word must be applied in ways that are relevant to those meanings. What a person does in their own *culture* to honor God's Word will not be the same as someone's behavior concerning the same issue in a different *culture*. An example would be the teaching of God's Word for husbands to love their wives. The teaching is not obeyed with the same activity in every *culture*. So, while the truth of God's Word is absolute, its applications, though always required, are *culturally* relative to the behavior that fulfills the requirement. To not respect this is cultural legalism: the adding of another culture's required behavioral applications to the message of the Gospel. The opposite of cultural legalism is cultural relativism. (Compare with Legalism.)

Culture: A learned and shared, integrated system of values, beliefs, and assumptions for understanding, coping with, and relating to the world, which results in behavior characteristic of a group of people.

Delayed Gratification: *Cultures* that value delayed gratification of needs and desires are focused on the future. These are often non-*Western* wisdom and Confucian background cultures. They see life through a more qualitative lens: good things are worth waiting for, and hard work and frugality are accompanied by patience. It is more important to have quality and virtue in life than the immediate accumulation of material things. (Compare with Immediate Gratification.)

Disregard for Social Respect: Western people like US Anglo-Americans do not value formal social respect. In fact, they have very few ways of showing respect at all. They, instead, value informality and *egalitarianism*. Based on these values, they display friendly personalism. When meeting and greeting people, Western individuals use the most familiar terms from the start. It is considered friendly to do so. They are interested in the new person's vocation and social and material standing. It is not usually for discovering what respect to accord them, but, rather, to fulfill curiosity about a person's worth and identity since it is attached to what they do. Knowing this, they may try to size up their competition with the new person, guess their motives for behavior, discern their level of friendly openness, and for some, size up how the new acquaintance can help them. Social discrimination for friendship is then based on these findings. (Compare with Social Respect.)

Doing Orientation: In addition to being task-oriented, people of this orientation must always be moving in a direction, causing some change, fixing some problem, being productive, and planning to continue doing something in the future. They must never be without some form of activity. They find it hard to relax, stop and sit still for a while, or be meditative. That is not doing something. They may have anxiety about the unpredictability of people and events, interruptions, wasting time, and not getting enough done each day. Being busy is a matter of self-worth and identity. It is usually the first thing they will say about themselves when meeting others. This is generally found in Western cultures and in the US specifically. (Compare with Restrained Orientation, Being Orientation, Monochronism)

Egalitarianism: Egalitarianism is a value that engenders a strong preference for equality, independence, and *individualism*. People who value egalitarianism like decision-making on their own and feel freedom when authority is kept in its place. Duty and submission are rare motives for behavior. Informality is the expectation for all interactions. They believe that apparent hierarchical gaps in the social order should be closed. (Compare with Social Hierarchy.)

Ethnocentrism: Ethnocentrism describes the level to which a person feels their ethnic group is central and superior to any other group. Though people in all cultures display some level of ethnocentrism, those who are strong in it usually do not take other cultures seriously. They see their own *culture* as the only viable one. *Cultural* diversity causes anxiety for them, and they may condemn other *cultures*. These people tend to feel that people of other *cultures*, deep down, want to be like people in their own *culture*. People who are low in ethnocentrism may not feel like they fit in well in their own society. They champion minority groups. They may be unhappy with traditional values. They are critical of their own *culture* and may feel people of other *cultures* have a better life. They are against demonstrations of loyalty to their country and diminish its accomplishments. People may be closer to one end or the other in ethnocentrism, but some are closer to the middle with respect for their own culture and its values, but also respecting other cultures.

External Locus of Control: Describes people who feel that many conditions in life are predetermined and built into the nature of things. There are limits beyond which people cannot go, which cannot be changed and must be accepted. Life is what happens to you. Your success is learning to manage under your circumstances, getting around difficulties, and waiting for good fortune. This value tends toward low initiative in problem-solving and planning for the future. It is more characteristic in Non-Western cultures. (Compare with Internal Locus of Control.)

God-Centered Orientation: People of this orientation have a worldview with God at the center. For them, he is the God of creation and grace, the God of all power and love as he is revealed in the Bible. He provides the way back to the original good he created that humankind spoiled through their selfish unbelief and lack of trust. That way is through the death and resurrection of Jesus Christ. All the suffering humanity has brought on itself is to be ended one day, and his people will spend eternity with him in heaven. In this life, people must trust him and his providence in their lives in a broken world. It is here they must serve his purposes and relate to others with compassion. People who know God are identified by lives that are motivated by love and grace. By the evidence of their good works and their message of the truth, they become salt and light, bringing life to others in the world. (Compare with Natural Orientation, Supernatural Orientation.)

Harmony: Harmony is a deep-seated value characteristic of *collective, face-saving, non-assertive, hierarchical,* and Confucian background *cultures.* People in a *culture* that values harmony are not interested in competing with others but in smoothing over relational difficulties while fulfilling their social obligations—sometimes called social lubrication. Maintaining relationships and respecting other people's status in society are more important than personal achievement and, if done well, give feelings of self-worth and personal identity within the group. Not doing so brings loss of *face* or *honor* which may be overwhelming. (Compare with Results Orientation, Achieved Status.)

High-Contact: This value difference has to do with touching in social settings. High contact *cultures* value touching frequently and feel it communicates friendliness, warmth, and genuineness, such as in Puerto Rico. Not touching often expresses coldness, disinterest, or anger in these cultures, while not touching at all may communicate respect in other cultures.

High contact cultures are usually *collective* and *polychronic*. (Compare with Low-Contact.)

High-Context: This term describes people for whom most of the information in communication is either in the physical context or is implicit in the people in their shared values, beliefs, assumptions, and experience. They rely on this context more than the words in communication. Detailed information regarding a matter is rarely communicated directly, and feelings are seldom expressed verbally. They usually value *harmony* and *saving face* in social relationships. They are indirect, less exhaustive, and more *holistic* than people of a *low-context* approach to communication. This preference for depending more on the shared context makes the listener more responsible for the meaning in a conversation. In contrast, the *low-context* style makes the speaker more accountable to construct the meaning with words. Examples of high-context *cultures* would be Japanese and Native American cultures. (Compare with Low-Context.)

Holistic: In a holistic *culture,* people are more concerned about the big picture than analyzing the parts of any situation or concept. It is the opposite of being *compartmental* or dichotomistic in thinking, breaking down the whole into parts and then organizing them into categories or cognitive domains. Beliefs and norms in one area of life are connected and related to every other area of life in the culture such that a value on honesty or on saving face would spread out to touch all other areas of a person's life. Examples of holistic cultures are Native American and Central African. (Compare with Compartmental.)

Honor and Shame: This is an understanding held by *collective* groups. They are usually more formal and *tradition*-bound, such as the Ancient Middle East and many present-day non-*Western* cultures. Each person tries to maintain an honorable status in the eyes of others in the family or larger social group. Each is responsible for their own honor, but it is actually granted by the group as they observe how one's behavior meets or does not meet their expectations. In most groups, loss of honor reflects on the entire group and, in some cases, must be avenged. Therefore, there is a good deal of social pressure on each person to maintain social respect. Being honorable in the eyes of the group gives one feelings of self-worth and a sense of belonging. If an individual does not meet the expectations of the group, they are shamed. This loss of honor is strongly felt by the individual and, because it is public, it is extremely difficult to re-establish. It is sanctioned in terms of social marginalization, expulsion from the group, or death. Enduring shame in the eyes of the group can be overwhelming for the individual. (Compare with Innocence and Guilt.)

Immediate Gratification: Cultures that seek immediate gratification of needs and desires are focused on the present. They see a correlation between effort and relatively quick results. Since they see life through a more quantitative lens and are achievement-oriented, they are concerned about more effort resulting in more reward and the fairness of the distribution of rewards. Money is a means to be used liberally in the expression of this achievement. (Compare with Delayed Gratification.)

Individualism: Individualism is a belief in the primary importance of the individual and in the virtues of self-reliance, independence, self-*assertion*, and personal achievement. It incorporates private ownership and privacy values, an individual social identity, and a "me-centered" outlook on life. It encourages individual and social freedoms and includes a preference for freedom from government regulation and an *internal locus of control*. The self is independent of the group, while in *collectivism,* the self is interdependent. Personal values and goals do not harmonize naturally with those of the group for individualists as they do for the *collective* person. Also, individualists dislike and skirt social obligations that are welcomed and obligatory for *collective* people. Individualism is perhaps the most significant value in Western culture from which many other cultural values emanate. (Compare with Collectivism.)

Innocence and Guilt: This understanding of behavior and social control is held by *Western, individualist* groups. Each person has personal feelings about whether their behavior meets society's moral and ethical expectations, a religious standard, or his own standard. He will have an inner sense of guilt if it does not, even if no one sees him fall short. We refer to these feelings as having a good (clear) or a guilty conscience. A guilty conscience can be a strong motivator for behavior. Each person is individually responsible for their conscience. If the breach of moral or ethical code affects others in the group, the act will be punished or forgiven by those affected or by those responsible for social justice. (Compare with Honor and Shame.)

Instrumental Values: Values referring to broad modes of conduct as means to desired ends. The desired ends are called *terminal values*. For example, a *terminal value* might be strong and healthy family members.

People with this goal would have instrumental values on the importance of eating healthy food, exercising daily, strong family relationships, and helping others in the family to see the importance of this terminal goal. (Compare with Terminal Values.)

Internal Locus of Control: Describes people who feel that few things or circumstances in life have to be accepted the way they are and cannot be changed. There are no limits on what a person can do or become if he sets his mind to it and makes an effort. Life is what you make it. (See *Optimism*.) Therefore, achievement is an indication of character and worth. Internal locus of control can go beyond circumstances to manipulate other people to achieve personal survival goals. (Compare with External Locus of Control.)

Legalism: Legalism is the adding of human rules and regulations to the teaching of God's Word to avoid possible worldly influence in the expression of the Christian faith. A typical example is when God's Word instructs us not to be drunk with wine; the legalist says being a Christian means not to drink wine at all. Another example might be the call to modesty for women that Paul gives Timothy in 1 Timothy 2:9–10. A legalistic view might be that all women in the church must wear ankle-length dresses of plain color and no buttons. A biblical example would be the oral Torah of the Pharisees that Jesus confronts in the Gospels. The opposite of legalism is *syncretism*, which adopts *cultural* standards as normal expressions of biblical standards without critical thought. Legalism is about doing something, and freedom in Christ is about being something. (Compare with Syncretism.)

Limited Good: This is "the socially shared conviction that the resources enabling a community to realize its range of needs [survive] are in finite supply and that any disruption of the social equilibrium can only be detrimental to community survival. …all goods exist in finite, limited quantity and are always in limited supply."[1] Things such as honor, wealth, land, food, health, children, status, and power are in limited quantities, in short supply, and already distributed. There is no way to increase the available quantities. Envy arises in such a system when someone seems to have more than their share. It is a zero-sum situation where whatever one person gains is at the expense of someone else. The understanding

---

1. Malina, *New Testament World*, 81–107,112–113. Pilch and Malina, *Handbook*, 122–127.

puts the survival of the social group at risk if some obtain more good than those around them. The two actions promoted by this in the biblical Middle East were the evil eye to settle the score when nothing else could be done to balance the scales and requesting help from a patron through a trusted mediator. (See Patron and Client System. Compare with Unlimited Good.)

Low-Contact: Low contact cultures feel touching is inappropriate and disrespectful in social settings such as the British or Thai cultures. People in these *cultures* express greetings and genuineness in other ways. In England, it is by verbal indication, and in Thailand, it is by non-verbal gesture, silence, or carefully chosen vocabulary. The US is toward the middle of the scale between high contact and low contact values, with some people at both ends of the continuum, but most in the middle. (Compare with High-Contact.)

Low-Context: This term describes people for whom most of the information in communication is entrusted to the verbal message. They are direct and detailed in communication and have difficulty understanding *high-context* communication. A low-context culture is one in which verbal information is objective and explicit. Feelings are discussed freely, and expectations are referred to openly. They usually value directness in relationships. This preference for depending less on the context makes the speaker more responsible for the meaning in a conversation. In contrast, a *high-context* style makes the listener more accountable to construct the meaning using the non-verbal context. Examples of low-context *cultures* would be German and US-American *cultures*. (Compare with High-Context.)

Monochronism: This value describes people who think there is a limited amount of time, and therefore it is necessary to use it wisely and not waste it. There is a premium on efficiency. Time is the given; people and events are unpredictable. Highly monochronic people prefer to do one thing at a time and finish each before starting another. Interruptions are an annoyance. To maintain these values, people prefer systems and order. They stand in line single file to wait for service. They generally let another person finish speaking before they offer their own comments. These people may tend toward systematics in their theology. (Compare with Polychronism.)

Natural Orientation: People of this orientation believe the *supernatural* to be superstition. The laws of nature are the laws of physics and the survival of the fittest. Magic is fun entertainment, and *chi, karma,* or *feng shui* are imaginary but sometimes chic ways of talking about things. Reality is objective and can be explained by science. People who believe in religious explanations are weak and need more education about the reality around them. (Compare with Supernatural Orientation, God-Centered Orientation.)

Non-Assertive Orientation: Non-assertive cultures are more cooperative in social relations. Competition is friendly, and they have values on caring for others and qualitative enjoyment in a peaceful society. Equality, nurturing, and empathy are essential values. Self-assertion is seen as negative. (Compare with Assertive Orientation.)

Non-Urgency Orientation: Cultures characterized by non-urgency norms have a different cluster of values than those oriented toward *urgency*. Their response to a need is no less genuine, but it is less urgent. The central part of the cluster seems to be an attachment to interaction with people, which gives them a penchant to search out those opportunities despite a list of things waiting to be accomplished. Without a value on time, there is no need for achievement, no sense of efficiency in completing something within a particular time, no sense of logic that causes a feeling of urgency. Problems never trump being with people if a decision has to be made about using one's time. (See *Polychronic*.) (Compare with Urgency Orientation.)

Non-Verbal Communication: Essentially, any form of communication other than the spoken word is called non-verbal communication. These might be listed as the use of kinesics, proxemics, paralinguistics (including silence), time, physical characteristics, tactile behavior (haptics), artifacts, and optical and olfactory signals. These are generally referred to as forms employed to communicate or to assist verbal communication. Non-verbal behavior provides the analog expression of attitudinal, emotional, and relational meaning accompanying digital, verbal information. According to Edward Hall,[2] some ninety percent of our communication is non-verbal, and half of that is done unconsciously. When there is a conflict between verbal and non-verbal communication, non-verbal is

---

2. Hall, *Dance of Life*, 4.

more reliable—the less conscious the use of non-verbal behavior in communication, the less distortion in meaning.

Objective Culture: Some *cultures* are more insistent on the objective world in thought and deed, though they cannot be entirely independent of the subjective elements in life. Life seems more black and white under *universal* standards and can only be understood using *rational logic*. In their low-context approach, these people are more decisive, detailed, quantitative, and specific, and emotions have little credibility. This value is found in more Western cultures and is based on the rationalism introduced by the renaissance. It is often a strong component in the expression of legalistic Christianity. (Compare with Subjective Culture.)

Openness to Vulnerability: Levels of willingness to show vulnerability are on a continuum from complete transparency to absolute aversion. The value of exposing vulnerability is connected to *individualism* and *egalitarianism* but can be seen outside strong tendencies in these directions. A willingness to be vulnerable allows people to "shoot from the hip," use "trial and error" methods, and say things like, "You never know until you try." These people feel they can learn from their mistakes, and everyone makes them, so we are alike in that way. No one suffers long-term embarrassment unless it is well known that the course of action in question has been attempted many times before and has consistently failed. Otherwise, "nothing ventured, nothing gained." "You can't make an omelet without breaking a few eggs." (Compare with Saving Face.)

Optimism: General approaches of optimism and pessimism in life rest on worldview assumptions about the nature of man and the world and beliefs about the potential for success in life that grows out of those assumptions. If humans are free to act with an *internal locus of control* and are part of a world of *unlimited good*, it puts them in a different place than people who do not have these benefits in their favor. Hard work and determination are seen to put any potential benefit within reach. People in these "fortunate" cultures or groups within cultures will tend to be optimistic. (Compare with Pessimism.)

Particularist: Particularist people feel that family and friends should be favored in decisions. What is right in each situation depends on the circumstances. People are not equal; there are always exceptions. Relationships are more important than right and wrong. Who someone is determines the value of what they do. People who hold this value may tend toward an expanded level of grace in their theology. (Compare with Universalism.)

Patrilineal Kinship: Patrilineal (father's bloodline) and matrilineal (mother's bloodline) kinship systems are unilineal systems instead of bilateral lineage systems as we have in the West. This is important in that they carry meanings and values that we in the West do not embrace. Unilineal kinship affiliation means belonging to a group with descent from a common ancestor through one sex only. In patrilineal societies, both males and females belong to their father's kinship group but not their mother's. Only males pass on their family identity and heritage to their children. A woman's children are members of her husband's patrilineal line. The system is the foundation of social life in the collective, patrilineal society. "The family or kinship group is central in social organization; it is the primary focus of personal loyalty and holds supreme sway over individual life."[3] Members of a lineage may have political, religious, and legal rights based on their descent from a common ancestor. All members are equal in these rights to all others in the lineage group. What you are obligated to do for a father is also required for a son in a patrilineal society. The son acts in his father's name. Status, prestige, authority, reputation, and factors of honor or shame and property ownership follow these lines of descent.

Patron and Client Social System: This social system for the support of the needy had three main players. The client was the person without wealth, power, or status in a world of *limited good* with an overwhelming felt need. The mediator or broker had influence with a patron as one of their servants, stewards, disciples, relatives, etc. Then there was the patron him or herself who was wealthy, powerful and the grantor of status to whom the client had no access except through a mediator of influence. The client would have a strong sense of gratitude and indebtedness to the patron, who was under no obligation to be generous. In a world that believed in *limited good*, this was far more meaningful than in a world that believes in unlimited plenty and equal opportunity. In a world of *unlimited good*, success depends on personal initiative and hard work, insurance often handles downturns, and welfare and social security systems help the needy. The language of the patron and client social system is an analogy

3. Malina, *The Social World*, 45.

Paul uses of the concept of God's grace in the New Testament. (Compare with Personal Initiative Social System.)

People Orientation: See *Polychronism*. (Compare with Doing Orientation.)

Personal Autonomy: People who are high in personal autonomy maintain a strong sense of personal identity, personal values and beliefs, respect for themselves and others, and confidence in their own decisions in situations dominated by those of an alternate belief and value system. They may set these values aside to learn another culture or assert their own cultural expressions in that culture. People who are low in personal autonomy lose their sense of personal identity, values and beliefs, respect for themselves and others, and confidence in their own decisions when dominated by an alternate belief and value system. They blend into the new cultural influence around them either because they desire to or through social pressure, sanctions, and the fear of rejection in the new situation.

Personal Initiative Social System: Personal initiative systems are based on *individualism* and its accompanying values of personal *achievement, unlimited good, optimism*, competition, *internal locus of control*, and free choice. Political-economic systems like democratic capitalism are based on individual initiative. For people who are disadvantaged or disabled in these systems with economic stability, there are accompanying social systems of welfare and Social Security benefits provided through taxation of those who flourish in the system. This system is highly in contrast with patron and client systems in biblical cultures. (Compare with Patron and Client Social System.)

Pessimism: Those who see themselves as living in a world of *external locus of control* and *limited good* do not have control over their circumstances and, therefore, have little chance to better their situations. This generally results in pessimism about life. In these *cultures*, people talk about luck and fate instead of completing a project. A worldview, for example, that incorporates moody ancestral spirits and unpredictable nature spirits causes fear of these powers and pessimism, even fatalism, regarding accomplishing anything of personal benefit. The potential of success hangs on the whim of the spirits, and they are difficult to figure out and manage. Pessimism may also be attached to economic barriers that seem impossible to overcome, social or religious discrimination, or a caste system fixing one's place in life. Whole *cultures* or sections of *cultures* can tend toward this pessimism just as entire *cultures* or subcultures can tend toward optimism. (Compare with Optimism, Internal Locus of Control.)

Polychronism: This value describes people who think there is always more time and never too busy for others. Schedules and deadlines are flexible as they depend on the circumstances. Life often requires doing many things at once, and a person does not have to finish one thing to go to another. There is no such thing as an interruption. Systems and categories are not bounded. Order is not necessary to accomplish a task or for life in general. They are people-oriented, and relationships are more important than time. These may tend toward relaxed and flexible views of theology. (Compare with Monochronism.)

Progressive Cultures: People in progressive *cultures* have a high degree of flexibility. The term describes people who can accept different ways of thinking and acting with tolerance, a lack of rigidity, and an interest in and level of comfort with the diverse people involved. People feel good about progress and trying various new and different solutions to achieving goals. Change, trial and error methods, and taking certain risks is part of progress. "Nothing ventured, nothing gained." There are some progressive people in all *cultures*, but it is more characteristic of some *cultures* overall. It is prominent in *Western* cultures where change and development are seen as positive. (Compare with Traditional Cultures.)

Rational Logic: Some cultures use rational logic based on propositional truths, information, and the law of non-contradiction. Most people of this kind of value system are *monochronic*—desiring order and process and preferring one thing at a time. This approach attempts to disallow who people are and relationships with others to interfere with judgments and decisions, though people in these cultures do not always accomplish this. Occasionally decisions are made emotionally and others on intuition, but there must be objective logic for most of life. Things must make sense and fit in a system that can be organized in compartments. (Compare with Relational Logic.)

Relational Logic: Aligning with values on *individualism* and *collectivism* as well as on *honor and shame, innocence and guilt*, is the value on and kind of logic employed in a culture. Some cultures are said to have no logic in their decision-making processes. But that is never the case. All people make decisions based on reasons that make sense to them in their cultural system. People in non-Western cultures make decisions based on what we call relational logic. It is both rational and emotional, but the reasons causing the choice of optional courses of action have to do with the people involved and potential benefit or collateral damage to those relationships. Damage might be a possible loss of face in not honoring those people in their social position: authority, power, or other influence. A person might accept terrible costs to themselves if they can save face with the people who matter to their social and emotional survival. That makes sense to them. (Compare with Rational Logic.)

Saving face: A value on saving face involves fear of failure regarding the social expectations of one's group or society in general. Loss of face is the shame a person feels from others when they fail to meet these social expectations. It is connected to values on *collectivism,* personal *honor,* and empathy for others. Concern for avoiding loss of face may look like insecurity to the outsider. Careful attention is given to appropriate be-havior and speech to meet these expectations. Self-awareness is of ex-treme importance. Knowing the boundaries is essential, and structure in society serves this purpose. With a value on saving face, there may be a reluctance to try new things involving others because of the risk of failure and loss of face that can bring. People of this orientation would say, "The nail that sticks up must be hammered down." (Compare with Openness to Vulnerability.)

Social Hierarchy: A value on hierarchy causes people to appreciate, and highly prefer, hierarchical social order and use of authority in their cul-ture. Strong leadership and supervision are natural and expected. Submis-sion is without question. People are not all equal, and they are insecure without this structure and formality in social relations. They are reluctant to make their own decisions. The average person prefers following to leading and is *collective,* valuing the group more than themselves. Jewish society in biblical history had strict social roles for people but became more hierarchical than God intended. (Compare with Egalitarianism.)

Social Respect: Values on social respect are highly attached to those on *hierarchy* and *collectivism.* But it also has aspects outside those categories. It is the value of showing respect for others regarding their relationship to yourself or not needing to do so based on the level of familiarity and trust. Social respect will be noticed in cultures where one pronoun must be used with a person until a certain level of friendship has been established. At some point in the relationship, the two people may become less formal and use the more familiar pronouns in greetings and conversation. This is seen among French and German people, where pronouns are used to distinguish how well people know one another. Social respect in Great Britain is controlled with formalities of understatement and non-verbal behavior. In Central Africa, pronouns of family relations are used when an outsider gains trust. These behaviors show respect for social status and levels of familiarity among people and are accompanied by a sense of social discrimination to sort out those worthy of that respect. (Compare with Disregard for Social Respect.)

Structured Society: This value describes a society where people need clarity regarding objective goals, quantifiable activity, traditional customs, and limited ingenuity and change. They are willing to work hard to obtain this. They prefer the security of rules and regulations over too much freedom of action. There is anxiety about ambiguity and a desire for formality and clear categories. Christians owning this value may tend toward *legalism* or highly structured theological systems. (Compare with Unstructured Society.)

Subjective Culture: People in some cultures highly value subjectivism, though they cannot function without many objective elements in life. Unlike an *unstructured society*, they are usually a part of a society with an ordered *social hierarchy*. These people do not seek to avoid ambiguity. Life is subject to each individual's needs, place in it, or ability to negotiate it with powers outside themselves. People are *particularistic* regarding the circumstances for each situation, are *high-context* in communication and relations, typically employ *relational logic,* and are not decisive, objective, or detailed in their descriptions. Subjective culture is often attached to religious frames of reference such as Hinduism, Taoism, and Buddhism (Compare with Objective Culture.)

Supernatural Orientation: This describes people who feel the world is full of power and forces such as *chi*, magic, *karma*, amulets, spirits, luck, witchcraft, etc. Good and bad things do not just happen: someone or something causes them. If you offend someone, they can curse you. If you offend an ancestor or nature spirit, it will be angry with you and harm you. These people believe specialists can manipulate power to help or harm them. All of life is spiritual and is ruled by fear of power and magic. (Compare with Natural Orientation, God-Centered Orientation.)

Syncretism: Syncretism is when one belief or value system is mixed with another to become a new system. When *cultural* values and beliefs contrary to the Bible are combined with Christianity, the result is syncretism. At best, the outcome is a culturally influenced Christian conscience that is only partially biblical. At worst, biblical absolutes become mixed with *cultural* absolutes creating a religious system that is counter biblical. The distinctions of the truth are blurred by *cultural* understandings and preferences. Proper contextualization of the Bible prevents syncretism, while over-contextualization encourages and implants syncretism. (Compare with Contextualization.)

Task Orientation: See *Doing orientation*. (Compare Polychronism.)

Terminal Values: Values referring to desired end-states of existence, goals to accomplish in life. These are achieved through the application of *instrumental values* to that end. For example, a terminal value might be to foster a biblical worldview among evangelicals in America. An *instrumental value* used for progress toward this goal might emphasize the importance of encouraging training for ministry that includes a study of *culture*, its influence on people, and intercultural issues in ministry in addition to Bible and Theology. (Compare with Instrumental Values.)

Traditional Cultures: People who feel good about tradition and uncertain and skeptical about trying new and different things make up traditional cultures. This gives people in these cultures a low degree of flexibility. They simply prefer doing things the way they have always been done such that new or different ways of thinking and acting can be threatening. There is rigidity and a lack of interest in and level of comfort with people who are different. Religion often plays a prominent role in the expression of strong attachment to tradition. There is one way to do something, and everyone should do it the same way. All *cultures* have some members that are more traditional than others. (Compare with Progressive Cultures.)

Universalism: Describes people who feel that the laws and standards of society apply to everyone. Right and wrong can be universally and categorically applied to all situations. To be fair, you must treat everyone the same. One size fits all. No one is above the law. Decisions regarding right and wrong are black and white. These may tend toward *legalism* in their theology. (Compare with Particularism.)

Unlimited Good: This understanding of life is more common among Western people in the world today. It is the belief that good is not limited and everyone has an equal chance to possess resources and, in some *cultures*, a great deal of resources. For these people, this understanding depends on the willingness of the person to work hard, compete effectively, and manage his resources well. In *cultures* that believe good is unlimited, certain people are disadvantaged by circumstances outside their control. They do not possess the available resources, but this does not negate the belief that the resources exist. (Compare with Limited Good.)

Unrestrained Orientation: Though some *cultures* are known for their attachment to doing, accomplishing, and achieving, others show a *restrained orientation* and are known for their emphasis on self-discipline, personal development, self-control, and wisdom. Western cultures value their self-expression, individual freedom, *and internal locus of control* in the here and now over self-awareness and self-discipline. Many non-Western cultures value the significance of their social role and personal honor in the here and now. These may keep the past in mind as they believe who they are is connected to their ancestors' status and worth or a previous incarnation. (Compare with Doing Orientation, Being Orientation, Polychronism.)

Unstructured Society: This describes people who desire informality, reduction of traditional regulations, and the acceptance of diversity and risks in life. They have a tolerance for ambiguity, change, and deviation from cultural norms. They do not feel life is so black and white in its order causing resistance to preset categories, systematic organization, and authority that limits individual freedom to set boundaries. (Compare with Structured Society.)

Urgency Orientation: Several factors enter into an orientation of urgency to act as well as one of *non-urgency*. For urgency-oriented cultures, values on time, efficiency, material concerns for loss of property or money, status concerns for one's identity based on achievement, values on doing and accomplishing tasks, etc., are uppermost. These values compel a person to act as quickly as possible in his own interest or someone else's behalf to save the item, the situation, even the person him or herself. They feel people must prevent potential crises—to avoid what might go wrong tomorrow. To know there is a possible predicament or emergency and not do anything about it is scandalous. This often means fixing things before they are broken or deep investment in insurance. (Compare with Non-Urgency Orientation)

Warm in Relations: Some cultures are considered warm in their relations. They are more emotional, and relationships matter a great deal. Friendship knows no bounds. They are somewhat compulsive and *unrestrained*. They can be described as *polychronic*, needing to enjoy their interactions more than to accomplish tasks or watch the clock. They often reveal a lot about themselves in a superficial way. When these people confront others, they do so emotionally. (Compare with Cold in Relations, Cautious in Relations.)

Western – Non-Western: Western *culture* refers to Western European, North American, White Australian, and other such *cultures* shaped by the influence of the renaissance toward values on logic, objectivity, science, philosophy, individualism, etc. Non-Western *cultures* have been influenced by other movements such as Hinduism, Confucianism, Buddhism, Animism, and Islam. The resulting differences are too numerous to count, but the generalizations that can be made are very helpful. Western *cultures* are considered, for example, *cold in relations*, while non-Western are considered *warm* or *cautious in relations*. Western peoples are *individualistic* and *monochronic;* non-Western are generally *collective* and *polychronic*. The social controls by which Western people measure good and bad behavior are feelings of *innocence and guilt,* while non-Western *cultures* are attached to *honor and shame* or are motivated to behavior by fear of the powers of spirits and magic.

Appendix 1
Cultural Value Profiles

There is an enormous potential for confusion when we assume other cultures see the world and interact socially by the same values, beliefs, and assumptions as we do. The shaded boxes below indicate the cultural values for each culture under consideration. The contrast between the cultures is seen in the comparison of the figures. Examples here are Western contexts, such as the US Anglo-American culture, compared to Biblical Middle Eastern and Japanese cultures. This way of highlighting the differences between cultures is highly simplified, and not all possible cultural values are included. There are many differences in the expression of the same value between people of different cultures, but their attachment to a value and the detachment of another culture from that value are noted here as an aid showing the major contrasts between cultures. Some cultures are not attached to values in their extreme as listed here. These fall somewhere in the middle of a continuum between the extremes. The USA, for example, is neither high contact nor low contact but falls in between the generalizations. The same would be true for Japan in their urgency orientation or on the monochronic/polychronic scale. If a culture is not marked as owning either of two opposing values, both are shaded to reveal an approximately equal emphasis on both, and neither is shaded if neither is particularly prominent. Please refer to the glossary for the definitions and descriptions of terms used in this illustration.

Unlimited Good	Traditional	Doing Orientation	High Context	Honor & Shame	Internal Locus of Control	Open to Vulnerability	Hierarchical	Wisdom Orientation
Collective	Guilt & Innocence	Ascribed Status	Assertive Orientation	Delayed Gratification	Need for Information	Low Contact	Task Orientation	Cold in Relations
Low Context	Structured	Individualism	Relational Logic	Urgency Orientation	Mono-Chronic	External Locus of Control	Event Orientation	Social Respect
Particularist	High Contact	Restrained Orientation	People Orientation	Limited Good	Unstructured	Progressive	Optimism	Warm in Relations
Egalitarian	Non-Assertive Orientation	Achieved Status	Being Orientation	Pessimism	Universalist	Immed. Gratification	Rational Logic	Disregard for Social Respect
Face Saving	Subjective Culture	Time Orientation	Harmony Orientation	Non-Urgency Orientation	Poly-chronic	Results Orientation	Objective Culture	Cautious in Relations

US Anglo-American cultural values.

Unlimited Good	Traditional	Doing Orientation	High Context	Honor & Shame	Internal Locus of Control	Open to Vulnerability	Hierarchical	Wisdom Orientation
Collective	Guilt & Innocence	Ascribed Status	Assertive Orientation	Delayed Gratification	Need for Information	Low Contact	Task Orientation	Cold in Relations
Low Context	Structured	Individualism	Relational Logic	Urgency Orientation	Mono-Chronic	External Locus of Control	Event Orientation	Social Respect
Particularist	High Contact	Restrained Orientation	People Orientation	Limited Good	Unstructured	Progressive	Optimism	Warm in Relations
Egalitarian	Non-Assertive Orientation	Achieved Status	Being Orientation	Pessimism	Universalist	Immed. Gratification	Rational Logic	Disregard for Social Respect
Face Saving	Subjective Culture	Time Orientation	Harmony Orientation	Non-Urgency Orientation	Poly-chronic	Results Orientation	Objective Culture	Cautious in Relations

Biblical Middle-Eastern cultural values.

Unlimited Good	Traditional	Doing Orientation	High Context	Honor & Shame	Internal Locus of Control	Open to Vulnerability	Hierarchical	Wisdom Orientation
Collective	Guilt & Innocence	Ascribed Status	Assertive Orientation	Delayed Gratification	Need for Information	Low Contact	Task Orientation	Cold in Relations
Low Context	Structured	Individualism	Relational Logic	Urgency Orientation	Mono-Chronic	External Locus of Control	Event Orientation	Social Respect
Particularist	High Contact	Restrained Orientation	People Orientation	Limited Good	Unstructured	Progressive	Optimism	Warm in Relations
Egalitarian	Non-Assertive Orientation	Achieved Status	Being Orientation	Pessimism	Universalist	Immed. Gratification	Rational Logic	Disregard for Social Respect
Face Saving	Subjective Culture	Time Orientation	Harmony Orientation	Non-Urgency Orientation	Poly-chronic	Results Orientation	Objective Culture	Cautious in Relations

Japanese cultural values.

Appendix 2
Alternate Model of Culture

THE PYRAMID MODEL HERE SHOWS clearly how behavior is the result of all the lower levels of culture:

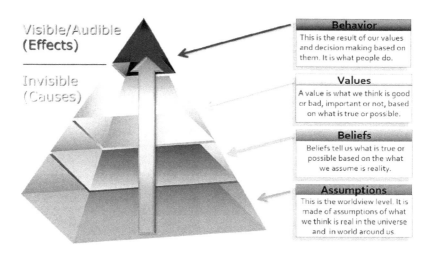

Behavior
This is the result of our values and decision making based on them. It is what people do.

Values
A value is what we think is good or bad, important or not, based on what is true or possible.

Beliefs
Beliefs tell us what is true or possible based on the what we assume is reality.

Assumptions
This is the worldview level. It is made of assumptions of what we think is real in the universe and in world around us.

Visible/Audible
(Effects)

Invisible
(Causes)

Pyramid model showing the developmental flow of behavior.

Bibliography

Agar, Michael. *Language Shock: Understanding the Culture of Conversation*. New York: William Morrow, 1994.

Anderson, Mark Robert. *The Qur'an in Context: A Christian Exploration*. Downers Grove: InterVarsity, 2016.

Armstrong, Chris R. *Medieval Wisdom for Modern Christians*. Grand Rapids: Brazos, 2016.

Ayegboyin, S. Deji and Ademola Ishola. *African Indigenous Churches: An Historical Perspective*. Lagos, Nigeria: Greater Heights, 1997.

Bailey, Kenneth. *Jesus Through Middle Eastern Eyes*. Downers Grove: Intervarsity, 2008.

Barnlund, Dean. "Communication in a Global Village." In *Intercultural Communication: A Reader*, edited by Larry A. Samovar and Richard E. Porter, 27–35. 8th ed. New York: Wadsworth, 1997.

Beck, Roger. "Zoroaster, as perceived by the Greeks." Encyclopedia Iranica, online edition, 2012, https://www.iranicaonline.org. Accessed March 12, 2021.

Boyce, Mary. *A History of Zoroastrianism*. Vol. 1. Leiden: Brill, 1975.

Brown, Colin, ed. *The New International Dictionary of New Testament Theology*, Vol. 2. Grand Rapids: Zondervan, 1976.

Carney, Thomas. *The Shape of the Past: Models and Antiquity*. University of California: Coronado Press, 1975.

Confucius, "The Doctrine of the Mean." In *A Source Book in Chinese Philosophy*, translated by Wing-Tsit Chan, 95–115. Princeton: Princeton University Press, 1963.

Confucius and James Legge. *The Analects, The Doctrine of the Mean, and The Great Learning*. Independently Published, 2020.

Conn, Harvey. *Eternal Word and Changing Worlds*. Grand Rapids: Zondervan, 1984.

Connors, Roger and Tom Smith. *Change the Culture; Change the Game*. New York: Penguin, 2011.

Corduan, Winfried. *Neighboring Faiths: A Christian Introduction to World Religions*. 2nd ed. Downers Grove: InterVarsity, 2012.

Curtis, Edward M. and John J. Brugaletta. *Discovering the Way of Wisdom: Spirituality in the Wisdom Literature*. Grand Rapids: Kregel, 2004.

deSilva, David A. *Honor, Patronage, Kinship & Purity: Unlocking New Testament Culture*. Downers Grove: InterVarsity, 2000.

De Waard, Jan and Eugene A. Nida. *From One Language to Another: Functional Equivalence in Bible Translation*. Nashville: Thomas Nelson, 1986.

Doyle, Tom. *Dreams and Visions: Is Jesus Awakening the Muslim World?* Nashville: Thomas Nelson, 2012.

Earhart, H. Byron. *Religion in the Japanese Experience: Sources and Interpretations.* Encino: Dickenson, 1973.

Friesen, Garry. *Decision Making and the Will of God.* Rev ed. Sisters: Multnomah, 2004.

Frost, Robert. "The Road not Taken." In *Selected Poems of Robert Frost*, 72. New York: Barnes and Noble, 1993.

Geertz, Clifford. *The Interpretation of Cultures.* New York: Basic Books, 1973.

Gershevitch, Ilya, "Zoroaster's Own Contribution," *Journal of Near Eastern Studies* 23.1 (1964) 12–38.

Gilliland, Dean. *Communicating Christ in Animistic Contexts.* Grand Rapids: Baker, 1991.

Gudykunst, William B. "An Anxiety/Uncertainty Management (AUM) Theory of Effective Communication." In *Theorizing about Intercultural Communication*, edited by William B. Gudykunst, 281–322. Thousand Oaks: Sage, 2005.

Hall, Edward T. *Beyond Culture.* New York: Doubleday, 1976.

———. *The Dance of Life*, Doubleday, 1983.

———. "The Power of Hidden Differences." In *Basic Concepts of Intercultural Communication*, edited by Milton Bennett, 53–68. Yarmouth: Intercultural, 1998.

———. *The Silent Language.* New York: Doubleday, 1959.

Hedinger, Mark R., Terry Steele, and Lauren T. Wells, "The Culture Tree: A Powerful Tool for Mission Research and Training," *Global Missiology* 4.17 (July 2020). www.globalmissiology.org.

Hiebert, Paul. *Anthropological Reflections on Missiological Issues.* Grand Rapids: Baker, 1994.

———. "Critical Contextualization." *International Bulletin of Missionary Research* 11.3 (July 1987) 104–11.

———. *Transforming Worldviews: An Anthropological Understanding of how people Change.* Grand Rapids: Baker, 2008.

Hofstede, Geert. *Culture's Consequences.* Thousand Oaks: Sage, 2001.

Howell, William. "Class Lecture Notes." University of Minnesota, Date unknown.

Keller, Timothy. *Counterfeit Gods.* New York: Penguin, 2009.

Kidner, Derek. *The Proverbs: An Introduction and Commentary.* Downers Grove: Intervarsity, 1964.

Kim, Min-Sun. *Non-Western Perspectives on Human Communication.* Thousand Oaks: Sage, 2002.

Klyukanov, Igor E. *Principles of Intercultural Communication.* New York: Allen and Bacon, 2005.

Kotter, David. *For the Least of These: A Biblical Answer to Poverty.* Tysons: Institute for Faith, Work & Economics, to be published, 2021.

Kraft, Charles. *Anthropology for Christian Witness.* New York: Orbis, 1996.

———, ed. *Appropriate Christianity.* Pasadena: William Carey, 2005.

———. *Christianity in Culture.* New York: Orbis, 2005.

———. *Issues in Contextualization.* Pasadena: William Carey, 2016.

Kwast, Lloyd E. "Understanding Culture." In *Perspectives on the World Christian Movement, A Reader*, edited by Ralph D. Winter and Steven C. Hawthorne, 397–99. 4th ed. Pasadena: William Carey, 1992.

Lewis, C. S. *The Four Loves.* New York: HarperOne, 2017.

————. *George MacDonald.* New York: HarperOne, 1973.

————. *The Lion, the Witch, and the Wardrobe.* New York: Harper, 1978.

————. *Mere Christianity.* New York: HarperOne, 1980.

————. *The Problem of Pain.* New York: MacMillan, 1953.

————. *Reflections on the Psalms.* New York: Harvest, 1958.

————. *The Silver Chair.* New York: Harper, 1981.

————. *Surprised by Joy.* New York: Harvest, 1966.

————. *The Weight of Glory.* Revised. New York: Harper One, 1980.

Lewis, Richard. *The Cultural Imperative.* Yarmouth: Intercultural, 2003.

Longman, Tremper, III. "Fear of the Lord." In *Dictionary of the Old Testament: Wisdom Poetry, and Writings,* 201–205. Grand Rapids: InterVarsity, 2008.

Luzbetak, Louis J. *The Church and Cultures.* New York: Orbis, 1988.

MacDonald, George. *Unspoken Sermons: Series I, II, III Complete and Unabridged.* CreateSpace, 2016.

Malina, Bruce J. "Faith/Faithfulness." In *Handbook of Biblical Social Values,* edited by John J. Pilch and Bruce J. Malina, 72–75. Peabody: Hendrickson, 1998.

————. *The New Testament World: Insights from Cultural Anthropology.* 3rd ed. Louisville: Westminster, 2001.

————. *The Social World of Jesus and the Gospels.* New York: Routledge, 1996.

————. "Understanding New Testament Persons." In *The Social Sciences and New Testament Interpretation,* edited by Richard L. Rohrbaugh, 41–61. Peabody: Hendrickson, 1996.

Malina, Bruce J. and Richard L. Rohrbaugh. *Social-Science Commentary on the Gospel of John.* Minneapolis: Fortress, 1998.

Malinowski, Bronislaw. "Man's Culture and Man's Behavior" *Sigma Xi Quarterly* 29.3 (October 1941); 30.1 (January 1942) 182–96.

————. *A Scientific Theory of Culture and Other Essays.* Chapel Hill: University of North Carolina Press, 1944.

Maslow, Abraham H. *Motivation and Personality.* 2nd ed. New York: Harper & Row, 1970.

McVann, Mark. "Change/Novelty Orientation." In *Handbook of Biblical Social Values,* edited by John J. Pilch and Bruce J. Malina, 19–21. Peabody: Hendrickson, 1998.

————. "Communicativeness." In *Handbook of Biblical Social Values,* edited by John J. Pilch and Bruce J. Malina, 27–30. Peabody: Hendrickson, 1998.

Moore, Glen and Cassandra Atherton. "Eternal Forests: The Veneration of Old Trees in Japan." *Arnoldia* 77.4 (2020) 24–31. https://arboretum.harvard.edu.

Murdock, George Peter. *Social Structure.* San Diego, CA: Andesite, 2015.

Newkirk, Dennis. *No Gods But God: Confronting Our Modern-Day Idolatry.* Edmond: H. H., 2015.

Neyrey, Jerome H. "Equivocation." In *Handbook of Biblical Social Values,* edited by John J. Pilch and Bruce J. Malina, 63–68. Peabody: Hendrickson, 1998.

Nicholls, Bruce. *Contextualization: A Theology of Gospel and Culture.* Vancouver: Regent College, 1979.

————. "Towards a Theology of Gospel and Culture." In *Down to Earth: Studies in Christianity and Culture,* edited by John Stott and Robert Coote, 53–62. Grand Rapids: Eerdmans, 1980.

Nida, Eugene A. and William D. Reyburn. *Meaning Across Cultures.* Maryknoll: Orbis, 1981.

Ono, Sokyo. *Shinto the Kami Way*. Boston: Tuttle, 2004.

Packer, J.I. *Knowing God*. Downers Grove: InterVarsity, 2016.

Pearcey, Nancy. *Total Truth: Liberating Christianity from Its Cultural Captivity*. Wheaton: Crossway, 2004.

Pew Research Center: Religion and Public Life. "America's Changing Religious Landscape." Last modified May 12, 2015. https://www.pewforum.org/2015/05/12/americas-changing-religious-landscape.

————. "In U.S. Decline of Christianity Continues at Rapid Pace." Last modified October 17, 2019. https://www.pewforum.org/2019/10/17/in-u-s-decline-of-christianity-continues-at-rapid-pace.

Pilch, John J. and Bruce J. Malina, eds. *Handbook of Biblical Social Values*. Peabody: Hendrickson, 1998.

Plevnik, Joseph. "Honor/Shame." In *Handbook of Biblical Social Values*, edited by John J. Pilch and Bruce J. Malina, 106–15. Peabody: Hendrickson, 1998.

Priest, Robert J. "Experience-Near Theologizing in Diverse Human Contexts." In *Globalizing Theology: Belief and Practice in an Era of World Christianity*, edited by Craig Ott and Harold A. Netland, 180–95. Grand Rapids: Baker, 2006.

Qureshi, Nabeel. *Seeking Allah, Finding Jesus: A Devout Muslim Encounters Christianity*. Grand Rapids: Zondervan, 2014.

Richards, E. Randolph and Brandon J. O'Brien. *Misreading Scripture with Western Eyes*. Downers Grove: InterVarsity, 2012.

Rohrbaugh, Richard. "Introduction." In *The Social Sciences and New Testament Interpretation*, edited by Richard Rohrbaugh, 1–15. Peabody: Hendrickson, 1996.

Rokeach, Milton. *The Nature of Human Values*. New York: Free Press, 1973.

————. *Understanding Human Values: Individual and Societal*. New York: Free Press, 1979.

Rots, Aike P. *Shinto, Nature, and Ideology in Contemporary Japan: Making Sacred Forests*. New York: Bloomsbury, 2017.

Sacks, Jonathan. *Morality: Restoring the Common Good in Divided Times*. New York: Basic Books, 2020.

Schirrmacher, Thomas. *Culture of Shame, Culture of Guilt: Applying the Word of God in Different Situations*. Eugene: Wipf and Stock, 2018.

Singer, Marshall R. *Perception and Identity in Intercultural Communication*. Yarmouth: Intercultural, 1998.

Smith, Charles R. *Can You Know God's Will for Your Life?* Winona Lake: BMH, 1977.

Smith, Donald K. *Creating Understanding*. Grand Rapids: Zondervan, 1992.

Sowell, Thomas. "Cultural Diversity: A World View." In *Intercultural Communication: A Reader*, edited by L. A. Samovar and R. E. Porter, 398–404. 11th ed. Belmont, CA: Wadsworth, 2006.

Stewart, Edward C. and Milton J. Bennett. *American Cultural Patterns: A Cross-Cultural Perspective*. Rev. ed. Yarmouth: Intercultural, 1991.

Storti, Craig. *The art of Crossing-Cultures*. 2nd ed. Yarmouth: Intercultural, 2001.

Tennent, Timothy. *Invitation to World Missions*. Grand Rapids: Kregel, 2010.

————. *Theology in the Context of World Christianity*. Grand Rapids: Zondervan, 2007.

Ting-Toomey, Stella and Leeva C. Chung. *Understanding Intercultural Communication*. Los Angeles: Roxbury, 2005.

Triandis, Harry C. *Individualism and Collectivism*. San Francisco: Westview, 1995.

Van Rheenen, Gailyn. *Communicating Christ in Animistic Contexts*. Grand Rapids: Baker, 1991.

―――, ed. *Contextualization and Syncretism: Navigating Cultural Currents*. EMS Series No. 13. Pasadena: William Carey, 2006.

Waltke, Bruce. *Finding the Will of God: A Pagan Notion*. Grand Rapids: Eerdmans, 1995.

―――. *The Book of Proverbs: Chapters 1–15*. Grand Rapids: Eerdmans, 2004.

Wright, Christopher. *The Mission of God*. Downers Grove: InterVarsity, 2006.

Yamakage, Motohisa. *The Essence of Shinto: Japan's Spiritual Heart*. New York: Kodansha, 2012.

Zaehner, Robert Charles. *The Dawn and Twilight of Zoroastrianism*, New York: MacMillan, 1961.

Zvanaka, Solomon. "African Independent Churches in Context." *Missiology: An International Review* 25.1 (January 1997) 69–75.

Printed in the USA
CPSIA information can be obtained
at www.ICGtesting.com
JSHW011715191023
50456JS00013B/145